Value-Based PRICING

Drive Sales and Boost Your Bottom Line by Creating, Communicating, and Capturing Customer Value

Harry Macdivitt and Mike Wilkinson

New York   Chicago   San Francisco   Lisbon   London
Madrid   Mexico City   New Delhi   San Juan
Seoul   Singapore   Sydney   Toronto

To Aileen and Lizzie
For their patience and support, and not insisting
that all these little DIY jobs get done. Ever.

Contents

Acknowledgments

There is a wonderful saying in Scotland that "twa heids are better than yin" (two heads are better than one). We have been privileged to meet, in the course of the three years it has taken us to write this book, some really marvelous people and to have the benefit of their critical but kind comments. We truly have discovered that "a hunnert heids are better than twa" (a hundred heads are better than two). The "twa" in this case being the authors. So to everyone who has contributed in one way or another to the writing and content of this book, we offer a big, collective thank you.

We would like to single out for special thanks a number of individual.

Our colleagues Ricki Coussins and Professor Ian Thomas kindly offered some suggestions and ideas when looking over drafts of early chapters. We acknowledge their contributions with thanks. Thanks are also due to a colleague of many years, Roy H. Hill, who kindly agreed to make available some material on contribution analysis that appears in Chapter 3. Our good friend and colleague Jack Matton has consistently offered good ideas, suggestions, and valuable criticisms based on his enormous experience in value work and led us in fact to make some very substantial changes to the running order and content of this book. Thanks, Jack, and keep working on that handicap! We owe a big thank you also to Barry Rodger, professor of law at the University of Strathclyde, for checking over the final draft of Appendix A.

Harry's daughter, Laura, applied her eye for detail in reviewing several chapters of this book and for working her magic on many of the graphics—usually at the end of a long day as a copy editor. Thank you, Laura.

In the course of preparing Chapter 10, we interviewed executives from a number of companies who had progressed some distance along the VBP journey or who provided content and ideas for other cases. We have promised to keep their companies confidential, but we mention them here again with our thanks for the time they spent with us and for the insights they gave us from their experience. So John, Simon, Frederic, Gary, Roland, Alan, Phil, Tom, Steve, and Marcus, you know who you are. Thank you.

Finally, we would like to express our appreciation to Niki Papadopoulos at McGraw-Hill for both her wise counsel, particularly in the final stages of preparing the manuscript and for actually believing that it would arrive. Eventually. We very much appreciate and acknowledge the careful—in fact, meticulous—editing of our scribblings, translating them into American English, and imposing a solid logical flow to our arguments by McGraw Hill's editing team – Ron and Joseph Martirano and Jospeh Kurtz. In fact, Ron and Joseph helped us turn our prose into a *real* book. Thank you, guys!

Over many years, we have met thousands of managers from hundreds of companies. We have met them on courses, at seminars, at management and board room briefings, in consulting projects, and at conferences. We also want to acknowledge the insights and ideas offered freely by participants in special interest groups on the Web. It is truly fascinating to realize that so many people across the planet are so deeply interested in pricing in general and in value-based pricing in particular and are willing to share their ideas and insights with fellow professionals. We never cease to be amazed at the interest that people have in our ideas on pricing and value, and always we come away from events and discussions with some exciting new concept or idea. They are too many to mention by name, but they genuinely have contributed in some way or another to the ideas in this book. We have written this book for them and those many souls who, like them, are grappling daily with tough challenges.

Value-Based
PRICING

Introduction

Over the past 20 years, we have delivered hundreds of seminars and training events throughout the world on pricing and value. One recurring theme is how poorly people understand value—what it is, why it's important, how it should be communicated, and what its role is in determining pricing strategy. Delegates at training courses frequently want to "deep dive" into the literature. Sometimes this happens because they discover an unexpected fascination with the subject; sometimes, quite simply, they need sound, practical, and sensible advice and ideas for their own businesses. Their interest and their need provided the stimulus to write this book.

This book will be of interest to managers responsible for planning, setting, or negotiating prices. This includes chief executive officers (CEOs) of Strategic Business Units (SBUs); marketing, sales, and finance executives; product/brand managers; key account and major account managers; management accountants; specialists in business analysis and pricing; and management consultants. It is also likely to be of interest to owner/managers of small and medium-sized businesses (SMBs), who often have very attractive value-adding products and services but damage their businesses by seriously undercharging for them. We also believe that many people in specialist masters of business administration/masters of science (MBA/MSc) programs and students preparing for professional business qualifications at the postgraduate or professional diploma level will benefit from the ideas presented here.

While we have identified what we believe to be "probable" users of this book, we may have missed a few categories. If so, that is entirely our fault, and we apologize right up front! It is our hope and belief that everyone with an interest in introducing and using *value-based pricing* will find something of interest and of use.

We present some pretty fundamental ideas in Chapters 1 through 5, which comprise Part I: Key Concepts. Readers familiar with conventional pricing methods may wish to skip Chapters 3 and 4, although the critical review of these methods may be quite useful and informative to them, especially if they are seeking to build some arguments to introduce value-based pricing into a conventional pricing situation. Chapters 1, 2, and 5 contain core concepts that are picked up and used in Part II. Readers especially need to understand our ideas around the value triad in Chapter 1, how to create and use value maps in Chapter 2, and how to measure value in Chapter 5.

Part II deals with important value-based pricing practicalities and should be of interest to practitioners, particularly those seeking to implement a value-based pricing strategy in their organizations. Chapter 6 demonstrates how to apply the value-triad concept in building a value-based price. Chapter 7 reviews a number of value-based pricing methods that have been reported in the literature or which we have encountered in our training and consulting work. Chapters 8 and 9 deal with the vitally important issues of creating the customer value proposition and selling this proposition to customers. In Chapter 10 we summarize results from case studies of current practice in implementing a value-based pricing approach. This chapter is a "must read" for senior managers who need to be familiar with the key issues. Chapter 11 addresses some contemporary issues in pricing, and we summarize important legal issues that have an impact on pricing in Appendix A.

We have written this book from the perspective of customer value. While many of our examples come from business-to-business (B2B) businesses, reflecting the experience of the authors and the nature of our clients, the ideas are relevant in both B2B and business-to-customer (B2C) businesses. We hope that executives from both sectors will be able to use the ideas of value to inform marketing, selling, negotiation, and pricing decisions. Creation, communication, and recognition of value remain central issues in both B2B and B2C businesses. Misunderstand value and, however clever our metrics and mathematics, we still will get the pricing wrong!

This book is about value-based pricing. In our view, every price can be considered to be a *value-based* price. Even if the product or service offers no incremental value over alternatives, or if the buyer is a consumer or a business, provided that the buyer is prepared to pay for it, then clearly it offers some value to him or her. If it did not, it would not be purchased! We are particularly interested in the idea of pricing on *incremental* value. Products and services must offer some differentiation around either functionality or emotional contribution. Without this differentiation, there would be no incremental value, and value-based pricing would be impossible.

Pricing decisions are often based on cost or competitors' prices for apparently similar items. Neither of these approaches takes due account of value to the customer or to the end-user consumer. Sometimes pricing is delegated to colleagues in accounting and finance who have little knowledge of customer value. This leads to incorrect pricing decisions, premature commoditization, obsession with specification and "product," and a chronic tendency to "leave money on the table." Such approaches also provide sales staff with few or no arguments to overcome price objections such as "too expensive," "the same as everyone else," and so on. When customers genuinely reject our offer, it is usually because they have not understood the real value of our offer *to them* or because a competitor has worked harder to build its proposition.

Many industries today face price pressure. Managers may blame the problem on their companies' or industries' pricing methodologies. Nevertheless, problems rarely lie in pricing methods. These, after all, are normally basic arithmetic. In almost every case, inadequate attention to value and what this means to the buyer lie at the heart of the issue. Solve this, and the rest will follow.

When confronted with a customer challenge on price, the sales response is often to discount. Discounting enhances *one* element of value, and it is easy for the salesperson to do if he or she has been delegated that freedom. However, it actively prevents other aspects of value from being raised, much less discussed. Worse, discounting on demand establishes a pattern of behavior, damages brands, encourages and rewards customer greed, and even may drive products toward commoditization. Initiatives such as Total Quality Management (TQM), Supply-Chain Management, Lean Manufacturing, and even Six Sigma, undertaken for other reasons, are used as the basis of cost-reduction programs, but the hoped-for margin growth eludes us. We cut our costs and provide our salespeople with another opportunity to discount. Aggressive buyer behavior, especially if coupled with a box-shifting mentality by the seller, leads almost inevitably to discounting to "win the work," and the product becomes almost instantaneously commoditized.

This process prevents useful discussions of the real value of the offer. As a result, the buyer fails to recognize the worth of what he or she has purchased and fails to gain, through lack of awareness, the full benefits from the products and services procured. A poor selling process means that the correct decision makers never hear the value proposition. The people who do—usually the procurement team—may well claim not to care about value, only price. The result of all this is poor results, poor morale, and increasingly contentious relationships with customers.

There is no shortage of challenges facing contemporary business, and we could write a whole book about these alone. Today's business managers—particularly those "out there" in the market—are confronted with unprecedented competition, incredibly fast-paced technology change creating market-disrupting products and services, hostile global trading conditions, and rapidly changing business models that render traditional methods and routes to market obsolete. How on earth do we keep up and keep on reinventing ourselves? With difficulty, particularly if our focus—maybe even our obsession—is exclusively on product technology and the drive to incorporate ever more clever functionality into our products. This focus—and this obsession—while understandable (and perhaps even highly laudable in earlier times), is wrong today. The focus is and must be on applying similar genius to a deeper understanding of customers' needs and how we can meet them uniquely and elegantly and be rewarded for doing so. In short, the new focus and obsession *must* be on customer value and doing everything in our power to identify it minutely and use it creatively. This "sea change" lies at the very core of this book. Dealing with these issues, which in our experience are ubiquitous, is what this book ultimately is all about.

Now more than ever before, it is essential for businesses to reexamine the reality of the value they offer to their customers. If the value is absent or marginal, businesses must find ways to enhance the value they deliver—and to develop strategies to ensure that they are rewarded adequately for the value they *do* deliver.

This is the purpose of value-based pricing.

This book shows you how.

PART I

Value-Based Pricing
Key Concepts

CHAPTER 1

What Is Value?

What is a cynic? A man who knows the price of everything and the value of nothing.

—Oscar Wilde

The word *value* is used so often in business and so loosely that it is in danger of losing whatever meaning it had. In short, the concept of value itself has become devalued! In reality, value is the core driving force underlying every business decision. Therefore, it is important that we know what it is and how it is defined and used in order to yield real insights into our daily work.

Although easy to ask, this question is really difficult to answer. We discovered just *how* difficult when we challenged managers from different companies to come up with a robust definition. Here are just some of the answers we heard:

- "Value is getting more than I paid for (or expected)."
- "Value is the perception that I need your solution more than someone else's."
- "Value is perceiving I've had a good deal."

- "Value is getting a feel-good factor from a transaction."
- "Value is making my life a bit easier."
- "Value is a mystery!"

Alan Watson, a London taxi cab driver and greengrocer, had this to say about value:

> My family has owned and operated a fresh fruit and vegetable stall in London for more than 90 years. We have come through two wars, a great depression, and a deep recession. We are about to go into another recession. We survived all of these, and we will survive the next one too. How? By listening carefully to what people want, doing our best to give them it—and even a little bit more. People are more interested in value than price, and that's just what I give them. I have customers who have been coming back to me for more than 40 years!

Alan's message is simple, durable, and actionable: "Understand exactly what people want—and give them it!" This is the complete theme of this chapter. The message is simple, but we need to interpret it in the context of the complex, technology-driven, and intensely competitive corporate world of the twenty-first century.

COMMODITY OR NOT A COMMODITY?

Most of us probably would agree that when it comes to commodities, water is a fairly basic one. When we turn on the tap, we expect water to come out. Here in the United Kingdom, that water is potable and, according to Thames Water, very inexpensive, at around 0.002 cent per liter at the time of writing. On this basis, why would anyone want to pay any more for what is, after all, just H_2O? Clearly, a lot of people do. The U.K. bottled water market is worth close to £1.5 billion per year—a high price for something that is so inexpensive from the tap. Somehow the bottled water companies have succeeded in differentiating their offering against tap water—and their other competitors—very effectively. In doing so, they have created benefits in the minds of consumers, perceived or real, to which consumers clearly attach some value. This perceived value is both tangible and intangible. Customers justify their purchases generally on the basis of logical arguments—it's convenient, it has fewer chemicals in it, it's purer, and it's healthier.

How much of this is actually factual and how much is the result of marketing efforts is open to debate. However, value is derived from convenience (you can't take a tap with you!), perceived health and taste benefits (despite Thames Waters' tap water coming in first in a blind taste test some years ago), and image (if the people at the next table in the restaurant are drinking volcanic water from New Zealand, your jug of tap water is going to look a bit sad! Claridge's Hotel in London now has a water menu to sit alongside its wine menu). And the price of a bottle? Anything from a few pennies a liter to $75 and more. For water! Simple H_2O with a little extra—brand image, cachet, a bottle designed by Jean Paul Gautier. So what is water really worth? Is it 0.002 cent a liter, or is it $75 or more? Or even … how much would you pay for a liter of water in the desert?

If a basic commodity such as water can be differentiated so broadly and effectively, imagine what you could do with your own products and services.

SOME INTERPRETATIONS OF VALUE

Let's drill down a little into this thing called *value* and try to pull out a few important truths that will help us on the way to creating a robust definition.

Value as a *Perception* and an *Expectation*

When we compare one offer with another, we select the offer that captures most completely whatever we are looking for. Our belief in its ability to actually deliver what we expect is based on perceptions alone if no other objective source of information is available at the time of purchase. In this scenario, the buyer is conditioned by the messages received prior to or at the same time as the purchase. Objective reality does not "kick in" until rather later when the purchaser has had time to reflect on the transaction and to observe performance in use.

Value as a *Quid Pro Quo*

In this situation, we expect a fair transaction in which the worth to us of the item purchased is at least equal to (and certainly not less than) the sum of the sacrifices we make in procuring it—time to search for and choose from among options, cost of money to purchase, the price itself, and any associated psychological risk factors. The sacrifice is not of a monetary nature alone; it also reflects our time and effort in seeking out the good in question and is logically the best use of the limited resources at our disposal. In short, this is a *rational buyer's* expectation.

Value as an *Enhancement of Our Situation*

A consumer or a business manager will invest his money in ways that will improve his life in some meaningful manner. While he might be willing to accept a quid pro quo offer, he is delighted if he actually receives more than he expected, especially if what he does receive genuinely enhances his situation.

WHY DOES VALUE MATTER TODAY?

From our work with many companies, we have learned that clear advantages accrue to businesses that apply a value-based approach to their thinking. A focus on value is really a focus on understanding the actual needs of customers and finding a unique and differentiated way of meeting those needs effectively and efficiently. As soon as we identify a unique approach or create a clever solution, it will be copied quickly. Consequently, a value approach demands single-minded commitment to innovation and creativity—and a sustained and single-minded search for uniqueness. Managers of value-oriented businesses are constantly on the lookout for new ways of meeting, perhaps even anticipating, their customer's needs and doing so in a manner that permits them to exploit their uniqueness.

A frequent challenge salespeople hear is that their products are "just commodities." While this may be true in some cases, it is usually put forward by a shrewd buyer as a ploy to extract some undertaking from the salesperson, usually in the form of a discount or some other deal "sweetener." If we have genuinely incorporated into our product-development processes and our service-delivery activities a real focus on customer value, this should enable us to respond in a manner that repudiates any assertion of commoditization. In short, a value-based approach to business provides an excellent counter to the challenge of commoditization. Differentiation is not just about doing something different. It is about doing something different in a manner that really matters to your customer. By clearly focusing on your customers' needs and pain points, you can uncover novel ways of serving them.

A value-based approach generates lasting customer relationships that are more difficult to dislodge than relationships based solely on price. In this sense, product and service life cycles reasonably can be expected to be significantly longer than those which are not based on understanding and delivering real customer value.

THE VALUE TRIAD

Value means different things to different people. Even for the same person, different contexts may create different value perspectives. For instance, the executive traveling on business may opt to fly British Airways because of her perception of superior service, access to business lounges, and perhaps even prestige. However, if she travels at her own expense, cost becomes a more compelling factor, causing her to choose a budget carrier instead. The purchasing context and who is paying have a profound impact on the decision.

Value can mean perception, an exchange, or even an economic enhancement. A single, simple definition is inadequate to capture this completely. For this reason, we developed the Value Triad concept as a practical tool to capture as much as we can of the richness and variety of meaning encountered in value (Figure 1.1).

We define the three elements of the Value Triad as

- Revenue gains (RGs)
- Cost reductions (CRs)
- Emotional contribution (EC)

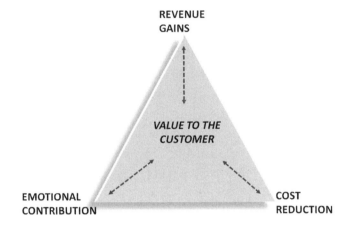

Figure 1.1   Value Triad.

Revenue gain and cost reduction both focus on the functional, tangible, and objective elements of value, whereas emotional contribution, as its name implies, focuses on the less tangible, more subjective measures.

Revenue Gains (RGs)

These are the improvements in revenue that accrue to a customer as the result of the purchase and use of your products and services. Outcomes such as superior yield from manufacturing processes or service-delivery initiatives or greater revenue streams perhaps through the ability to create and sell a better and more competitive service, the ability to charge a premium price for products and services in turn, or the ability to increase market share all generate revenue gains.

Cost Reductions (CRs)

These involve our ability to help a customer reduce costs through the use of our products and services. This is not merely about reducing the price of purchased goods and services. CRs for your customer also can be achieved by reducing direct labor hours, having longer periods between servicing, employing less expensive personnel, training staff in new skills, reducing short- and long-term capital expenditure, and so on. CRs must be achieved without compromising subsequent value delivery to your customer's customer.

Emotional Contribution (EC)

This arises from many sources and is in general linked closely to the "feel good factor"—for example, reduction of "hassle," peace of mind, increased confidence, greater safety, pleasing to the eye, personal gain, trust, self-esteem, absence of risk, and so on. There are lots of these, but to appreciate them fully, we need to put ourselves in our customers' shoes and see the world from their perspective! While there may be quite a high degree of alignment around the more tangible economic factors, executives often have quite different opinions about what affects them, personally, from an emotional perspective. This makes it very difficult to create a universally acceptable, objectively verifiable quantitative estimate of emotional impact. Emotional considerations have a profound but hidden impact on the overall attractiveness or even acceptability of a proposal. What may be an overwhelmingly attractive economic offer can be overturned by an adverse emotional viewpoint of a key decision maker.

VALUE DRIVERS

A *value driver* is any factor that, if a business acts on it, leads to an enhancement of competitive advantage. Business-to-business (B2B) drivers are mostly economic in nature. In business-to-consumer (B2C) situations, these are likely to be largely intangible. This is not to say that it is impossible to find intangible or even emotional drivers in a B2B transaction. After all, business is an interpersonal affair. Likewise, while many consumer purchase decisions may be emotional, perhaps even impulsive in nature, many are driven by economic considerations— increasingly so during times of recession or financial stringency.

Economic value drivers are factors that ultimately result in increased revenue or decreased costs. These factors tend to increase profitability or reduce/eliminate economic losses, and these factors can be measured or calculated with relative ease.

Emotional value drivers are factors that ultimately lead to some improvement in the customer's emotional satisfaction or the avoidance of a reduction of his emotional satisfaction. These "intangible" factors are much more difficult to measure or calculate. Nevertheless, we must try to assess the "worth" of an EC element to a customer in a given context and its relative importance in the buying decision. If there is little difference between competitors on RG and CR elements, the EC factors become very important drivers of the final decision and perhaps even a tie-breaker!

Some factors contribute to both. For instance, a company manager whose purchase decision leads to his company achieving or increasing profitability also will experience some feelings of satisfaction and improved self-esteem.

Later in this book (Chapter 5) we take a close look at how the Value Triad can be used to identify the principal value drivers of a particular proposition and how we might go about identifying suitable metrics to assess their impact on our customers' businesses.

In Figure 1.2 we identify the extent to which different Value Triad elements have an impact on a "typical" B2B transaction and a "typical" B2C transaction. Usually B2B decisions are based largely on economic factors. Managers tend to emphasize the CR consequences more than the RG consequences of a decision. It is relatively rare in B2B work that EC elements are considered explicitly. There are powerful EC impacts from what appears at first sight to be an economically driven choice. The offer is unlikely to be accepted unless it can be demonstrated objectively to have economic value. But we also must search diligently for any EC impacts while constructing a value proposition.

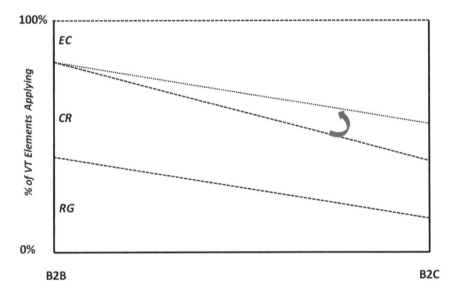

Figure 1.2   Value Triad in B2B and B2C transactions.

EC is dominant in many B2C transactions. CRs are also common in B2C transactions, for example, in relatively mundane transactions such as weekly supermarket shopping. Economic factors play a significant role and complement the EC created by packaging, branding, and advertising. Indeed, when money is scarce, as in recessionary conditions, cost awareness increases dramatically among some segments of the community and may dwarf EC factors. RGs are relatively uncommon but do exist, for example, in investments individuals make in their education, self-improvement courses, and services to facilitate job finding. During recessions, we might expect CR elements to become more dominant in the consumer purchase decision. The ideas we discuss here have a significant impact on our thinking about managing channels to market and how we might craft differential value propositions to different "players" in the channels. We look at this more closely in Chapter 8.

DIFFERENTIATION

Differentiation describes any aspect of our total customer offer that is different from that of the competition and, crucially, that is valued by the customer. It is a lot more than a mere difference in specification. Our product or service may well be different from that of the competition, but unless this difference delivers real value that the customer can identify with, understand, acknowledge, and be willing to invest in, then it is merely a point of difference—nothing more. If we can manipulate some aspect of price or performance in a way that mobilizes our unique capabilities and in a way that no competitor can possibly emulate and as a result create an elegant—perhaps even unique—solution to a customer's problem, then we have a winning proposition. This is infinitely easier to say than to do. Never underestimate your competitors' abilities to surprise you. And never, ever make the assumption that your differentiation will make the competition irrelevant. This is both foolish and dangerous. The question you need to ask is, "What can we do, in relation to our total customer offer, to encourage the customer to choose us and remain with us?"

This distils down to, "What are the critical differences between us and the competition, and how do they influence the relative value the customer perceives?" Note that this absolutely must be from the customer's perspective—not ours. Our views are irrelevant—we are not the buyer! Our success in meeting a customer's requirements is based, at least in part, on listening to (and fully understanding) the customer's context, value-adding processes, and "pain and pleasure points" and how we can mobilize this information in the creation of a product or service that offers real differential advantage from that customer's perspective.

If delivering value is about enhancing our customer's competitive advantage, and if competitive advantage is about our customer's ability to leverage her differential value in turn, then delivering a differentiated value is about our ability to enhance our customer's differentiated value better than anyone else. A minor specification change is not a differentiation unless we can demonstrate credibly how it adds real value. A change that, for instance, makes a product easier for us to produce or a service easier to deliver is *not* a differentiation from the customer's perspective. However, if this change can make the customer's life easier or her business more profitable, it *may* be a differentiation. It only becomes one once we can demonstrate that it *will* enhance our customer's business in economic or emotional dimensions or both. We *must* resist the temptation to make changes in specification merely because we have the technology or know-how to do so. Clever technology can be incredibly seductive, particularly if we have a large technology portfolio. The Philips company, for example, has a wonderful track record of technology development and an impressive stream of new-product introductions over many years. Marketplace success, however, eluded the company in many cases because its products had not been built around real customer insight. The products often were before their time and were withdrawn long before the market caught up. Consumer insight was what was needed, and it took a change of chief executive for a consumer focus to be introduced throughout the whole organization—a dramatic shift in emphasis from technology push, and not one that was easy to implement either.

Beware of falling into the trap of believing that your products are commodities. This is a fast highway to a self-fulfilling prophecy. If you start to believe that your product is a commodity, your thinking will change subtly, and so will the way you approach the business. You will ignore, or discount, the value of any differentiation you do possess.

You will not promote the product, and you thus will leave the customer with a clear impression that you are just one of the crowd. The way to counter this is to challenge any assertion that the product is "just like everyone else's." Demand justification of this assertion, and look for and present strongly rebutting arguments. Of course, your product may be heading toward commodity land. If so, this is time for a thorough root and branch assessment of the product and its relevance in the market, a search for potential differentiators (existing or new), and a strategy to reposition the product in the mind of your market. In one well-documented case, Rhone Poulenc was able to find a new use for silicon dioxide (sand) as a component of car tires to reduce rolling resistance and improve fuel consumption.[1] Never stop looking for customer and product insights that can lead to new routes to differentiation.[2]

In any work you are doing in differentiation, you *must* think in Value Triad terms—and ask the famous *So what?* question: "So ... what advantages will this change make in the customer's overall product or service experience?" If the answer is "None," or "Negligible"—*Don't do it!* All you are doing is increasing your cost and reducing your margin.

Value-based pricing (VBP) is about pricing on *differential* value. If your product or service has no differential value compared to the competition, you simply cannot price on value and must instead choose one of the other alternative conventional pricing approaches.

ROUTES TO DIFFERENTIATION

The complex, technology-packed products in today's markets come with a host of potential differentiators. Here are a few ideas (not by any means a comprehensive list) to think about.

Consistency

Have you ever had the experience of taking your car for service at your local garage? The first time you go, the job is done perfectly. The car is clean and performs well, and the bill is reasonable. You are delighted and resolve to use this garage in the future. Next time, however, the car is returned in a disgusting state. Half the work is not done, the mechanic couldn't care less, and the bill is outrageous. The service delivery here is inconsistent. There is clearly little or no quality control in operation, so the standard of service you receive is a lottery depending on the professionalism of the individual mechanic.

You can differentiate your service by ensuring that your customers receive consistently great service—not just once but every time. Dependable, reliable service breeds dependable, reliable customers.

Convenience

A European chemical company carved out a large slice of the market for its specialized materials used in many B2B applications. This market is dominated by huge companies such as Hexion, Bayer, and DuPont and is in large measure commoditized. The standard approach was for suppliers to ship product monthly, in hundreds of tons, and for the material to be stored in huge tanks on site until required. This process locks up millions of euros and thousands of square meters of prime space. The supplier's logistics guaranteed just-in-time delivery—a feature that at that time could not be emulated by its competitors. The effect was that customers were able to reduce the size of the storage facilities required and unlock both working capital and space for expansion.

By enhancing the convenience to your customer of using your product or service, you may be able lock them in—especially if your competitors cannot copy your methods.

Customization

Delivery of a customized service demands deep understanding of your customer's value-adding processes or production operations. Deep understanding can come only from a proper discovery process and will demand in-depth examination of the client's business. McKinnon & Clarke, a company operating in the energy-efficiency consultancy market, routinely undertakes detailed site assessments of their clients' energy consumption. As a result of the deep understanding that results, the company offers highly customized recommendations for energy cost reduction. The service provider and the client share in the cost reductions achieved through implementation of the recommendations. The client pays nothing up front for the service, which is undertaken at the service provider's risk. Customer loyalty is ensured through major cost reductions—often hundreds of thousands of dollars—that the client could never have achieved independently. The service is difficult to copy because the consultant has years of experience, an encyclopedic knowledge of energy costs from all suppliers, and a robust analytical process undertaken by highly qualified and skilled consultants.

By clearly and thoroughly understanding your customer's value-adding processes and pinpointing where your company's unique skills can be applied, you can create a mutual dependency that yields benefits to both client and service provider.

Combinations

Virgin Mobile, a mobile virtual network operator, was exploring opportunities in the fiercely competitive U.S. mobile market. This market at the time was dominated by the big players such as Sprint, Verizon, and AT&T. There seemed no way in. Virgin set about searching for a poorly served sector and discovered it in the youth market. At the time, the typical offer for young mobile phone users was exactly the same as for adults. No other supplier had differentiated the offer to their young customers, the standard offer being a monthly contract, tied handsets, peak and off-peak call rates (which, confusingly, changed frequently), and premium-priced services such as Internet connection. Virgin, long experienced in serving the youth market in its music businesses, understood the needs of young people much better than the competitors, none of whom had made any meaningful inroads into this market. Furthermore, Virgin's excellent contacts in the entertainment sector afforded an opportunity to provide unique, specialist content that could not be copied by competitors. The operator constructed a specifically targeted youth offer. It eliminated the monthly contract (a real bone of contention); provided an easy-to-use and easy-to-understand billing structure in which customers paid only for what they used, thus eliminating monthly billing and statements that parents might see; and incorporated a host of "cool" features such as music, wallpapers, ring tones, and even concierge services. A particularly popular feature was the "get out of a bad date for free" service, where a prearranged phone call could provide an escape excuse if a date was going badly! Virgin was the first to succeed in this market.

You can differentiate your offer by truly understanding the real needs and motivations of your customers—and responding to them.

Characteristics

The characteristics of your product or service may be sufficient to differentiate it. Such factors as size, speed, color, components, bundles, or add-ons all may confer distinctiveness—and make it hard for competitors to emulate. Sony, for instance, has a long history of creating clever consumer products through miniaturization of electronic circuits and has introduced such disruptive innovations as portable televisions and the Walkman.

Bundling of discrete product elements into a solution is today a popular method of creating differentiation. It can work only if the bundled elements genuinely add real "triad value" and are difficult or impossible for competitors to emulate, for example, Microsoft's Office packages and Fresenius Medical Care's online purification cascade.

The key issue for success is to be able to create a solution that genuinely meets customers' needs in a way that cannot readily be copied by others. This means listening carefully to what the market is saying, designing your product in such a way that it can be assembled differently for different requirements and tested to demonstrate that the assemblies work in any given customer's context, and ensuring that the components are carefully sourced, selected, or developed uniquely for your solution. Merely throwing together "bits and pieces" from off the shelf and calling this a "solution" is not only unlikely to work but also will incur real wrath and deep cynicism from buyers. When a real solution emerges, they will migrate en masse to the new supplier.

We have reviewed only a handful of possible ways to differentiate our product or service. There are many, many more. However you decide to differentiate, you will need to follow these steps:

1. Learn as much as possible about the customer, her company, and her market. There is lots of information in the public domain, and it need not take a lot of time or effort to collect it. It is simply not possible to know too much.
2. Consider what your research says about your customer's context. Where are the sources of pain and difficulty she is suffering that no one else seems to be addressing?

3. Find ways of using your own unique capabilities, contacts, technologies, or other resources, and weave them into a solution that is difficult for competitors to copy—and easy for the customer to buy.

4. Build a powerful value proposition, and learn how to deliver it persuasively and compellingly. We offer detailed guidance on building the value proposition in Chapter 8.

COMMUNICATING AND DEMONSTRATING VALUE

You are not finished yet! However cleverly you believe that you have created a differentiated product, service, or solution, the final arbiter is, of course, the customer. Communicating your differentiated solution in a clear, compelling, and persuasive manner is vital. What buyers and users want to know are the following:

1. Does it work the way the salesperson tells us?
2. Can it be used/implemented in *our* organization?
3. Does it deliver the results we want and need?
4. What evidence can we be given?
5. How can my risk (psychological and financial) be reduced or eliminated?

The first two questions are part of the salesperson's *discovery process*—that is, before coming up with a recommended solution, the supplier needs to satisfy himself that the solution is appropriate for the specific customer. And if you cannot meet their need, be honest and say so! We have more to say about this a little later in this book (Chapter 9). Questions 3, 4, and 5, however, are crucial in value-based pricing (VBP). From our research among companies that have implemented VBP successfully, it is clear that a central part of the sales process is the ability to identify and, where possible, quantify the real benefits to the organization as a whole and individually to the members of the *buying center*—the team of managers and influencers who usually make up the decision-making unit. Thinking about measurable performance and economic factors is good, but it is not enough. You also need to think through how the purchase will affect individuals. This part is often overlooked. Yet it is so important. It is about understanding and managing psychological risk, on the one hand, and presenting an attractive, inspirational vision, on the other.

The Value Triad can help us here. It may be possible to estimate or even to pinpoint the exact operational or economic impact (RGs or CRs) of a purchased product or service on the customer's processes. In complex B2B situations, this requires technical analysis. Should this be the case, much of this work should be done by staff in the supplier's "back office" by appropriate specialists such as management accountants, product managers, business analysts, or technology experts.

Often these details cannot readily be estimated sufficiently accurately by the supplier's people. In this case, the salesperson's role is to collect as much operational information as possible. This is part of the discovery process.

Some companies, for example, Xerox, Alstom Power, Akzo Nobel, and Michelin, to offer a few examples, have developed point-of-sale pricing tools that have, built into their architecture, all the variants in customer needs that are likely to appear in routine day-to-day selling activity. These models are designed to be easy and straightforward for salespeople to apply during customer meetings and can be very powerful in enabling sales staff to engage the customer, collect critical customer data, and instantly demonstrate economic impacts of different product and service configurations. The best data of all come from the customer.

In more complex cases (or in the case of very new technology), external experts may be needed to make the necessary assessments and even then may not be enough to encourage adopters to "cross the chasm."[3] Professionally sourced data or reports carry much more weight than those created by your own people. As far as the customer is concerned, "You would say that anyway, wouldn't you!"

However this assessment is carried out, it needs to be done with care, rigor, and a deep understanding of both the customer's value-adding processes and how your product or service fits into them. It is not a task that casually can be left to the salesperson.

Management should never permit sales staff to present a value-based price unless they have been given—and understand completely—a thorough briefing on the impact of the product or service on the customer's business.

Failure to justify fully the value-adding elements of the product or service proposition will lead to instant rejection of the total proposition.

In speaking to senior executives in companies that have implemented VBP, we identified failure to create believable and acceptable customer arguments as one of the major obstacles to effective implementation of VBP.

Quantifying the Value Triad elements as they apply in a given customer situation is crucial if you are determined to implement VBP successfully in your organization.

FOUR STEPS TO BUILD VALUE

What follows are four steps any sales organization can take to build value.

Understand Your Customer

You can never know too much about your customer. Every scrap of information you collect may have a profound impact on your understanding of the customer's business, context, strategy, or aspirations. Value diversity—Be aware of it! Everyone is different. Even in the same segment, each company is different. Value is different for every customer and even for the same customer under different circumstances. Therefore, to identify value properly, you first have to know and understand—really know and understand—your customers. You must learn everything you can about their RG, CR, and EC value drivers.

Know Your Differentiation

Make it your business to know—at a deep level—how and why you are different from your competitors in order to identify your competitive advantages and disadvantages. In virtually every buying decision, customers have choices. They will make their decision on what product or service to buy based on the perceived value to them of these competitive differentiators. In Chapter 2 we introduce a powerful yet intuitive method of representing your products' differentiation. The customer value line can offer real insights into how to develop business and pricing strategy and how to enhance the perceived significance of your products in the minds of customers.

Quantify the Differentiators

You need to be able to quantify the RG, CR, and EC differentiators in the customer's own financial terms or other metrics. This is probably one of the most difficult aspects of VBP and can present a real obstacle to its effective implementation. It is important that this is done correctly and from the customer's perspective—not from your own!

Communicate Your Differentiated Value

This task is crucial and enormously demanding, especially on your sales-people, who may need to relearn their trade completely. The differentiated message needs to be presented both compellingly and sensitively in such a manner as to persuade your customers that they need the value you offer—and that you are the right people to deliver it.

CHAPTER 2

Mapping Differentiated Value

There is no such thing as absolute value in this world. You can only estimate what a thing is worth to you.
— Charles Dudley Warner (1829–1900)

A s a young man, Harry spent many happy days walking among the Scottish moors and mountains. During one of those rambles, fog came down very suddenly, as it does in Scotland, and it became impossible to see the way ahead. He lost his bearings and became utterly and hopelessly lost. This is very dangerous in mountainous country. Fortunately, he had had the forethought to bring with him a compass and a map. After the initial panic, logical thought kicked back in again. With use of the map and compass, Harry could take sightings on landmarks once the fog lifted a little and came safely back down off the mountain. So it is in business. The value map is a great tool to help you to understand the competitive landscape. It can help you to identify where you are and where your competitors are. By using customer value as a "compass," you can plot a course toward where you want to go—new business opportunities and new profits and maybe even "blue oceans."

Value maps are excellent tools to help you to "visualize" markets. But they are only models of the business reality "out there." Nevertheless, armed with a properly constructed chart of the market, it becomes easy to share, interactively, ideas with colleagues, debate strategies, and even estimate timelines. We introduce the idea of value mapping in this chapter to help you to lift the fog! Value maps can help you to build reasonable and practical models of your own markets, help to craft options for pricing decisions, and enable you to make reasonable assessments of the impacts of alternative choices.

PERCEPTUAL MAPPING

Market researchers use perceptual mapping tools with market survey data in two and more dimensions (*multidimensional scaling*) to enable them to identify innovation opportunities or to generate other insights. Although the analyses can be quite complex, they rely in principle on comparing our performance scores with those of competitors across a range of attributes. As a simple example, in our courses and briefings, we present delegates with a simple exercise: "Select a brand of car and, without thinking about it too deeply, position it on this two-dimensional diagram." We ask them to exclude sports models, 4 × 4s, and sport-utility vehicles (SUVs) to ensure like-for-like comparisons.

Each delegate, in turn, comes up and places his chosen brand on the graph depending on where he *perceives* it to be positioned in terms of quality and price. This may not be quantitatively accurate in terms of positioning the brand based on actual performance characteristics or price—that is not the objective. In populating the diagram, people make a subjective judgment on what they know about, hear about, or experience from the brand they select. It is this subjective judgment we are trying to capture. This is a powerful determinant of subsequent buying behavior. Respective positioning of brands proposed by course delegates varies quite considerably across Europe, and the exercise is great fun to carry out. We have used this exercise hundreds of times, and Figure 2.1 illustrates typical responses.

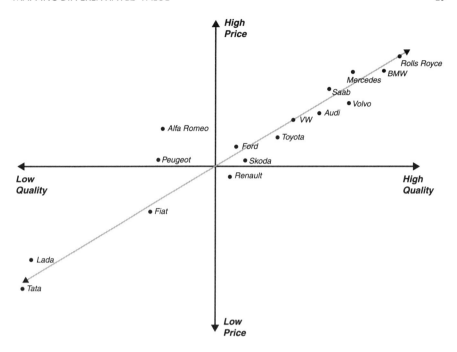

Figure 2.1   Perceptual map—sedans.

What does the diagram tell us? First, there appears to be a more or less linear relationship between price and quality. These concepts, admittedly, are very loose (we shall tighten them considerably a little later). In simple value-mapping thinking, any brand of sedan that falls on the line has equivalent customer value to any other brand falling on or close to the same line. This is a simple customer value map. On this basis, a Rolls-Royce has the equivalent value to a Ford, a Fiat, or a Lexus—assuming that they too fall on the line. This seems slightly counterintuitive because we often refer to a luxury car, such as a Rolls-Royce, as a high-value car and the Tata as a low-value car. This apparent ambiguity arises from the rather precise way in which we are using the term *value*. In reality, the Rolls-Royce is a car that delivers many attractive benefits to the user. Because of this, we expect to pay much more than average. It also follows from the value map that "we get what we pay for." Of course, if we get more than we pay for, this represents higher value; if we get less than we pay for, this represents poorer value.

Assuming that we could choose as a gift any car we wanted, we might choose a Rolls-Royce perhaps because this sends a message to others about "me" or quite simply because we like the car. We might soon realize that practical, mundane considerations such as ease of parking, fuel consumption, servicing and repairs, insurance, and so on may make the aspiration uneconomical. While, aspirationally, we still might yearn for the Rolls-Royce (or some other dream car), our pocketbooks do not. Unfortunately, in the real world, we do not often receive the gift of a Rolls-Royce or any other car. Therefore, we are compelled to buy. What we choose depends on our pocketbook, our life context, running costs, our list of priorities, and perhaps much further down the list for most of us, our aspirations.

SIMPLE VALUE MAP

Figure 2.2 presents a simple version of the value map. As in the perceptual map above, the axes are labeled *Price* and *Quality*. The round black dots represent products competing for share of a specific, well-defined market segment. Although we have shown fairly close alignment between the products and the line running through the map (which we call the *customer value line* or CVL), this need not be the case. In practice, you should expect to see a fair degree of variation. The degree of variation may be less in more mature markets that have had time to settle down; in less mature markets, where the correlation between price and quality is still evolving, one might expect to see more variability.

The second thing to notice is that as we have drawn the map, products are clustered around the bottom, in the middle, and at the top, representing the bottom end of the market, the midmarket, and the top end of the market, respectively. The "clouds" around each group indicate relative market sizes. Top-end market subsegments typically will be relatively small and consist of customers with a taste for quality or, in business-to-business (B2B) situations, a need for high or unusual performance for which they are prepared to pay a sizable premium. Bottom-end customers, in contrast, will be much less choosey about performance and perhaps more sensitive to price, trading off performance for low cost or having requirements that can be met adequately

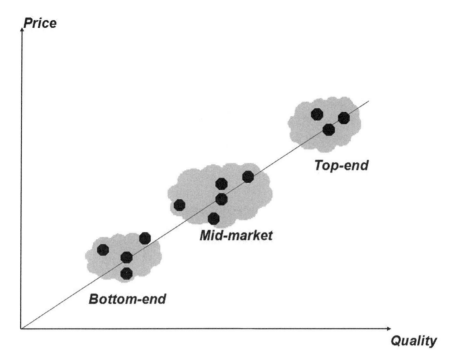

Figure 2.2   Simple value map.

by a low-end product. This group, too, will be relatively small in size under normal conditions. Midmarket customers exhibit a variety of price-quality combinations, with performance expectations varying quite considerably. In most markets, the midmarket represents the greatest volume and, not surprisingly, attracts the largest number of suppliers and offers.

If we wish to apply this kind of approach in analyzing the positioning of our products, we must be careful about how we define the segments we target. For example, in the car brand exercise earlier, we were careful to say "sedans on sale in Europe." We did not say 4 × 4s or sports cars because these appeal to quite different customer segments with quite different product and service performance preferences. Inclusion of brands such as Bugatti, Porsche, and Hummer would lead to completely incorrect analyses and dangerously misleading results. A laptop computer can be used by financial analysts, gamers, and engineers. Each segment has different expectations from the machine they use, and different machines will meet those needs differently. What may appear hopelessly overpriced, for instance, for a gamer may be ideal for an engineer and represent superb value for money.

Although inherently a simple idea, the value map concept can help us to develop strategic responses to competitive actions and also to reposition poorly performing products. A number of consultancy organizations have developed this idea more fully to illuminate product management, strategic marketing, competitive selling, and value-based pricing decisions.

POOR CUSTOMER VALUE

Let's now examine the scenario illustrated in Figure 2.3.

The line that runs through A, B, and C and represents average value for this industry is the *customer value line* (CVL). Any product that sits on this line has equivalent value on the somewhat limited dimensions of price and quality, even though the price and quality may be quite different. D_1, which purports to address this target segment, lies *above* the line and represents poor value for the customer. It is priced at P_2 but is delivering only a level of quality equal to Q_1. From the CVL, we

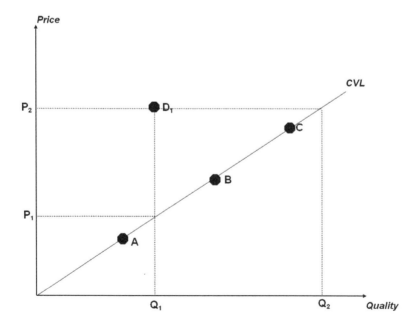

Figure 2.3   Poor customer value.

would expect to pay P_1, which is significantly less than P_2. In effect, sellers of product D_1 are perceived to be overpricing their product and potentially will reap the rewards of poor sales and brand damage. If the sellers of D_1 are to remedy the situation, they must move the product quality to the right or reduce the price or some combination of each. Remember that we are still talking about *perceptions*, so to remedy the situation, we need to create a *perception* of better quality or a *perception* of lower price or both. This is an important principle in pricing work. Every significant price adjustment must be accompanied by a marketing communication of some kind.

GOOD CUSTOMER VALUE

Now let's consider a different scenario. In this scenario, product D_2 is positioned *below* the CVL. In order to purchase D_2, customers need to pay P_1 and at this price would expect to have quality of Q_1. The *perceived* quality of D_2, though, is higher than expected at Q_2. The buyer, in effect, is gaining a significantly better deal than buyers of A, B, or C and, of course, very much better than buyers of D_1. Sellers of D_2 accordingly probably will gain greater market share than direct competitors in the vicinity—B or C. Sales of A probably will remain largely unaffected, at least in the short term. Another way of looking at this is to realize that the price of D_2 is significantly lower than we might expect. The value line suggests that the higher price P_2 should apply.

D_2's positioning is in fact quite aggressive and may not be sustainable unless its suppliers are attempting to leverage a competitive advantage, such as protected and unique intellectual property, and are able to do so for a significant period. Alternatively, D_2 simply may appear to be too good to be true, and if D_2 is performing a mission-critical task, customers may distrust the innovation until others in the market adopt and "beta test" the innovation. Positioning on or even slightly above the CVL may be both a more believable strategy and less likely to provoke aggressive competitor response (Figure 2.4).

B's and C's options at first sight may seem limited. Confronted with this challenge, a typical reflex action is to reduce price to the level of D_2. The trouble with this strategy is that, in a very competitive market in particular, this will erode profits, compelling cost reductions to restore

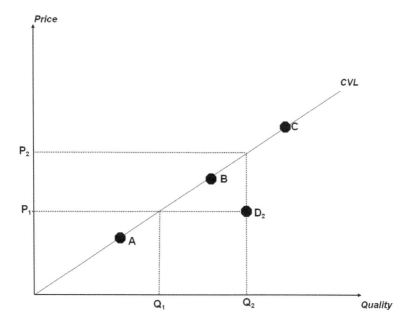

Figure 2.4 Good customer value.

margins. These cost reductions potentially could destroy any residual competitive advantage.

A price reduction is easy to do. Pushing price back up again at a later date is much more difficult. We also should not forget the impact that a price reduction might have on brand perceptions. Suppliers of *B* in some cases may lose share. Indeed, there may be a case for offering additional inducements to customers to continue to use this product. The best approach, however, is to determine how the product is perceived in terms of customer decision drivers and to redefine the value proposition in line with those drivers.

One option might be to take out unnecessary functionality and to repackage the product as a "fighter brand" to retain customers who otherwise might migrate to *A* or D_2. If we are fortunate enough to have our own versions of *A* and D_2 in our portfolio, we should seek to promote them vigorously to retain customers we otherwise might lose.

There is another way—*B* and *C* can focus on the key (tangible and intangible) elements of the offer and enhance them. These enhancements must be communicated to the market. The question is, "What enhancements are most likely to restore competitive equilibrium?"

To do this, we need to look rather more closely at the simple value map and refine it in a way that enables us to identify and model strategic options.

BUILDING THE CUSTOMER VALUE LINE

We started off this chapter by describing a perceptual map in which we used the axes of *Price* and *Quality* and positioned a variety of sedans in the diagram. Price and quality, however, are not really the best labels for this chart. Price is not the sole economic determinant of purchase unless we are competing in markets where every product is genuinely identical to every other product. Thus we need to look more closely at what is meant by *price* and *quality*.

Price is a surrogate for a range of economic factors that include, for example, invoiced price, discount, payment terms, running costs (e.g., fuel, insurance, and registration), installation, training, recruitment, residual value, and so on. This list is quite extensive. In any particular situation, only a subset of these factors will be really important—even for the same product.

Quality has a precise meaning to engineers—the degree to which a particular product or process conforms to specification. Our use of the term thus far has been rather loose. If economics is one part of the buying process, then how the product performs in the task for which it was "hired" is the other part. Quality can be recast into the package of benefits and advantages the customer obtains through procurement and use of a product or service. In B2B markets, these benefits and advantages become drivers of the purchasing decision process. Professional buyers will examine alternative suppliers in terms of these drivers. The drivers can be tangible and intangible. For instance, tangibles might include compliance with quality or regulatory standards, emissions levels, uptime, maintenance intervals, and so on. Intangibles might include reduction of hassle, peace of mind, avoidance of psychological risk, aesthetics, brand value, comfort, safety, and so on. The list of intangibles is even more extensive than that of the tangibles.[1]

For the economic factors, we use the term *total cost of ownership* (TCO). For the benefit factors, we use the term *total customer benefits* (TCBs). For a given market, the elements of TCO and their relative weightings may be more or less constant in a given instant of time. Similarly, the elements of TCBs and their weighting will be pretty constant during the same period. The CVL is a snapshot of the status of a given market and the expectations of members of this market. This picture can and will change rapidly.

Returning to the familiar CVL model, we can use our new thinking on TCO and TCBs to help us to create realistic strategies for B and C in dealing with the challenge posed by D_2 (Figure 2.5). If D_2 represents a significant change in value for money through breakthrough product design or clever technology, it creates a new CVL that will lead in time to value migration as competitors seek to participate in the new opportunities for growth presented by the change (e.g., Dyson, iPhone, Walkman, etc.). If D_2 is based on disruptive technology, it typically will redefine existing market parameters and lead to new opportunities for growth.[2]

This new CVL is now the target, and existing approaches become immediately obsolescent or even obsolete depending on the pace and intensity of adoption of the novel product. Such a change may happen

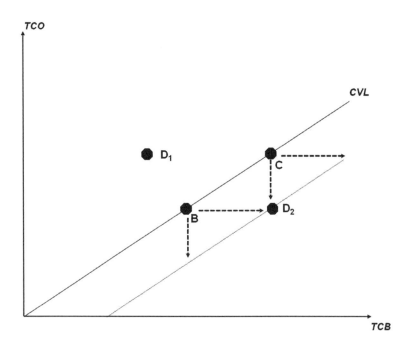

Figure 2.5 Options for action.

slowly over time, giving incumbents time to change (assuming that they see the threat and are willing to move to neutralize it), or very quickly. If D_2's positioning is opportunistic, that is, offering a very low bargain-basement price, this could signal the start of a price war.

In the case of D_1, the selling company must find a way back onto the CVL. There are two extreme options—either reduce TCO (or at least change the perception of TCO) or change TCBs by selecting and strengthening one or more intangibles or, and perhaps easier, change the way in which buyers perceive the benefits package. This might buy the company time to develop necessary competitive technology. In practice, it should be possible to manipulate both sets of parameters.

While price reduction may be an option, it is not the only one. Manipulation of payment terms, making the investment easier to manage (e.g., through leasing deals and case studies demonstrating better cost in use through reduced downtime or other efficiencies), and other approaches are also available. Price reduction is a last-resort option because of the effect on brand and profit. Similarly, massaging the TCB package may render the offer more attractive—perhaps even as attractive as D_2. The challenge for TCBs is that we may find ourselves making adjustments to the offer without knowing what matters to customers. Furthermore, even though we have made the adjustment, the customer may not acknowledge or recognize it. This is a marketing communications and selling challenge.

CVL IN RECESSION

During "normal" conditions such as those experienced during the 1990s and early 2000s, the volume of customers in a given market will peak against the most popular price. A relatively small, discerning group of customers at the top end will continue to be willing to pay premium prices for C. The majority of the market, however, is shared by suppliers of B, which is midrange on price and represents, in specification terms, an acceptable performance—albeit without the sophistications of C. Product A is the bargain-basement offer that appeals to the limited budgets and limited expectations of its clientele, who do not need or want the higher performance levels of B or C.

When customers are economically challenged, they review the products and services on which they spend their money (Figure 2.6). They reconsider their needs and seek alternative approaches or perhaps even decide to do without. *C*, and perhaps *B* also, will be perceived as too expensive. In the new circumstances, *A* will seem about right. *A* emerges as a better deal for customers and will gain share at the expense of *B* and *C*. Product *C* will experience some diminution of demand. This demand is unlikely to disappear entirely—there will always be customers willing to pay top dollar even in a recession. *B*, of course, will gain share at *C*'s expense. Some authorities suggest that the slope of the CVL itself is changed, with *A* emerging below the line and thus a very attractive deal for buyers.[3]

Product *A* therefore is highly likely to enjoy significant increases in demand as customers, affected by recessionary conditions, seek to fulfill their more modest requirements at a lesser cost. Much of this behavior is evident in consumer markets such as hotels, travel, and mobile phones, where performance expectations are "titrated" against price by more frugal consumers.

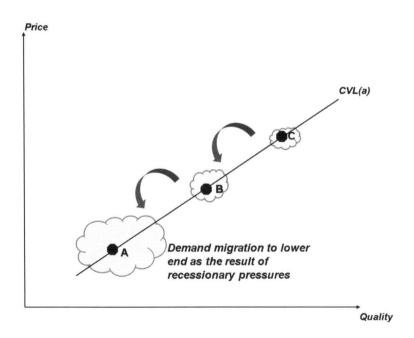

Figure 2.6   Impact of recession.

In B2C markets, for example, customers with less discretionary disposable income are abandoning foreign holidays for vacations at home, providing a welcome but unexpected boost to the home vacation market.[4] Cash-strapped couples are cutting back on meals out, choosing instead "to eat out at home." Various supermarket chains have responded quickly and cleverly to this trend and have assembled bundles for two, complete with appetizer, main course, dessert, and a bottle of good wine, all for £10.[5]

The situation in B2B markets can be expected to be analogous. The typical B2B customer does not have the flexibility of the consumer. Business processes are configured on the basis of specific product and material performances that will be difficult to trade down. The only remaining options, therefore, are intensified pressure on suppliers' prices or sourcing from a low-cost supplier, possibly offshore, with concomitant risk. As a consequence, suppliers come under increased pressure to drop prices without compromising quality delivered. Managers of B2B businesses across a wide range of sectors have confirmed this to us during our pricing training events.

IMPORTANT CAVEATS FOR VALUE-MAPPING WORK

The value map is a very useful tool. Its particular usefulness is in enabling us to present visually how our products compare in price and performance with those of competitors. With some added sophistication,[6] it also can help us to make both qualitative and quantitative judgments about product or service strategy and price changes.

Data Compression

Anyone who has tried to create a summary of comparative specifications, features, and price options for competitive products offered to a given market will recognize that anything other than a large, comprehensive spreadsheet cannot do justice to the diversity and complexity of the products on offer. To create a map, we must trade off complexity for simplicity, and this means creating subsets of attributes that we think are important. Inevitably, important data will be lost, and what is lost may well be very important in a purchasing decision.[7] Detailed and careful customer research is crucial in identifying the right attributes and allocating their correct weightings.

Number of Attributes

The smaller the number of attributes we can identify that are really important, the more relevant our map will be. If, for instance, a particular product has 50 attributes, and 30 of these are important, then a value-mapping approach is very difficult—the weighting of any one attribute will be tiny. However, if the set of attributes is much smaller, and it is possible to recognize, say, five to ten attributes as critical factors, then the weighting process will yield much more meaningful results.

Segmentation

As we commented earlier in this chapter, a value map can be valid only if it is applied to a clearly defined customer segment. An individual product or service can have fairly catholic appeal across a whole market, but only specific facets will be relevant to any given segment. If we are clever enough to create a proposition with broad multisegment appeal, this can be achieved only if certain aspects of the proposition are so compelling that buyers are willing to pay for functionality they neither need nor want in order to acquire the facets that *do* matter.

Differentiated Value

Every product for which there is customer demand has value. The issue is, What kind of value? If the value merely is that the product performs generically—its *commodity* value; according to some authorities,[8] it is neither better nor worse in common performance characteristics than any other product addressing the same market segment—then there is little differential benefit, and the product will attract minimal market share. If, however, the value is differentiated—that is, it performs better than other products in its class in attributes that *are* relevant to the customer—then it will achieve greater market share and a higher price. In creating a value map, therefore, we need to identify, first, that the product *does* actually perform adequately on a generic basis. If it does, these attributes can be taken for granted and eliminated from the map. This will leave the attributes that offer differentiated value. These are the ones on which a map should focus—the kernel of differential advantage to its supplier.

Emotional Contribution

The CVL covers only the tangible elements of a customer's decision making. One key element of the Value Triad—emotional contribution (EC)—is missing. Various figures have been passed around as to the relative importance of EC in decision making—all the way from 80 percent to zero. Whereas in a business context efforts are frequently made to reduce subjectivity, as long as people buy from people, the EC factor will remain. A perfect example of emotion overriding functional reasoning is provided by Apple. A lot of Apple's appeal is in its design—an emotional consideration. This isn't to say that Apple doesn't deliver functionally. Of course it does. But there are many other suppliers moving into Apple's space that provide all the functionality and in some cases more (e.g., Samsung, HTC, LG, Sony Ericsson, etc.), often at significantly lower prices. Nevertheless, Apple's reputation for innovation, design, and desirability still allows it to charge premium prices for its products.

Case Study

Let's look at how the CVL model can be applied in the U.K. multifunction office product (MFP) market (which includes high-capacity copiers for corporate offices). This market is exclusively B2B. Major suppliers in this market include international companies such as Xerox, Minolta, Kyocera, Ricoh, Sharp, and Canon. These are diversified companies with sophisticated technology, well-organized and well-developed distribution networks, and carefully selected channel partners. Technology innovation is a core competence that in large part dictates each company's ability to create products with attributes attractive to

(Continued)

channel partners and end users. When one company innovates, others follow suit very rapidly. Pursuit of market share is fierce.

Figure 2.7 shows typical routes to three main macro segments—public sector and government, large corporate and commercial, and small corporate and small/medium-sized businesses (SMB). Systems integrators are another specialist route to market. Sector 1 end users generally are served either directly by the manufacturer, a large distributor with an exclusive arrangement, or independents with nonexclusive agreements. There is little that manufacturers can do to control market prices because these are recommended rather than mandatory. An end user may choose to go through a major independent or a systems integrator to access the seller's abilities to assemble bundled solutions (perhaps using components from other suppliers). In general, cost-effective supply contracts are in place for sector 1 end users, who usually procure through a tender and submission process. In this sector, value is equated to overall solution cost, and differential performance is less important than cost.

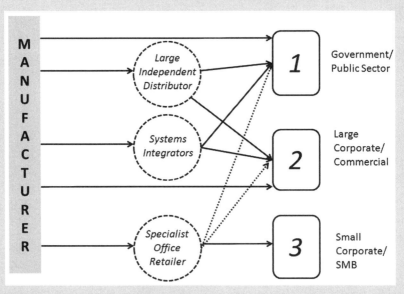

Figure 2.7   Market map: U.K. photocopiers.

Price comparisons down to component, consumable, and support levels become very important in product/solution selection.

Price comparisons can be extremely detailed, with component costs significant to 0.0001 cent.

Sector 2 end users have a very similar route of supply. While price is important, other factors also come into play, such as suppliers' abilities to construct very specific value-adding packages that meet the diverse needs of different businesses. The compelling argument in this sector is around product and solution efficiency. Technology, market insight, close cooperation, and sound competitor intelligence are required to succeed in this sector. Customers in both sector 1 and sector 2 purchase in high volume and may have very complex requirements demanding broad technical specification and extensive sales and technical support.

System integrators assemble components from multiple manufacturers and package them to meet their clients' specifications. These can be very big companies with in-depth expertise in hardware and software management, facilities management, and solution engineering.

Sector 3 end users' needs generally are much simpler and print volumes are very much smaller than those of sector 1 and 2 customers. There are many more of these. SMBs are much smaller (and even may be tiny) local businesses whose needs can be handled by smaller, less sophisticated suppliers and simpler (possibly even desktop) equipment.

In this short case study, we look at sector 1 issues in which suppliers market to large corporate customers directly or through partners.

Commercial Challenges for the Manufacturer-Dealer Partnership
The overriding imperative for dealers is profit maximization. This translates into being able to offer really competitive solutions that are easy to sell at a premium price. Differentiation drives product competitiveness and is a mix of a number of technical, design, and support elements. Assembling a viable solution for a portfolio of demanding corporate customers necessitates deep understanding of their diverse needs and applications. Even for a large dealer, this is a challenge that can be met only through strategic partnership with the supplier. A compelling customer proposition depends crucially on the manufacturer-dealer partnership's ability to deliver the correct combination of key factors in a cost-effective "wrapper."

(Continued)

From the customer's perspective, a trouble-free solution with predictable costs and return on investment (ROI) over the copier's life traditionally has been the most important driving factor, and TCO, accordingly, is examined very closely. However, there is increasing interest in—and demand for—environmentally friendly, energy-efficient products and solutions. Companies that are able to demonstrate a commitment to environmental protection through sustainable manufacturing strategies, product policies, and green marketing are likely to gain share from non–environmentally aligned competitors. The third factor in the mix is the degree to which a collection of solution elements can be assembled into a customized approach to meeting the customer's specific needs. This is a very complex and technical matter that demands a careful audit of the customer's print needs, processes, and associated energy costs. Much depends on the seller's ability to understand deeply the customer's business, how print fits into this, and where the pain and pleasure points lie in the value-adding chain. The better these needs are known, understood, and measured, the more likely it will be that the range of options assembled will be correct. Unless these needs are communicated effectively from a customer value perspective, though, it is likely that an inferior offer will succeed if the TCO is lower. Ultimately, the supplier that presents the best combination of TCO, solution effectiveness, and environmental impact is the one that will consistently gain traction in the market.

Using data from the Buyer's Lab Web site, we can construct a CVL for a segment with relatively unsophisticated copier needs using reasonable weightings for each of the identified attributes. Even with a small subset of comparative data, the weightings are quite small. We assume a four-year scenario, a fairly typical contract duration in this industry. We are also assuming a scenario of 15,000 copies per day over a four-year period, approximating to 15 million copies. Toner and parts replacement are included in the consumables costs. Table 2.1 shows the attributes selected for Figure 2.8.

Table 2.1 Importance Scoring of Selected Attributes—Copier Products

Selected Attributes	A	B	C	D	E	F	Weight
Digital	10	10	10	10	10	10	0.08
Quality of print color	10	10	10	10	10	10	0.08
Toner yields	8	8	10	8	8	8	0.06
First copy time	10	9	6	10	7	8	0.08
Maximum paper capacity	6	9	10	8	7	5	0.09
Service response time	10	10	10	10	10	10	0.10
Duplex	10	10	10	10	10	10	0.10
Green product design	10	7	6	5	6	8	0.08
Technical solutions service	8	8	5	4	5	6	0.08
Multiplatform performance	10	10	10	10	10	10	0.06
Overall energy efficiency	10	0	0	0	0	9	0.08
Speed	10	10	10	10	10	10	0.11
TCB score	9.36	8.51	8.16	8.02	7.85	8.71	
Cost elements							
Capital cost	20,940	16,530	17,250	17,819	15,050	15,799	
Consumables	285,000	255,500	262,000	270,000	245,500	277,500	
TCO Score	305,940	272,030	279,250	287,819	260,550	293,299	

In Table 2.1 we have identified a number of attributes that are relevant in the selection of a copier product capable of providing color and black-and-white output in both A4 and A3 formats at 50 prints per minute. There are many, many more attributes to choose from, and a buyer probably will examine a range of attributes that are relevant to her specific requirements. Even with a very restricted number of attributes, individual weightings are quite small, and there is a tendency for the numbers to be close to one another.

(Continued)

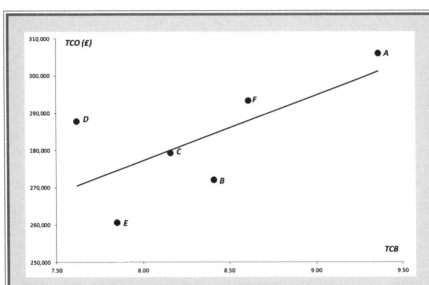

Figure 2.8   Customer value line: large list of attributes.

The spread of points around the CVL is pretty typical of a mature industry, as is the TCB spread, which is small, only a matter of about 2 points (7.5 to 9.5) separating A and D. In a "younger" market, the spread will be much wider. As a market grows older, products become more and more homogeneous, and prices converge. Unless participants take steps to avoid it, the result will be a tight cluster of competitive products that are more or less the same in performance and more or less the same in price.

The larger the number of attributes, the smaller the individual weightings are likely to become. In a market in which there is fierce competition and rapid technological catch-up, the reality is that there is little to choose between offers, at least at a specification level. For the seller, deciding what to emphasize and what to ignore or downplay becomes virtually impossible. Continued competitive focus on these factors increases the number of choices available to the customer (without necessarily simplifying her selection) but also increases the manufacturer's development costs. It also creates an expectation of ever more sophisticated equipment (well beyond most users' ability to utilize fully). The customer's decision will default to brand, previous experience, or some other factor because she cannot discriminate on technical features alone. Clever manufacturers will take every opportunity to lock customers in, either by tailored packages or even replacement of part of the customer's machine "fleet" at advantageous terms.

Instead of obsession with technical features, companies in this industry need to act rather more cleverly. Today there are more than 250 options for a relatively routine piece of equipment. Technology continues to drive product proliferation.

The reality now is that "on the edge" performance is not about how many features a product has. It is about how that equipment can add value to the mission-critical functions of a company around reprographics or, better still, around its overall business strategy. Manufacturers need to think more deeply about the real value they are delivering to their customers. Certain key functions are taken as ready for any copier worth its money. There is no point in promoting these—everyone has them. Instead, we need to look at the package that we can assemble that meets the customer's identified strategic needs in a manner that no competitor can match and that, ideally, costs us very little. Therefore, we need to construct a CVL based on the differentiating elements of a solution. And it needs to be a *solution*—not merely a randomly assembled package of bits that the marketer calls a solution. The clever part of this is to be able to see beyond the huge parts list, sold and priced on an individual basis, to a much bigger picture where a selection of these parts is transformed, collectively, into a vital element of a solution.

Where a number of suppliers can meet a range of basic customer requirements, these no longer merit comparison one with another. They become the "table stakes" that everyone delivers to the same basic standard. The search is for other differentiators that the customer will find really valuable from her point of view. The CVL is a useful tool to assist in this search and to assess the relative importance of these differentiators. This calls for a level of salesmanship or a sales process that has an outstanding discovery process at its heart. We call this *value-based selling.*

(Continued)

We constructed this case study to demonstrate the method of assembling a data set and the CVL. The underpinning thinking is exactly in line with the Value Triad—there are elements of all three Value Triad elements in the case. For your industry, you should be able, with the correct data, to assemble exactly the same analysis for yourself and use this analysis to improve your business's overall performance.

CHAPTER 3

Cost-Based Approaches

I have never known a concern to make a decided success that did not do good, honest work, and even in these days of fiercest competition, when everything would seem to be a matter of price, there lies still at the root of great business success the very much more important factor of quality.
—Andrew Carnegie (25 November 1835–11 August 1919)

At its simplest, cost-based pricing is based on our assessment of the total costs we incur in manufacturing a product or delivering a service. This method is the most popular method of pricing in use today, and in our experience is the default pricing methodology adopted by most companies. It is usually applied in conjunction with competition-based pricing[1,2,3]. We identify and add up all the unit fixed and variable costs and then add a percentage to this figure (*markup*), which then becomes the price. Different companies use different formulas for this calculation, including typically

- Percentage on direct labor
- Rate per labor hour

- Rate per unit of product
- Percentage on prime cost (i.e., direct materials plus direct labor plus direct expenses)
- Rate per machine hour
- Separate rates applied to various elements of the costs

How these costs are allocated can have a profound impact on the apparent profitability of different members of the product portfolio. This is shown in Table 3.1.

Figure 3.1 is a general model of the cost-based pricing approach. Of course, the calculations and analyses lying behind this model can be incredibly complex and detailed but ultimately the price building approach is relatively straightforward.

Put simply:

$$Price = variable\ cost\ per\ unit + fixed\ cost\ per\ unit + planned\ profit\ element$$

Planned profit simply may be a markup set by custom and practice, or as a fixed target percentage of the final price, or simply as a target cash figure that must be achieved in each transaction.

Table 3.1 Consequences of Rigidly Applied Cost-Based Pricing

	Year 1	Year 2a	Year 2b
Expected sales units	100,000	75,000	75,000
Total factory fixed cost	200,000	200,000	170,000
Direct costs per unit	2.00	2.00	1.70
Fixed costs per unit	2.00	2.67	2.27
Full cost	4.00	4.67	3.97
Markup, %	10.00	10.00	10.00
Markup value	0.40	0.47	0.40
FCRP	4.40	5.13	4.36

Note: In case (Year) 2a, FCRP leads to serious overpricing. In case (Year) 2b, FCRP leads to serious underpricing.

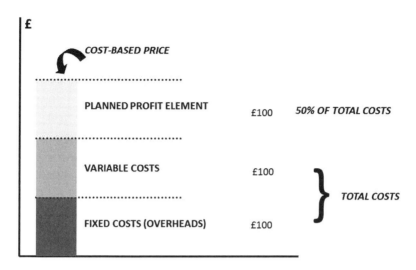

Figure 3.1 Cost-based pricing process.

The assumption is that since we have considered all the costs, we have guaranteed that the product or service will be profitable. Because the accounting department has full details of the costs of every element of the product and has the necessary skills and resources to manipulate these figures, the responsibility for price setting in a cost-based model often ends up with accounting. This practice tends to divorce price policy from the value proposition and from the customer. It adds a layer of decision making—and hence delay—to price negotiations.

Calculating a realistic price that will yield the planned and hoped-for profit depends on achieving or exceeding projected volumes within the cost envelope identified. If the unit volume sold is less than that projected, we would be required to spread our costs over a smaller number of units and apply the same percentage markup as before. This makes no sense whatsoever if the reason for poor sales is high price. Achieving the target price/volume mix is essential if the rest of the logic is to fall into place. Unfortunately, the market does not always cooperate with us, and we often find ourselves having to cut our prices to make the planned volume, which, of course, invalidates the strategy. This is one of the biggest problems with cost-based pricing.

A major attraction of cost-based pricing is its simplicity. It is conceptually and arithmetically an easy process. This simplicity perhaps goes some way toward explaining why it is such a prevalent—and popular—

pricing method. The problem is that this simplicity conceals several real problems that lie within the assumptions made in the calculations. In addition, we have come across several Web sites advising business managers that cost-based pricing guarantees profit success. This is dangerously misleading and overly simplistic. We explore these assumptions a little later in this chapter.

COMMON VARIANTS OF COST-BASED PRICING

What follows are descriptions of some of the more popular cost-based approaches in use today. They are used widely primarily because they are relatively easy to apply and work adequately in relatively simple pricing situations. They indeed may be the only options that do work in a commoditized market. Some methods are better than others. Whatever cost-based pricing method we adopt may be fundamentally flawed if it fails to take into account customer demand (and how this varies with price), knowledge of a particular product's costs and selling situation, and, of course, value delivery to the customer.[4]

We will look at the main criticisms of cost-based pricing a little later in this chapter.

Full Cost Recovery Pricing (FCRP)

Full cost recovery means recovering the full costs of a product or service. In addition to the costs directly associated with the product, such as labor, materials, energy, direct services, and so on, full cost recovery also will seek to estimate costs incurred elsewhere in the organization attributable to the creation, production, and delivery of the product. Finance, human resources, management, and information technology (IT) systems are all part of the chargeable overheads and must be recovered. The full cost of any product therefore includes an element of every overhead employed, allocated on a comprehensive, robust, and defensible basis. As we shall see a little later, this is fraught with difficulties. Nevertheless, this form of pricing is still very popular.

Imagine a manufacturing company launching a new product (Table 3.1). At market entry, the fixed and variable costs together give a full cost recovery per unit of $4.00. Applying a 10 percent margin, the norm in this particular market, gives a full cost recovery price of $4.40. Managers estimate demand at this price of 100,000 units for the full year.

At the end of the year, actual sales unit volume was 75,000—75 percent of what was budgeted. Fixed and variable costs have not changed, and recalculation, using 75,000 for the forthcoming period, leads to a full cost recovery price of $5.14—17 percent more than last year. If a price of $4.40 was not acceptable last year, $5.14 certainly will not be possible in the coming period. In this case, full cost recovery pricing leads to an unrealistically high price.

On the other hand, imagine that during year 1 the company had invested in new production technology, reducing variable costs by 15 percent per unit, and had reduced overhead costs by $30,000. Recalculation of the full cost recovery price would yield a price for year 2 of $4.37. In this case, FCRP, if applied rigorously, would lead to a price reduction of around 1 percent. In other words, efforts to reduce costs would be rewarded by a smaller margin. In this case, the company's efforts to reduce costs have enabled a small price reduction and no profit return for the effort of reducing costs. Strenuous cost reductions have enabled the company to go backwards. The company still might win in a competitive, price-sensitive market by gaining some market share at the slightly lower price.

Target ROI Pricing

In *target ROI pricing*, we attempt to build in recovery of the investment costs over a period of several years. The calculation uses as input fixed and variable costs and the figure, established by company policy, of an acceptable minimum return on investment (ROI). This may be related to the costs of borrowing or return from lending. The intention would be to calculate the minimum number of units and the associated sales price per unit required to achieve recovery within the specified time period. If there is serious competition or a lot of technical innovation, this will cause a reduction of the expected product life and may challenge the viability of the product. Managers therefore need to be confident of the robustness of their intellectual property protection, technical superiority, or other differentiator to be sure of an acceptable income stream to achieve payback. If the product *does* offer demonstrable performance advantages, we should instead consider value basing the price rather than using a cost-based method such as target ROI.

Simple markup pricing tackles the short-run return on trading through short-term profit but does little to recoup longer-run investment costs. Many companies establish price policies that seek to recover development and other investment costs.

The company establishes price levels in order to generate a target ROI. The time scale taken is the shortest anticipated product life. Sales unit levels are estimated and prices set at a level to return the target ROI. ROI pricing attempts to link the target margin to the capital employed and to set a price that includes a return on capital as well as to recoup the initial capital invested.

This is a rather more rational approach than merely deciding on and applying a "fair" markup because it links directly into the company's investment policy objectives. There are a number of assumptions lying behind this method, any one of which can invalidate the results. Although the target contribution is prescribed by the upfront investment costs and the company's expected return on this investment, it may be too high for the market to bear, and the pressure then will be either to relax the expected return, to write off part or all of the investment, to cut variable costs per unit (perhaps compromising product quality and acceptance), or to spread fixed costs differently. This method assumes that the company will have a clear "playing field" with no or minimal competition during the planned product life. In the intensely competitive conditions that many businesses are facing, this is obviously unrealistic. Competitor entry at an early stage in particular will lead to the company "sliding down" the price. The temptation here is to consider the investment costs as sunk and remove them from the price calculation. Such a strategy will fail to recoup the upfront development and other costs, which will need to be recovered elsewhere. New or disruptive technology might render the product obsolete at any point in its planned life cycle—a problem shared with all pricing methodologies. Target ROI pricing is a cost-based pricing method and hence suffers from the same drawbacks as simple markup or FCRP.

Contribution-Based Pricing

Contribution-based pricing is based on maximizing the contribution per unit of a single product or service. *Contribution* is the difference between the price of a product and the total variable costs of one unit of that product. Variable costs are assumed to be constant per unit (but total variable costs obviously will increase with output). The total contribution to profit from all of a company's products and services less the company's fixed costs equals the firm's operating income. Using a contribution approach, it is possible in theory not only to achieve the company's budgeted total contribution but also to adjust the contribution of each individual product to take account of market conditions.

The key issue with contribution-based pricing is how we identify and allocate overheads. We usually have a number of options, but frustratingly, what we might discover is that under one scenario, one product shows a healthy profit but others do not. So how do we realistically allocate overheads to show the "true" situation? This allocation can have profound implications on the apparent profitability of given products and lead us to make wrong—perhaps dangerously wrong—decisions. In the process, much management stress and conflict are created. The underlying reality is unchanged in each of these alternatives.

Example

A small company manufactures three different products—platinum, gold, and silver. The management accountant has forecast costs for each product at planned budget sales level. To keep the calculations simple, we assume that each product requires separate manufacturing locations within the small factory. The challenge is to calculate the profitability of each product. Table 3.2 shows how this is done:

(Continued)

Table 3.2   Calculating the Profitability of a Company's Products

US $000				
Product	Platinum	Gold	Silver	Total
Sales	150	500	650	1300
Materials	40	140	180	360
Labor	30	150	100	280
Other direct costs	40	30	150	220
Total direct costs	110	320	430	860
Area allocated to product (ft^2)	800	1700	7500	10000
Contributions	**40**	**180**	**220**	**440**
Total indirect costs/overheads				360
Operating profit/(loss)				80
Scenario 1				
Indirect costs allocated in proportion to total direct costs				
Contributions	40.0	180.0	220.0	440.0
Indirect costs	46.0	134.0	180.0	360.0
Operating profit/(loss)	−6.0	46.0	40.0	80.0
Scenario 2				
Indirect costs allocated in proportion to total labor costs				
Contributions	40.0	180.0	220.0	440.0
Indirect costs	38.6	192.9	128.6	360.0
Operating profit/(loss)	1.4	−12.9	91.4	80.0
Scenario 3				
Indirect costs allocated in proportion to factory floor area				
Contributions	40.0	180.0	220.0	440.0
Indirect costs	28.8	61.2	270.0	360.0
Operating profit/(loss)	11.2	118.8	−50.0	80.0

In the preceding example, we might be tempted to stop producing one of the loss-making products. Whichever one we select will
be the wrong choice depending on the overhead allocation scheme.
The company at present is profitable (although not spectacularly so)
at 6.2 percent net margin on sales. Not unsurprisingly, management
wants to try to increase this and expand production of one of the more
profitable lines perhaps by releasing some floor area. If, in reality, we
elected to stop producing one product—let's say silver (because based
on scenario 3, it is making a loss of nearly 8 percent)—paradoxically
the profitability of the whole company would drop, in this case quite
dramatically (to a loss of nearly $250,000), because the relatively high
volume of sales is absorbing more overhead, which now needs to be
recovered by the remaining product lines.

Direct (Variable) Cost or Marginal Cost Pricing

At the breakeven point, the total revenue received by a firm from sales
of a given product exactly covers the cumulative total of fixed and variable costs. At this point, the company's total fixed costs for the whole
of the trading period are covered. Moving forward assuming that the
product has been costed correctly, demand continues as predicted,
and no other unexpected changes take place, every sale will be profitable. This provides management with the opportunity to price *on the
margin*, that is, to ignore the fixed-cost element of the product and use
only the marginal variable cost as the basis for pricing. Marginal cost is
the cost to the company of producing one extra unit of output. For as
long as input variable costs are controlled within budget, the marginal
cost will remain constant, at least in the short run, assuming that there
is no investment required to expand capacity. This enables companies
to offer products at a lower price (thus exploiting any inherent price
elasticities of demand), to stimulate demand across the whole market,
or to initiate local price-reduction tactics in areas where demand for
their products is weak.

Companies with high market share need to be particularly cautious
if contemplating this strategy because they may be perceived to be
exploiting a dominant position. Obviously, this approach should be
considered only once the fixed costs for the year have been covered.

If the company relies on this method, fixed costs will not be covered, and a lower than expected contribution will result.

MAJOR ASSUMPTIONS IN COST-BASED PRICING

There are many assumptions regarding cost-based pricing that should be reviewed.

Assumption 1

Accurate and reliable costs can be collected.

We assume that the cost data are factual and not subject to challenge or to change. We also assume that we know which cost data to collect. In reality, even if we have identified the relevant costs, the actual purchase cost per unit may change depending on volume purchased. Furthermore, if purchase costs are linked to intrinsically volatile producer prices, such as petrochemicals, or based on the assumption of stability of exchange rates, such as the $/£ or $/€, this also could bring about dramatic changes to the cost-based price. Some companies find this very difficult to pass on and therefore have to take a margin "hit" in order to avoid losing customers.

Assumption 2

If costs do vary over the period during which the price is applied, any changes in costs will be incorporated as soon as they are known.

In practice, this is unlikely to occur. American companies change their prices roughly twice a year and Eurozone companies change their prices approximately once a year on average. Changes in the costs of inputs to the pricing model, such as labor rates, raw materials, energy costs, volume changes, and so on, are likely to be carried until the next pricing change, conceivably as much as a year ahead. Even if a company's systems were able to accommodate cost changes immediately, the sheer physical task of making these changes, particularly for a large product portfolio, would be prohibitive. Cost-based pricing therefore leads to price *stickiness* (the resistance of a price to change despite changes in the market or economy generally that might indicate that a different price should be applied) and encourages a global adjustment to price using a spreadsheet, especially with a large price list. This approach completely ignores the effects of price elasticity, perpetuates "dumb pricing" (i.e., failure to identify pricing errors at an early stage), and as a result magnifies them year upon year. Price control regulations, commercial contracts, and competition law factors all may conspire to maintain price rigidity. Conventional cost-based approaches to pricing do not take into account the customer's costs—they only consider the supplier's costs.

Assumption 3

The allocation of overheads within the business is fair, equitable, and prudent.

As we have seen, this is difficult to ensure, and disproportionate overhead allocation may be particularly onerous for new products. There are several ways of spreading fixed cost—on a per-capita basis, as a percentage of revenue, on the basis of volume, and on the basis of floor area of the business premises allocated to the product, to name a few. All these approaches are arbitrary and may unfairly load too much (or too little) cost, leading to an incorrect price. Activity-based costing (ABC) would seem to be a more equitable method because it allocates costs incurred to the activity that incurs them. ABC can be bureaucratic and time-consuming and requires significant resources to implement properly. Quite a few companies maintain armies of cost accountants to calculate product cost and overhead allocation. There may be, in such companies, only one executive with a part-time role in pricing. This creates a powerful but unspoken message that cost management matters much more than effective price (or value) management.

Assumption 4

Noneconomic matters have no intrinsic importance to the buyer.

Noneconomic elements such as brand recognition, reduction of pain or discomfort, and elimination of hassle and conflict, although not directly measurable, nevertheless may be worth a lot in cash terms to the buyer. A cost-based approach does not place any importance on these issues, and they are, in essence, ignored.

Assumption 5

Alternative competitor offers are not important to the customer.

No buyer, particularly of a purchase of major importance, is likely to ignore alternative offers, although his preferred brand may overlay a powerful emotional bias to the choice. Professional buyers will examine all relevant aspects of every alternative before making a final selection. For this reason, when cost-based pricing is the core pricing method, most pricing managers still will adjust their price in line with competitive prices to ensure at least some consideration of the competition.

Assumption 6

The customer will recognize that pricing on a cost basis is fair.

If we are challenged on price, it is relatively easy, with cost-based pricing, to show how we built up the price from cost elements and added a reasonable markup to arrive at the price figure. The pricing approach appears to be transparent and fair and should be easy for a customer to accept. For most of the time, if we believe this, we are deluding ourselves. Customers may commiserate with us when we discuss with them our company's input costs. If, however, we seek to pass on some of these costs, we will meet strong resistance and feigned disbelief! Customers care much less about our costs than about their own. Therefore, they are concerned primarily with *our* price to *them*. They are perfectly happy for us to absorb our own costs but very unhappy if we try to pass them on.

A cost-based approach to contract costing provides no incentive for a supplier to operate cost-efficiently. It is not unknown for contract costs to be "loaded" in order to boost the gross profit to the supplier, an approach that leads, in some industries, to excessive cost overruns (e.g., defense contractors). There is another issue. If we are foolish enough or compelled by the crude application of raw buyer power to open our books to the customer (and thus reveal in dangerous detail the individual component costs of a product or offer), every single item then becomes subject to challenge by the buyer on the pretext of "fairness." Any subsequent attempt we make to increase our prices because of our increased costs will be met with fierce resistance— "Remember, we *know* your costs."

Assumption 7

Both the market and costs are stable.

Many markets today are exhibiting serious volatility. For cost-based pricing to continue to deliver profit, all input costs must be monitored and prices adjusted as soon as they are spotted. Key factors to monitor include demand, fixed and variable costs, and the market acceptability of planned selling prices given the competitive situation. We know (from Assumption 2 and from experience) that this does not readily occur. This will compel frequent reappraisals of cost-based price, which may be impractical. The combination of infrequent price adjustments and chronic market volatility will result in systemic margin erosion and prices always being out of date.

Assumption 8

Manufacturers use similar production technology as their competitors.

In markets in which there has been little innovation over many years, this assumption is probably largely true and inevitably will lead to similar products with similar performance and similar costs. This is a prediction from classic economic theory and can lead to commoditization. Wherever this occurs, and in the absence of any unique differentiators, a cost-based approach leads to similar prices. Not too surprisingly, this causes buyers to challenge our offer, for example, by describing it as a commodity ("Your product is exactly the same as that offered by everyone else in the market"). Similarly, if our salespeople claim uniqueness or superiority and cannot, when challenged, justify the claim (and the high price), the buyer will adopt a strategy of point-by-point comparison on specification. This will "prove" that our products are identical to those of the competition and thus substitutable by them. And therefore we have no right to charge a higher price than our competitors.

Assumption 9

Demand is independent of price.

In the unusual situation where there is no price elasticity (i.e., our product is genuinely unique and meets a customer's compelling need), then demand will be independent of price. In other words, people will pay whatever it takes (up to a limit, of course). In all other cases, it is not independent of price, and demand will vary with price in line with the specific demand curve. It would suit our own requirements to eliminate the effect of price on customer demand, and we seek to do this through product and service differentiation. It is, however, highly unlikely that a cost-based approach will allow this to take place, especially in a market with little technological innovation.

TWO SERIOUS CRITICISMS

In principle, any price variation that may exist can be evened out through the process of discounting. Since value probably has not been taken into account in the price, the salesperson has no ammunition to defend her product. As a result, she ends up playing right into the buyer's hands and inevitably is forced to offer a discount. This is a slippery slope that destroys our brand value and damages our company's reputation and our salesperson's credibility. Worse, it sends the message that we are overcharging for a commodity product. We will be reminded of this at every subsequent opportunity. Worse still, in order to sweeten the deal for the customer, we end up "giving away" elements such as services and software. This, of course, is lunacy if these elements offer serious added value (and thus can be charged for on a value basis) and the tangible element has low or no margin. *We* know that our product is not a commodity. Probably our buyer knows it too. But try to climb out of the hole that we have dug . . .

Perhaps the most severe criticism of cost-based pricing is that it does not recognize (nor does it enable us to share in) the economic benefit we create for our customers. No part of the cost-based pricing formula takes account of the customer's value in use. The principal problem with price setting is not the arithmetic. For the most part, this is relatively trivial. The main problem is that companies have not properly worked out the real value they are offering. Therefore, they cannot articulate it. Hence, face to face with the customer, they cannot communicate it either. In cost-based pricing, this issue is not even considered. It is perhaps the strongest justification of all for the use of VBP where appropriate.

Table 3.3 Advantages and Disadvantages of Cost-Based Pricing

Advantages	Disadvantages
Easy to calculate—The calculation is straightforward and readily automated.	Automating price list data via spreadsheet may compound earlier pricing errors, especially with a large product portfolio.
Fair and transparent—It is possible to prove every element of cost.	Our fairness can be exploited if buyers choose to apply raw buyer power. *We* probably value our fairness more highly than customers do!
Minimal information requirements—Most or all of the information is available immediately.	Overly simplistic because critical data on competitors and customer needs are ignored. Indeed, in a cost-plus environment, managers may well challenge the need for these data as an unnecessary expense.
Easy to update variable costs—When these change, the model can be readily updated.	Updating in reality takes place only once or twice each year, so additional costs are carried with an adverse effect on margin.
Overheads data are available from accounts systems.	How overheads are allocated can distort profitability calculations.
For a low-cost supplier, cost-based pricing may offer some protection because of its position on the experience curve or through economies of scale.	A company with a dominant market share may be at risk under Article 102, TFEU (Treaty on the Functioning of the European Union), if there is evidence of exploitation of this position (see Appendix A).
	Takes no account of noneconomic factors, which can have a very major impact on demand and on willingness to pay.
	Prevents us from being able to share the economic gain we create for our customers because the sales negotiation becomes dominated by discussions about cost and discounts.
	Leads to debates about comparative specifications and potentially acrimonious price negotiations.
	The underlying assumption for cost-based pricing approaches to work is market and cost stability. When markets are volatile, this will compel frequent reappraisals of pricing, which may be impractical, leading to profit loss.

(Continued)

Table 3.3 Advantages and Disadvantages of Cost-Based Pricing—*(Continude)*

Advantages	Disadvantages
	Uses historical costs rather than replacement value.
	Uses normal or standard output levels to allocate fixed costs. These are based on forecasts that themselves are based on planned price levels, and the process becomes circular.

It is clear from the summary in Table 3.3 that while cost-based pricing may have some advantages, they are far outweighed by the disadvantages. An alternative approach is required.

CHAPTER 4

Competition-Based Approaches

Any connection between your reality and mine is purely coincidental.
—Anonymous

In competition-based pricing, we compare the features and specifications of our product with those of the competition and make a judgment about how the product should be positioned and priced. This is the second of the two chapters in this book dealing with conventional pricing methods. From recent research, it is clear that together with cost-based pricing, these conventional pricing approaches represent by far the majority of pricing decisions, at least in Eurozone companies.[1]

GOING-RATE PRICING (COMPETITOR PARITY PRICING)

Figure 4.1 illustrates the typical approach to *going-rate pricing*, a very common variant. Going-rate pricing recognizes that when a (rational) customer is deciding on a purchase, he will work systematically through a search process in which he will gauge price, performance, product specification, supplier reputation, support, brand, and other factors relevant to him. If the new purchase is the renewal of an earlier similar purchase, he probably will use this earlier purchase as a reference and seek in some way to benchmark the new alternatives against what he is already familiar with and values. This is in fact quite a key issue because if the product or service is not used or used very lightly, the chances of a repeat purchase are somewhat diminished.[2]

From the customer's perspective, P_{ref} represents this "package," and a new supplier will be required, at the very least, to match this in the view of the customer. In any given market, there will be a number of possible P_{ref} options, some of which are priced higher, others of which are priced about the same, and others priced at a lower level. Suppliers, seeking to position and price their products as accurately as possible, will evaluate their own product against the numerous alternatives. Where they finally position their own offer will be more guess than science in the absence of a more rational decision model, and positioning may be completely inappropriate because one or more of the underlying assumptions are invalid. The work we have already done and the ideas presented in Chapter 2 indicate the level of rigor that is required in mapping customer preferences.

Going-rate pricing is likely to yield a price a few percentage points above or below the competition because no one wants to "rock the boat." If every competitor based every price and product design on the existing

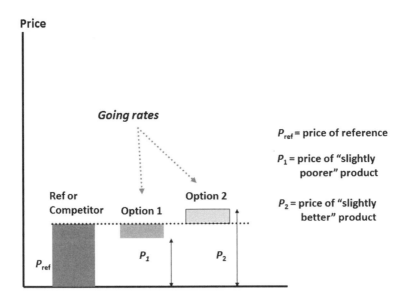

Figure 4.1 Going-rate pricing.

competition, we would end up in a situation in which there was very little difference between the various offers. Marketing communications would tend to say very much the same things across the market, and consequently, customers would be confused and perceive no difference. Under these conditions, it would be very difficult later to claim, "Our products actually are better than the competition—we just didn't tell you at the time we launched. Oh, and by the way, we now want you to pay more for them."

In going-rate pricing, products and services are priced at or around the average price for similar items in the market. Often this relates to commodity items for which pricing is highly elastic—small price increases lead to large demand reductions. In reality, every offer will be different, some by a little and some by a lot. What we are trying to do is take price right out of the equation and base the commercial argument on other factors.

The marketers' approach in dealing with a situation of this type is to create some advantage perceived as valuable by the customer. Factors such as reliability, delivery, customer service, technical support, and so on are good sources of differentiation and can form the basis of a really attractive proposition to customers. Needless to say, much creativity is required, as is the willingness (and courage) to break from the status quo.

Example

A long-established book seller with major market share refused to move to new premises to expand its range of titles, choosing instead to depend on long-established relationships with local schools and colleges. New competitors could not offer price advantages (because of the net book agreement then in place) and elected to take the risk and lease much larger premises to display a comprehensive range of titles (including books specified by local colleges) and set up an alliance with a coffee franchise to provide an attractive coffee lounge. Although the book seller eventually tried to emulate the competition, the original shop lost most of its market share and most of its college student patronage and was forced to close down. The business continued, however, by applying a niche strategy, repositioning itself both strategically and geographically inside college and university campuses and rebranding as "University Bookshops." The company also established niche markets supplying specialized publications (Her Majesty's Stationer's Office and Ordnance Survey Maps).

COMPETITIVE BIDDING

Competitive bidding (sometimes described as *contract bidding*) is a pricing approach used by buyers to solicit offers typically to undertake contract work or to deliver products or services over an extended period of time. The purchasing organization, often a government office or corporate organization, identifies a need for a third-party solution to a problem but is not certain who should be given the work. Additionally, the purchasing organization may be under legal pressure to open up procurement to a wider "church" of suppliers including SMBs. The purchasing organization therefore defines the requirements in significant detail and submits this variously in the form of a request for proposal (RFP) or a request for quotation (RFQ) or an invitation to tender (ITT) to qualified vendors. Government procurement processes must be fair and be seen to be fair. Therefore, the process must be transparent and the selection criteria clearly and transparently applied. There is always a defined process, but the narrative of the invitation may be unclear or even contradictory depending on the familiarity of the individual preparing it with the technical content of the request. Usually, especially with government tenders, the method of price calculation is prescribed precisely with requirements for individual elements of the bid to be priced separately to ensure item-for-item comparability. Normally, a cost-based pricing approach is prescribed, and often the price must have a sales tax or VAT added.

After the deadline has expired, the envelopes of all bidders are then opened and assessed on their respective merits, usually according to a set of guidelines decided in advance. Often (although not always), the lowest bidder wins the contract. For bidders, therefore, the key issue, after compliance with the specifications, is the likely prices of competitors.

This is a competition-based pricing approach, and all competitors' bids will be subject to the same constraints. It is often difficult to discover which of our competitors are being invited to bid (although obviously there will be the usual suspects, and we can make an educated guess). Creating a bid that emphasizes our competitive advantages over unknown competitors is extremely difficult. Preparing a bid takes a great deal of time. Unfortunately, there is no guarantee that our bid will succeed, even if we believe that we are the best supplier, have submitted the best possible price, and have spent significant time preparing it. For these reasons, many companies, although eminently qualified, simply refuse to take part in the bidding process unless they have good reason to believe that they are in a preferred position. Organizations may seek competitive bids simply to "make up the numbers" and (appear) to be offering a level playing field for all competitors. The reality may be rather different, and decisions in principle may be made well in advance of the tendering process.

Nevertheless, there are steps you can take to level the playing field and enhance the likelihood of success of your submission.

Hot-Wiring

Hot-wiring is a practice in which we offer to assist customers in constructing tender invitations that meet their needs. This might be attractive to small organizations and municipalities that do not have resident experts. In this scenario, we become quasi-consultants providing our services, possibly for free, in the hope that we will be considered favorably for any subsequent contracts. We can bias the outcome of the tendering process by including in the document specifications that we alone can meet. Of course, this approach may be considered unfair influence and may even be illegal in some jurisdictions.[3]

Customer Relationship Management

Customer relationship management (CRM) software tools enable sales and marketing people to track contacts with customers, monitor trends in usage, and identify key dates. Used thoughtfully, it should be possible to record previous bid invitations by customers and use this information to predict future bid opportunities. Using this insight, salespeople can start the process of creating awareness of their companies' products and services and ensuring they are seen as a credible supplier in advance of the next tender.

PREDATORY PRICING

Predatory pricing (sometimes called *destroyer pricing*) is used as an attempt to eliminate competition. It involves lowering prices to the point where competition is forced to withdraw.

Figure 4.2 illustrates the typical predatory situation. The unit cost curve describes the range of costs of all the competitors in a particular market. The average price line represents the average price of all competitors in the market at a given time. If prices are based on a going-rate approach, then most prices will be close to the average price line. Company 2 is the lowest-cost competitor in this market and may well be a dominant supplier. It has achieved this dominant cost position through higher cumulative experience (and probably will have higher market share than the competition). The price of its product typically will be very close to the average price line.

Company 1 is representative of the other competitors in the market, with a product cost that is significantly higher than that of company 2 but selling at a similar price. In the situation depicted, company 2 has a wide range of pricing discretion. A small price decrease still would keep it profitable but would disadvantage the competitors with higher costs. If company 2 wished to do so, it could drop prices dramatically to just above its unit cost. This would compel company 1 and others with higher costs to match company 2's price reduction or risk losing share, assuming a price-sensitive market. In this situation, company 2 has applied predatory pricing. If company 2 is a

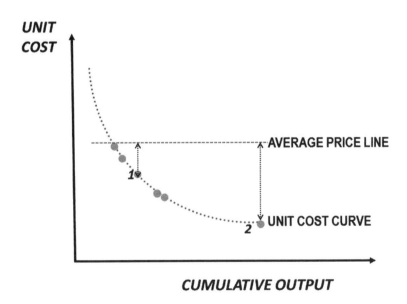

Figure 4.2   Predatory pricing.

dominant undertaking and it can be demonstrated that its reason for this pricing decision was deliberately to force other competitors out of the market, the company could be prosecuted for abuse of its dominant position.

THE PRODUCT-SERVICE-PRICE MENU

This menu is shown in Table 4.1.

Table 4.1 lists six competitive products. Each of these competitors has up to five product attributes and up to five separate service attributes. Each product is charted and the price identified (e.g., from price lists, Internet searches, market surveys, etc.). The baseline product, A, is a reference against which all competitors are measured. Price increments are identified from research. If we plan to introduce a new product, let's say with four product attributes and three service attributes, the table might lead us to "fit" product G between products E and F and to set a target price of, say, base + 44 percent. It should be clear immediately that there are a host of assumptions built into this approach. These assumptions are, in fact, the same core assumptions underlying most competition-based pricing methods.

Table 4.1   Product-Service-Price Menu

Product	Product attributes					Service attributes					Price
	1	2	3	4	5	1	2	3	4	5	
A	☐	☐				☐					Base
B	☐	☐				☐	☐	☐			Base + 15%
C	☐	☐		☐		☐	☐	☐			Base + 18%
D	☐	☐	☐			☐	☐	☐	☐		Base + 35%
E	☐	☐	☐	☐		☐	☐				Base + 38%
G	☐	☐	☐	☐		☐	☐	☐			**Base + 44%**
F	☐	☐	☐	☐	☐	☐	☐	☐	☐	☐	Base + 50%

Source: George Cressman, "Driving Profitability: The Price Connection," *PharmaChem*, January–February 2002.

MAJOR ASSUMPTIONS IN COMPETITION-BASED PRICING

There are many assumptions built into competition-based pricing. Some are relatively innocuous; others, however, are seriously dangerous and may lead the price setter to make wrong decisions. We spell out the more important assumptions here.

Assumption 1

We have selected the correct range of product and service attributes on which to base our decision.

This is an enormous assumption. The flaw in this thinking is that the selected attributes identified in the table may be irrelevant or unimportant to the customer. In fact, this kind of thinking leads to the creation of new products based on a kind of leapfrog mentality. Company 1 introduces a product with two product attributes and one service element. Company 2 goes one better and adds a further service element. Subsequent product introductions continue this one-upmanship with the overall result that there are a lot of clever, highly specified products in the market. The trouble is that in terms of what really matters to the customer, many of these clever add-ons offer little or no real enhancement to the customer's life experiences or competitive advantage. They are competitively irrelevant. The manufacturers have built these products because they can (or because they feel pressured to do so), not because they should. The result is an oversupply of overengineered products targeted at a finite market. The consequence? Premature commoditization with spiraling downward prices offered by suppliers in a panic effort to gain or retain market share. These suppliers will be the first to fail when, in recession, customers cut back and look for purchases that create, for them, real, provable value.

Assumption 2

The selected product and service attributes are of equal importance to the customer.

Even if we have selected the correct performance attributes, the methodology of Table 4.1 suggests that each of these is of equal importance to every customer. This is rather unlikely. Even if each of the performance attributes were of equal importance to the buyer, other factors, such as the reputation, brand, or other competitive advantages of the seller, are ignored when, in reality, they may be crucial to the buyer's decision. A major telecom network provider received competitive bids from a large American supplier of specialized components and a similar bid from a Chinese supplier. In every technical element of the bid, the Chinese supplier outperformed the American supplier—and at a price significantly lower than the U.S. company's bid. The deal really should have been "in the bag" for the Chinese company. What was the result? The American supplier won regardless of the higher price and lesser performance of its components. Why? The American company's brand and reputation were much better known than those of the Chinese company, and selecting the Chinese supplier would have represented an unacceptable (emotional) risk.

Assumption 3

We have estimated the prices correctly.

The reality, as most business-to-business (B2B) marketers know, is that price lists more often than not are works of creative fiction. In fact, there are many factors that may influence the actual price paid in the market. For instance, a construction company with high loading on its operational staff may charge a premium temporarily in a given situation. High demand in the market and the shortage of supply may place the seller at an advantage over the buyer. In another scenario, the situation is reversed. The level of discounting in one market may be completely different in another, some form of price discrimination may be in effect, and so on. In competition-based pricing, companies benchmark their prices against the competition on a product-by-product basis. If through benchmarking we realize that our product is a little poorer than that of the competition, we drop the price "a bit." If we think that our product is a bit better, we inflate the price "a bit." By how much, in either case, is a matter of judgment—there is no real science. What results from this activity is a series of competitive products, all of which are priced very similarly. Furthermore, the magnitude of "the bit" could have been estimated completely incorrectly, especially if its worth is estimated by us rather than by the customer.

Assumption 4

Performance and other data are available and accessible.

Finding meaningful comparative information is often a challenge. Companies with appropriate budgets may be able to source samples of their competitors' products and reverse engineer them to identify the manufacturing technologies applied, performance parameters, and so on. This is very easy to do in consumer markets and for low-cost industrial products and is in fact undertaken routinely. Trying to do the same in high-end capital goods is much more difficult. Even if the manufacturer had a suitable budget, competitors would not sell to them. Even if competitors did sell to the manufacturer, the task of reverse engineering a large, complex item would be prohibitive for all but the largest companies. Sourcing from customers is also unlikely to be successful because competitors' salespeople would want to follow up on the purchase and would quickly discover the subterfuge with adverse effects on the customer's future relationships with this vendor.

Assumption 5

Competition-based pricing won't rock the boat.

Market stability is important for many companies for strategic reasons. For instance, a company fighting a price war on one front will seek stable market conditions in its other market sectors. Competition-based pricing does tend to offer some measure of market stability. If, however, we want to come to the market with a brand new, perhaps even disruptive technology, then we really *do* want to rock the boat—vigorously! We even may wish to redefine the market's operating economics to our own competitive advantage.

Assumption 6

Customers buy only on the basis of price/specification.

Competition-based pricing does not capture for us the value created and delivered to the customer. If our product developers have done a really good job of building a product with highly competitive and highly valued features, competition-based pricing does not capture this in any way. This leads to frustration among product-development staff and business leaders, as well as disappointingly poor returns from the investment. Competition-based pricing is based on a comparison with competitors. If we do this, then we can hardly criticize customers for doing the same and using the information they have found to challenge our assertions about uniqueness and distinctiveness. In this process, not only is little or no account taken of the *real* value of our offer to the customer, but we also find our products being compared purely on features and specifications with adverse effects on our ability to price at a premium.

Assumption 7

There is no emotional component to a price decision.

This assumption is not true. In most cases, in business-to-consumer (B2C) markets, we know that emotion plays an enormous role. Even in a highly rational, objectives-driven B2B situation, there is always an emotional component, however small, whenever human beings are involved. Indeed, used wisely as part of the Value Triad, emotion can be a powerful influencer of a purchase decision. While competition-based pricing should minimize the risk of a price war and reasonably ensure a share of the available business, it does have significant disadvantages, again based on the underlying assumptions.

Table 4.2 presents a summary list of the advantages and disadvantages of competition-based pricing.

Table 4.2   Advantages and Disadvantages of Competition-Based Pricing

Advantages	Disadvantages
A lot of competitive data generally is available in the public domain.	The available data may be wrong, out of date, or irrelevant. The information we really need is much harder to obtain. The evolving specialism of competitive intelligence can help us to triangulate on key data and assumptions, but we are still in very difficult territory here.
It is relatively easy to position our offer in the context of the competition.	As a first approximation, we can position our offer easily, but this does not take account of customers' different priorities and variations between segments.
It allows us to focus on the attributes on which the purchase decision is based.	These elements may not in fact be the right ones from the customers' perspectives.
It maintains market stability.	Stability is achieved at the cost of suboptimal profits through conservative pricing.
It pretty much guarantees that we will win some share of the market, assuming acceptable brand and specification.	Our prices will be very close to those of the competition, which sends a signal to the market that there are few differences between competitors—an issue that may accelerate commoditization.
It enables us to collect the price and specification data as part of our pitch.	This leads directly to point-by-point comparisons on price and specification.
	This does not take into account the economic elements of value in use.
	This completely ignores the psychological or emotional qualities of our offer.

Case Study: Hansen Bathrooms

Hansen Bathrooms is a producer of bathtubs, washbasins, toilets, and bidets. The company has been in the bathroom market for over 50 years, and while sales have never been spectacular, the company has managed to withstand the impact of several economic recessions by prudent cash-flow management. Experts in the industry describe Hansen as a traditional, reliable producer that tends to follow market trends rather than lead.

As a response to changing times, Hansen recruited a 30 year old marketing director, Rob Vincent, and a 25 year old assistant, Susan Clements. Rob's responsibilities include suggestions for new bathroom designs, advertising and promotion, and formulating pricing strategies. The final decisions (except for day-to-day issues) are taken by the board of directors, which is headed by Karl Hansen, son of the founder of the company.

Rob Vincent and Susan Clements have been in their jobs for nearly two years and, at times, have found the work frustrating because of the board's tendency toward conservatism. However, an exciting development rekindled their enthusiasm. A technologist at the company had developed a special coating that could be applied to all bathroom items (i.e., bathtubs, toilets, washbasins, bidets, and tiles). The coating contains an agent that disperses the usual grime and grease that accumulates in bathtubs, washbasins, and so on. Susan Clements commissioned a market research study that showed that people cleaned their bathroom fittings on average once every week and that it was one of the most unpopular household chores. The new coating made this unnecessary. Product trials with a prototype bathroom incorporating the new coating showed that cleaning could easily be extended to once every three months. Respondents in the test were delighted with the reduction in workload. Hansen sought and obtained a patent on the new coating.

Rob felt sure that the board would approve the launch of a new bathroom product range using the new coating and was pondering what price to charge. As a starting point, Rob set about using Hansen's tried and tested pricing formula. This produced the calculation shown in Table 4.3:

(Continued)

Table 4.3   Per Bathroom (Washbasin, Toilet, and Bath)

	£
Direct materials	40
Direct labor	40
Total direct cost	80
Fixed cost (150% of direct labor)	60
Total cost	140
Profit markup (20% of total cost)	28
Basic price to retailers (BPR)	168
Allowance for promotional costs (10% of BPR)	17
Allowance for retailer discounts (20% of BPR)	34
List price to retailers (LPR)	219
Retailer profit markup (100% of LPR)	219
Recommended price to consumers	438

Rob felt very pleased. The price to consumers of £438 was very competitive with the price of other bathroom suppliers (e.g., the main two competitors charged £450 and £465). After the usual 25 percent consumer discount, this would mean that the Hansen bathroom would sell for £328 compared with £337 and £348 for its main rivals. "I wish all my marketing decisions were this easy," thought Rob. However, before making a final decision, he thought he ought to consult Susan.

If you were Susan, would you agree or disagree with Rob Vincent's proposal? What other factors do you think should be considered? What alternative strategies exist?

Source: David Jobber, *Principles and Practice of Marketing,* 4th ed. New York: McGraw-Hill, 2004.

HANSEN BATHROOMS: COMMENTARY

This case study illustrates the typical pricing approach adopted by many companies. A cost-based pricing formula offers a target from-the-factory price to the channel. Standard markup, in this case 20 percent, gives a basic price to the channel that together with trade allowances and standard retailer markup gives a Recommended Retail Price (RRP) of £438. Comparison with the competition places Hansen's price very comfortably at just below the prices of the main competitors but with a wafer-thin gross margin on the from-the-factory sales price.

Rob Vincent has made no attempt whatsoever to add anything to the price to represent the value added by Hansen's new coating. Rob seems perfectly satisfied with his calculation—the final RRP is well inside his comfort zone. Susan Clements, however, is not so sure. She is worried that this decision was too easy and was taken too quickly without adequate consideration of alternatives. For instance, Rob seems to have ignored the market study results that just came in this week—in particular the benefits that the new coating will offer and the premium that consumers would be prepared to pay for the added value. It seems obvious to Susan that there is a real gain. She spends a lot of time in her own flat cleaning the bathtub, toilet, and other surfaces and really resents the time spent on these tedious and repetitive chores.

As Susan reflected on this, she realized that there were lots of other possibilities that Rob hadn't even started to consider. The coating could make the job of cleaning bathrooms a lot easier and a lot more pleasant (and possibly also utility rooms and kitchens, if it could be applied to surfaces in these rooms as well). Of course, her only cost was time and the other ways she could use her time. In other potential markets, time is money (e.g., hotels and the hospitality industry, hospitals and care establishments, and commercial and government buildings). In all these buildings, people were hired to clean toilets. In some cases, the need is basic hygiene. In others, such as hospitals, dirty toilets represent a serious health risk—a topic that is never out of the newspapers these days. Surely Hansen's new coating not only could make that job a lot easier, but also allow managers to save a lot of money.

In each of these segments, there's a real opportunity to build a new and attractive market for Hansen's products and help the company to break out of the traditional B2C sector in which it has operated. Susan realizes that each segment has slightly different requirements.

Hospitality Sector

Hotels, bed and breakfast houses, boarding houses, and so on spend time and money on housekeeping labor and cleaning materials. The motivation, apart from hygiene, is the impression of clean, well-maintained, and inviting rooms and public areas. The benefits here would be maintaining or increasing room occupancy rates, contributing to a favorable and memorable experience, and reducing labor costs and janitorial supply costs.

Health Care Sector

Hospitals, hospices, nursing homes, and so on are high-throughput buildings often at the risk of poor hygiene. In addition to all the issues relating to the hospitality sector, the big issue facing managers is maintenance of high standards of hygiene and keeping hospital infections under control.

Commercial and Government Buildings

Factories, shops, retail premises, government offices, and so on are also high-throughput establishments with similar issues to health care, albeit without the infection problem.

Susan realized that it would be possible to structure quite different propositions for each segment. In every case, the Hansen SupaCote (as she was now describing it in her own mind) could reduce labor and material costs considerably and/or increase the productivity of that labor by freeing up operators to do other things. Because of the economic advantages—cost reductions and/or productivity improvements (which are readily measurable)—Hansen could argue for a much higher price and justify it on the basis of an economic argument. And this does not take into account all the emotional gains—reduction of hassle, greater convenience, peace of mind, enhanced aesthetics, and so on.

We summarize the Value Triad issues for each of these markets in Table 4.4.

As Susan was reflecting on these matters, she realized that maybe Rob was correct after all. Hansen's has no experience dealing with hospitality, health care, or industrial/commercial markets. To address any of these would require the company to move away from being a traditional bathroom products supplier to the retail trade to a much more marketing-focused business. The company is conservative and probably unwilling to learn the new skills necessary to succeed.

Table 4.4 Use of the Value Triad to Identify Value Components in Each Market

Market	Revenue gain	Cost reduction	Emotional contribution
Hospitality	Clean bathrooms contribute to maintaining/ increasing occupancy rates.	Cleanliness can be achieved at lower cost of cleaning labor and materials.	Aesthetics, avoidance of hassle, greater convenience, image, etc.
Health care	In public hospitals, not really a factor.	As above plus contribution to avoidance of transmission of hospital-acquired infections.	Avoidance of hassle, greater convenience, peace of mind, reduced infection risk, image, etc.
Government	Not really a factor.	Cleanliness can be achieved at lower cost of cleaning labor and materials.	Aesthetics, avoidance of hassle, greater convenience, image, etc.

Licensing the Intellectual Property

As she reflected further on the problem, Susan realized with a start that the new coating provided Hansen with a completely new opportunity—selling licenses to other similar manufacturers who wanted to incorporate the coating in their own products in exchange for a royalty. This would be a particularly attractive opportunity for Hansen because it would generate revenue for very little additional effort and could operate alongside the existing business if that was what the directors wanted to do.

Addressing all these new opportunities would force the company to change completely. Would the company do it? What was Susan going to say to Rob on Monday? "Oh well," she thought, "time to clean the apartment."

CHAPTER 5

Measuring the Value Triad

Not everything that counts can be counted, and not everything that can be counted counts.

—Sign hanging in Albert Einstein's
office at Princeton University

THE VALUE TRIAD REVISITED

Measuring the impact of value is a significant obstacle to the full and effective implementation of a value-based-pricing (VBP) approach. Without measurement, it is difficult to promote and sell our services, difficult to track how well we are doing, and finally, almost impossible to demonstrate the real impact we have made on our customers' businesses.[1] We use the Value Triad as our basic tool to assess customer value. There are many applications of this simple tool, but in this book we use it primarily to help us analyze customers' needs and, armed with this information, to construct a value-based price and a compelling value proposition. The key elements of the Value Triad—net revenue gain, net cost reduction, and emotional contribution—are used to identify the factors that really matter to the customer and then to quantify the advantages offered by the seller's product or service.

Some books examine the process of measurement and identify various specific metrics; others review important approaches to measurement in practical detail. We have assembled a selection of recommended titles in the Additional Reading section at the end of this book that employ those approaches, but here we'll be taking a rather different approach. We examine instead the important link between what really, really matters to a customer and how we can identify the measures that are important in such work.

Revenue-gain and cost-reduction elements are inherently measurable, and there are well-established measurement tools to assist us in this endeavor. The third element, emotional contribution (which is largely intangible in nature), generally is perceived to be more difficult to quantify. The key issue is to measure, as objectively as we can, the outcomes that matter to the customer. We recognize that this is a topic that some readers would like to dig into deeply, but there is not enough space in this book to explore these tools in detail. We therefore have provided a rather longer list than normal of additional reading sources that should satisfy the needs of most readers.

Many managers experience difficulty in making the link between the technical properties and qualities of their products and the impact they have on their clients' businesses. We encounter this among product-management, sales-management, and technical-support people. This is not surprising, of course, but it does constitute a real problem—how to map these attributes to real customer impact. For each dotted arrow in Figure 5.1, you need to identify the nature of the link, how it affects the client's organization, and how that impact can be measured with reasonable precision. It should be obvious that you do not need to map *every single element* in the design of our product or service to *every need*—only to the ones that matter most to the customer in her current context. Equally, some important but less obvious needs may be hidden behind those which are most evident. It is the job of the discovery process to find these and to assess their impacts.

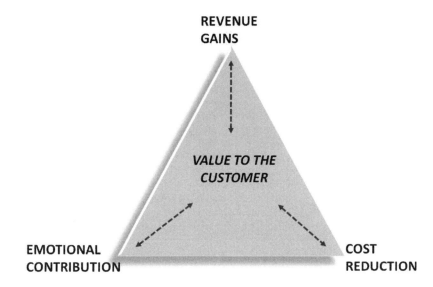

Figure 5.1   Value Triad.

CUSTOMER BENEFIT CATEGORIES

The range of products and services—and the benefits arising from all of these—is truly immense and quite impossible to categorize comprehensively in fewer than 20,000 pages. Instead, we suggest that you use customer benefit categories to help you to structure your own thinking about what really matters. See Table 5.1 below for a few ideas to think about. The simple classification of different types of benefits is a good starting point for your analysis. You should include only the characteristics of your organization and your products. For example, "consistency of results" is a *consequence* of the use and application of your product. It is a "So what?" *outcome* from the use of your product—not an attribute of your product itself.[2]

The attributes we have listed are in no way comprehensive—nor can they be, because every situation is different. Also, there is inevitably some overlap. They are intended to get you *thinking* about the wide range of attributes possessed by your *whole organization*—not simply the products and services you offer—and to encourage you to think as widely as possible about those attributes. When a customer buys from you, he is buying not just the product or service but the whole

Table 5.1 Customer Benefit Categories

Category	Some attributes
Product performance	Size, shape, attractive styling, color, reliability, ease of use, conformation to specification, conformation to standards, compatibility with other items used with it, robustness, durability, dependability, aesthetics, design, serviceability, environmental friendliness, upgradeability, etc.
Service performance	Competence, reliability, ability to relate to users, honesty, dependability, reassurance, encouragement, flexibility, responsiveness, consistency, geographic location, etc.
Timing	Punctuality, on-time completion, faster startup, just-in-time delivery, speed of response, reduction in operational cycle time, etc.
Credibility	Innovation, brand, experience, track record, product range, price positioning, skills portfolio, culture, flexibility of approach, etc.
Relationships	Relationship management, open access, ease of contacting, sharing of know-how, interpersonal relationships, etc.

package that your company represents. There are many cases in which a customer selected a slightly poorer product because he perceived the supplier to be offering a better total proposition overall. If your focus is exclusively on product design and technology, you would miss this important point—and possibly lose the deal. People in your customer organization are human beings—not automatons. So work hard to identify the soft factors. They may be just as important or perhaps even more so than the hard factors.

In training events, we frequently challenge delegates to identify as many characteristics of a ball-point pen as they can. We have found 29! We then ask them to take three or four of these and brainstorm how these attributes might be useful to particular types of customer. So, for instance, the plastic components allow the carrier to take the pen through airport security x-ray machines, the pocket clip allows it to be carried conveniently and securely in clothing but also might prevent it from rolling off a flat surface such as a map table on a boat, non-water-soluble ink prevents writing washing off in the rain, and so on. It is a simple and quick exercise, but it forces people to think broadly rather than narrowly about the item and sometimes come up with surprising results.

When you consider the effect of each attribute, it will become clear that there potentially can be an impact on two or even all three of the Value Triad elements. Recognizing this, you can start to construct richer value propositions at the segment, business, or even individual manager level. These arguments can be made by salespeople during a sales negotiation, by marketing people in constructing compelling arguments in marketing communications and collateral, and by product managers in their efforts to define new product concepts.

SO WHAT?

In Table 5.2, we selected a few of the attributes from Table 5.1 and identified their potential impact on your customer's business. The "So what?" question is a powerful tool to help your thinking here. Just imagine that you are in a discussion with a particular customer and are reading off a list of the attributes your product offers. Every time you utter a word, the customer says, "So what?" This challenge is the very essence of the transformation of some attribute of your business into something of real worth and significance to the customer. To answer the "So what?" question properly, you need to know quite a lot about your customer's business. It's best to have done your thinking before meeting the customer. Whether you are a product manager conceptualizing a new product or service, a marketing executive thinking about how to communicate the product, or a salesperson working face to face with the customer, get used to asking yourself the "So what?" question. And get your colleagues used to it too!

Each time you ask yourself the "So what?" question, think about your answer through the lens of the Value Triad—revenue gains (RGs), cost reductions (CRs), and emotional contribution (EC). Then force yourself—hard—to think about these items in your customers' terms—not your own! In Table 5.2 we illustrate the approach.

Table 5.2 Applying the "So What?" question to Product and service attributes

Attribute	What we do	So what? (potential impact using Value Triad)*
Ease of use	Less operator training required	• Faster to productivity → RG
	Eliminate user error	• Fewer errors in use → no rework → productivity improvement → RG, CR
	Simplicity of instructions	• Fewer errors in use → no rework → productivity improvement → RG, CR
		• Reduced operator frustration → EC
		• Less wastage → reduced raw materials and efficient use of operator time → RG, CR
		• More consistent results → improved quality control → less scrap/rework and better productivity → RG, CR
Robustness	Designed for rugged environments	• Peace of mind, cost reduction, improved productivity → RG, CR, EC
	Tested to destruction	• Peace of mind, cost reduction, improved productivity → RG, CR, EC
		• Last longer in routine use → requires less frequent replacement → CR
		• Requires less maintenance and support → gives user peace of mind, fewer repairs → EC, CR
Serviceability	Modular product design	• Easy access to service components → increases peace of mind → EC
	Established wide availability of spares	• Easy access to service components? eliminates search times and costs and reduces hassle → CR, EC
	Tight control of manufacturing costs	• Spare parts inexpensive → CR
	Well-written user maintenance manuals	• Avoids service engineer callout or other support → CR

Reassurance	Skilled, trained employees	• Understand process and associated issues → enhances peace of mind, builds confidence → EC
	Employees trained to deal with unexpected situations	• Enhances peace of mind, builds confidence → EC
	Demonstrates trustworthiness	• Enhances peace of mind, builds confidence → EC
Speed of response	Clear processes for customer support	• Keep interruptions to customer's business to a minimum → CR. RG
	Protocols for frequently encountered problems	• Keep interruptions to customer's business to a minimum → CR, RG
	Support guidance on Web site	• Enable customer to resolve simple problems quickly → CR, EC(?), RG
Ease of contact	24/7/365 access to key personnel	• Ability to contact night, day, and holidays → EC, CR, RG
	staffed with competent people	• Peace of mind → EC
	Dedicated phone and e-mail lines	• Avoid long queues waiting for service → EC, CR, RG
	staffed with competent people	• Peace of mind → EC
	Guaranteed response within specified period	• Confidence that problems are resolved quickly → peace of mind → EC

*Note that these are all from your customer's perspective—not yours.

We have coded some of these with what we think are likely to be the most typical Value Triad impacts. But *you* need to be sure, taking into account the context of your customer, just exactly what the impact really is in any given circumstance. Try to get into the habit of doing this. It will mean that you will miss fewer opportunities to enrich your value proposition, enhance your company's importance to your customers, and yield ideas for the metrics that really matter. Let's look at a simple example from consulting practice.

Example

A furniture manufacturing company was struggling to sell its up-market products. The company sold high-quality, high-specification furniture to international hotel chains such as InterContinental, Hilton, Starwood, and so on. The products—which included wardrobes, bedside cabinets, conference tables and chairs, cupboards, credenzas, and desks—were crafted from quality hardwoods such as oak, teak, walnut, mahogany, and beech, all from sustainable sources. The company took great care with its supply chain, securing only the best raw materials and auditing their provenance to ensure procurement from sustainable sources. It had invested heavily in computer-aided design (CAD) software and high-end machine tools that were linked to the CAD systems, employed skilled and experienced craftspeople, and maintained a panel of furniture designers (and active links with furniture design consultancies and training organizations). This enabled the manufacturer to create special-edition and customized items for specific clients. The company maintained adhesives and staining shops using low-emission materials and generally did just about everything it could to ensure what it believed to be a very high standard of product.

Despite all this, the company was losing sales and market share. The new chairman, a former consultant with one of the major firms, had invested personal money in the venture and was committed to turning the company around. Selling was handled through a geographically organized sales team, products were priced exclusively on a cost-plus basis, and selling was based almost entirely on features.

When we asked the sales manager to describe what the company sold, he asserted "High-quality furniture" and described the preceding approach in outline. When pressed to explain what the company *really* sold, he repeated the same litany but described in even greater detail the technology of the product. When we changed the question to "What does the customer buy?" exactly the same response was given—this time accompanied by a frustrated, "What part of FUR-NI-TURE don't you understand?"

The sales manager hadn't a clue, and neither did anyone else in the company. Why? No one had given a millisecond's thought to the customer. The prevailing assumption was that quality will sell. The company's idea of what was meant by *quality*, however, was vastly different from what the customer thought. When we asked for the most important benefit of the company's product, the answer was, "Quality." No one ever asked what that meant—or "So what?"

The dialogue went as follows:

Q: "What is the most important benefit of your product?"

A: "Quality."

Q: "What does that mean?"

A: "It's made well with all the best materials and in a very precise way."

Q: "So what?"

A: "I don't know what you mean."

Q: "So what? Does that matter to the customer?"

A: "It's good quality."

Q: "You've already said that."

A: "Erm, I don't know what to say."

It was a Dilbert discussion! The problem is that if you sell a product or a service on the basis of a product attribute and the customer is thinking, "Why should I buy this?" sooner or later the discussion hits a rock, and apart from sterile repetition, there is nothing left to say.

The answer lies in asking the correct question: "What are the most pressing worries that keep the customer awake at night?" The answer for the hotel manager probably is room occupancy and how to keep it as high as possible. The drivers of room occupancy include a good menu, a good location, friendly staff, and attractive public areas, facilities, and standard of decor of the guest rooms. At this point, the penny

(Continued)

dropped—for some. Alas, not for the sales manager. Room decor is only one of a portfolio of factors that collectively define a good—or excellent—guest experience. Room decor, or the decor of meeting rooms and public areas, of course, is exactly where high-quality furniture fits in. For the brighter individuals around that table, the lights went on. They immediately saw why their product-driven approach was failing. At the same instant, they also realized what they could do about it. Focus on the factors that enhance hotel guests' patronage and build up arguments to support those factors. There is in addition an economic argument about ensuring the viability of the hotel's investment over a prolonged period of time. The Value Triad helps us to build up all these arguments and, as we shall see in Chapter 8 weave them into a compelling value proposition. If there is no good answer to the "So what?" question, why even mention the attribute?

Table 5.3 presents an analysis of the situation using our thinking in Table 5.2

Table 5.3   "So what?" Analysis: Furniture Manufacturer

Attribute	What we do*	So what? (potential impact using the Value Triad)†
Robust products	High-quality materials Durable materials Built to exacting standards	• Look attractive for a long time → CR, EC • Last longer → resist wear and tear → minimize need to replace → RG, CR, EC
Product design	Ergonomic design Optimize aesthetic appearance Attention to detail Specialized design skills	• Easy and intuitive for users → minimizes fatigue → EC, RG • Pleasing to eye → nice to be in → RG, EC • Reinforces the quality image and brand → EC, RG • Distinctive and unique designs → reinforces high-end image → RG, EC
Environmental sensitivity	Materials from sustainable sources Low-emissions adhesives	• Enables the hotel chain marketing team to make an environmental claim → RG, EC

*From the supplier's perspective.
†From the hotel manager's perspective.

WHAT TO MEASURE

It should be pretty clear from the preceding that we can employ two different sets of measures—those which quantify the *efficiencies of the supplier* (operational measures) and those which measure their *impact on the customer* (outcome measures). Both are very important, and both should be measured as a matter of principle. In fact, the two sets of measures should be linked closely so that, for instance, we can estimate how a change in some part of our process will affect downstream customer value. In this chapter we are more interested in *how* we measure the Value Triad impacts on customers. How we measure customer value impacts should drive many of the internal measures that we are using to control our own internal operations.

A quick glance at Tables 5.2 and 5.3 will reveal that products or services have both *tangible* and *intangible* impacts. For instance, a consultancy firm's ability to drill down deep into a client's problems and come up with a good solution will yield tangible and intangible benefits. The changes enable the client to eliminate unnecessary steps, reducing cycle time (cost reduction); the same changes could deliver superior product consistency and productivity (contributing to revenue gain) and also eliminate operator frustration and inconvenience (which map to emotional contribution). There may be other knock-on, or second-order, consequences of such a change (e.g., reduced bought ledger costs, machine time released for other purposes, and better management morale, to name a few). These are worth identifying and measuring if they are considered significant. There are at least three obvious things in this example that can be measured to assess the impact of the intervention. They are also likely to be interconnected.

Cycle time. The time taken to produce a specified quantity of output before and after implementation of changes.

Wastage rate. The percentage of out-of-spec items before and after changes.

Operator frustration. The degree to which the operator is annoyed or inconvenienced by the processes he is obliged to use and how these frustrations are diminished or eliminated by our solution.

Undoubtedly you can think of many more!

Calculating the significance of these changes is the role of statistics. After all, you want to be sure that these changes did not simply happen by chance.

The first two are pretty easy and pretty obvious. They depend totally on your ability to collect accurate pre- and postimplementation measures and track them for long enough that you can assert that statistically significant changes have taken place. It is a simple calculation to turn these measures into actual revenue-gain and cost-reduction estimates. These are tangible measures and in general are fairly easy to track. Collecting the information can pose difficulties if the required information is not currently collected, is distributed across different databases, or annoyingly is "owned" by another department that chooses not to share it. We need to put in the time and secure the necessary management support to collect these data. Thomas Nagle, in *The Strategy and Tactics of Pricing*, advocates use of *economic value estimation*—a rigorous process designed to unveil the economic impact of a product or service.

The third item, operator frustration, is somewhat more difficult to measure given that it is intangible and subjective and will vary, operator to operator, depending on personal circumstances, health, level of fatigue, mood, and so forth. A surrogate measure such as absenteeism could suffice if we believe it to be closely correlated with operator frustration. However, such a measure just as easily could be linked to other unrelated factors, such as illness, morale, bullying in the workplace, and so on. The ideal is to try to find a metric that maps uniquely and exclusively to the issue you are trying to measure. It is far better to try to measure the direct effect of a change on individuals, and for this reason, tools such as Likert or semantic differential scales can be applied. These tools are used widely in marketing research to collect—and attempt to (semi-)quantify—intangibles such as attitudes toward products and so on. We do not review these methods here, but full details with practical examples can be found in good textbooks on marketing research.

Table 5.4 lists just a few of the customer impacts arising from the attributes identified in Table 5.2 and their nature (tangible or intangible). We also suggest performance measures that can be used to assess and track customer impact. This also is not comprehensive,

Table 5.4 Measuring Outcomes

Customer Impact	Nature	Measure(s) of relative performance (outcome measures)
Effective operator training	Tangible	Work output in units per time period
	Tangible	Time to complete specific standard task
	Intangible	Confidence in task performance
Reduced operator frustration	Tangible	Absentee days among staff performing this task
	Intangible	Staff annoyance/irritation
Less maintenance	Tangible	Number of visits by service engineer
	Tangible	Number of emergency calls to helpline
	Tangible	Time off for maintenance
	Intangible	Management hassle
Improved company image	Tangible	Enquiries received
	Tangible	Hits on Web site
	Tangible	Twitter followership
	Tangible	Employment applications
	Tangible	News articles
	Intangible	Employee morale
	Intangible	Management morale
Increased demand for product	Tangible	Shipment levels
	Tangible	Market share
	Tangible	Order intake
	Tangible	Revenue booked
	Tangible	Load on shop/service delivery staff
Earlier new-product introduction	Tangible	Time to first order
	Tangible	Time to money
	Tangible	Time to profit
	Tangible	Market share
	Intangible	Customer perception of supplier
	Intangible	Management "feel good" factor

and you will need to carry out a similar analysis for your own customers. Note that these measures may be absolute. In VBP, you should be motivated to make these measurements because you want to compare your product or service against your customer's next-best alternative (or current preference). The best results from this point of view are *relative* measurements. The suggestions in the table are merely our ideas based on what we know other companies have used successfully. You must create your own.

Any particular impact can be of a tangible or an intangible nature. When searching for ways to assess the overall worth of your product to your customer, you need to search for both types. Each impact can share a measurement method with another impact, which makes it difficult to isolate the contribution precisely. Try to find metrics that measure the right things, even imperfectly, rather than those which measure the wrong things right. Each measurement needs to be relative to the customer's next-best alternative. For example, if your product, service, or other contribution leads to your customer increasing her market share, this can only be measured over a period of time by comparing with historic data. You might need to make corrections for changes in the external market and other factors over which you have no control and that might influence the numbers you use. This is what makes the measurement of outcomes so difficult to do. It should not, however, prevent you from trying. And it certainly should encourage you to be creative in the measures you use.

SOME MEASUREMENT TOOLS

VBP analysts use many tools to measure customer outcomes. Table 5.5 describes briefly a number of these tools and indicates typical applications. Again, since this is such a massive topic, the list is not exhaustive. Find methods that work for you.

ECONOMIC VALUE ESTIMATION (EVE)

EVE is a robust and practical approach developed originally by Tom Nagle of the Strategic Pricing Group to estimating the economic value of a supplier's products. There are three components to EVE—studying

Table 5.5 Measurement Tools

Method	Description	Example of use
Conjoint/tradeoff analysis	A market research tool used to estimate the economic worth of tangible and intangible attributes by asking respondents to choose between different alternatives.	Product design optimization; assessing the respective importance of alternative intangible product or service options; market segmentation studies; etc.
Analytical hierarchy process[4]	In AHP, we create a hierarchy of decision elements (possibly product attributes). We then make comparisons between each possible pair, generating a weighting for each element.	Forecasting, total quality management, pricing, quality management, and the balanced scorecard
Perceptual mapping	Seeing how items compare with each other on the basis of attributes (usually selected two at a time). The CVL is an example of simple perceptual mapping.	Identifying market gaps and how these might offer business development opportunities; identifying clusters of customers; price positioning; etc.
Regression and correlation	A statistical tool to demonstrate how changes in variables are linked to changes in other variables.	Sales and demand forecasting; assessing how observed results are explained by different causative variables; assessing price-change impacts; etc.
Management estimation	Asking managers closest to the situation under study to make subjective guesses.	Forecasting; assessing impact of process changes; how people will react to initiatives; estimating response of customers to price change; etc.
Net promoter score	A method of summarizing a customer's opinion of the product or service used.	Measuring customer satisfaction with service provider after service delivered; etc.
Financial metrics	Net present value, return on investment, margin, revenue.	Analyzing the financial impact of initiative; usually data collected can allow drill down to permit measurements of segments, customers, salespeople, geographies, etc.
Likert scales	Asking respondents to place a numerical value on a variable between two limits.	Turning a qualitative response into a quantitative response

(Continued)

Table 5.5 *(Continued)*

Method	Description	Example of use
Semantic differential	Asking respondents to describe their experience by choosing one of a number of alternative phrases.	Attempting to capture emotional response to an experience
Simulation	Methods of assessing the likelihood of specific outcomes. Can be experimental or analytical.	
Elasticity	Measuring how volume demanded varies with price charged.	Forecasting the effect of price changes; measuring segment characteristics.

customer economics, quantifying value drivers, and estimating the differential Value. However you go about assessing and measuring customer outcomes, these are the key things to examine. Thompson, Coe, and Lewis advocate use of economic-value pricing models.[3] We have taken a slightly broader approach—the Axia Valgorithm—in line with our core thinking around the Value Triad.

THE AXIA VALGORITHM

We have noticed that there are broadly two different types of challenges. The first is obsession with measuring every aspect of one's own organization's processes and performance on the assumption that if the organization can do better managing inputs, its customers will benefit fully from the outputs. This can happen only when inputs and outputs are aligned properly. When customers do benefit, it is because, by plan or by choice, improvements in these internal processes lead to an improvement in what the customer sees and values. The second challenge is to know the right things to measure. This is a real problem because if the company has not undertaken even a rudimentary "So what?" analysis, as in the case of the furniture company described earlier, it has no clear idea of what it should be measuring, and any measure is likely to produce the wrong results. Wrong measures are endemic in business. For instance, government training schemes designed to help unemployed people back to work have employed the performance measure of "number of people attending events" as a measure of event success. By any standard, this is idiotic. Number of people attending merely may be a result of pressure on individuals to attend "or else," or they may be unable to benefit from the event because of illness or other factors, or the training may be poor, or the environment may be wrong. Number of attendees is a very crude and rather meaningless score. What surely must matter more is increases in the number of individuals entering employment—*as a consequence of* the training—or at least a better flow of employment opportunities. Developing strategies based on the number of trainees attending may be dangerous because it is based on flawed data. The microscope is pointing in the wrong direction.

Recognizing these issues, we developed the Axia Valgorithm—the value algorithm—originally as a consultancy tool to help focus on the things companies should be doing by asking questions of their customers in a structured way and then feeding the information back to decision makers in the supplying enterprise.

WHAT IS THE AXIA VALGORITHM?

The Axia Valgorithm is an audit process that will lead to the identification of company attributes, as in Table 5.1. It can be used as the basis of viable initiatives for value positioning (at the segment level) and value propositions (at the individual client/customer level). Simply stated, the Axia Valgorithm is a procedure designed to unearth the most important elements of (potential) value in companies at strategic business unit (SBU) level.

We advocate that the SBU is the appropriate level of an enterprise to examine, as at any level higher than this the focus will weaken and become more diffuse. Different SBUs in the same company probably will be focused on quite different markets/segments (otherwise, they would not need to be separate). At a lower level than SBU, we run the risk of not having enough engagement with the problem owners who can make decisions on their own authority. We can find derivative activities at marketing team and sales team levels, but the initiative must start with and be owned by SBU leaders who see the strategic significance of the activity.

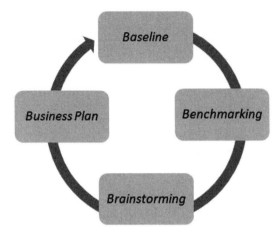

Figure 5.2 Axia Valgorithm.

Value is defined only by customers. There is a temptation to assume that a company's managers know the value they are delivering. Nevertheless, from our experience with the "So what?" question, there is still a lot of vagueness about this. More important, however, if the company is failing in its value delivery or in its pricing, we can safely assume that the managers *do not know* the value that their customers want. This is probably best assessed independently. We illustrate the approach in the flowchart in Figure 5.2.

The process consists of four phases typically undertaken over a number of months for any changes to be made to work through to the consciousness of the customer.

Baseline

Key question: How do customers assess the products and services we sell them, and are these assessments consistent with their expectations?

This is the starting discussion in which we work with the customer to identify the critical drivers that arise from the customer's value chain and business context. This is exactly the bit that the furniture company, as a supplier, completely missed. This should be an in-depth study examining the way in which your products are used, the positive and negative aspects of that usage, and collecting opinions from users. This also may include a search for the metrics that the customer is applying and attempting to identify the data that are used to calculate the metrics.

Benchmarking

Key question: Are your salespeople, marketing people, product managers, and company managers aligned on delivering the value demanded by their customers, and how is this measured?

The information collected from the customer is analyzed, summarized, and presented back to the internal team using a series of charts and diagrams to compare actual information (from the customer) with what internal people believe to be the situation. Spider charts and similar tools are applied to highlight divergences from customer expectations. The end result is generally a clear gap between what the customer ideally would like and what the supplier is actually delivering. This is best facilitated by someone not intimately involved in delivering the product or service.

Brainstorming

The supplier's whole team works together to ensure alignment on customer value delivered and commitment to a value based strategy.

The next step in the process is to explore how this gap can be bridged. Any necessary changes and adjustments to internal processes should be linked to the establishment of metrics that clearly link internal processes with customer outcome measures. Once the key changes have been identified and made, they must be monitored for long enough to ensure both that the right factors have been identified and that the correct measures have been created.

Business Planning

Review initial results and realign the team on segmental business objectives as necessary.

The final step in the process is to develop implementation plans for the remainder of the customer base and to roll this out over a period of weeks or months depending on the nature of the relations. The effectiveness of these changes needs to be monitored regularly to ensure continued alignment, particularly in rapidly changing markets.

The one reality of value is that customers' perceptions of it are constantly changing. As a result, you need to apply regularly the whole Axia Valgorithm process to your business relationships in order to monitor those changes and to respond accordingly.

PART II

Value-Based Pricing in Practice

CHAPTER 6

Building the
Value-Based Price

If you ask me how much something costs, I need to ask you, "Why do you want to know?"
—Gordon Shillinglaw, Professor Emeritus of Accounting,
Business Law and Taxation, Columbia Business School

We have already seen that conventional pricing methods fail to take account of the value delivered by well-conceived and carefully differentiated products and services. As a result, pricing discussions between buyers and sellers tend to become adversarial. The customer perceives that the vendor expects too much payment for a product that can at best only partially address his needs. The vendor, for her part, becomes frustrated and, in order to win a deal, compromises her position by discounting. The result is a win-lose situation, the winner being the one who exercises the greatest power in the exchange. Future discussions become increasingly contentious as the previous loser tries to redress the situation. Value-based pricing (VBP), in contrast, seeks to identify and reach agreement on the benefits created by the product or service—economic and emotional. Once agreement is reached, both parties then share in the gains created by the transaction. Handled correctly, VBP leads to win-win situations and to long-term sustainable relationships based on trust.

DEFINING VBP

We suggest the following definition:

> A value-based price is designed and communicated such that all parties understand, recognize, and accept the distinctive worth of products and services purchased in the transaction and participate optimally in the gains created by their use.

The first thing to note about this definition is that the price is specifically designed for each individual transaction based on our assessment of the critical mix of values to the customer. This mix consists of the net revenue gain to be achieved by the customer and the overall net cost reduction that he experiences as a direct result of adopting our proposed solution. This is not pricing on *perceived* value. We measure value as objectively as we can using, wherever possible, the customer's own metrics. Therefore, it is pricing on *objectively measurable* value so far as is possible in a given situation. In constructing the value-based price, we make the fullest possible use of Value Triad thinking.

Second, we should note the existence of multiple participants to the VBP transaction. The first two participants are obvious—the seller and the customer—and we shall examine these in a moment. Often there is also a third party involved, and if he is genuinely contributing to the value adding process, he is also entitled to benefit from the transaction.

The whole transaction is motivated by a desire to deliver a superior solution to a customer's problem (or enable customers to exploit a business opportunity). This solution must be unique if the supplier is to claim and benefit from the measurable differential value. The buyer must be a winner, and her choice of solution must deliver to her real value in line with her own definition of value. Ideally, the buyer should be engaged in the cocreation of a solution that generates mutual value.

VBP is not merely about delivering superior value to the customer. It is also about capturing a fair proportion of this value for ourselves. If all the value flows to the customer, there is no real point in our adopting VBP other than perhaps making the customer aware of the value that she has been enjoying and has come to expect. But then this is something our salespeople and our marketing collateral should be communicating anyway. The third element of the definition relates to the customer's understanding of the real worth of the value offered. Not every customer will acknowledge this worth. Some will seek to "rubbish" the assertions of the supplier or seek to denigrate the offer by challenging its uniqueness, performance, and so on. In such circumstances, the vendor needs to decide whether such a sale is worth the effort. He always should be prepared to walk away rather than compromise on price or yield to bullying behavior. There are, after all, other customers who will understand, acknowledge, and buy into a proposition. These *value buyers* are our target. For VBP to have any prospect of success, we need to deal with individuals who are willing to listen intelligently to our offer and have the vision to recognize the potential impact of this offer on their own value-adding processes. This will mean being willing on occasion to bypass procurement and go direct to the owners of the problem.

The use of the word *optimally* is important. VBP is not just about charging higher prices, nor is it only about better profit—it is about better business. It is about being rewarded for creative thinking and innovation and delivering propositions to the right customers that generate sustainable win-win relationships. VBP is not about profit maximization at the expense of relationships, and it is certainly not about "ripping off" our customers. These attitudes merely lead to adversarial relationships in the future. As one of our clients put it, "We need to have some skin in the game."

The final part of the definition relates to products and services. In VBP, we are trying to provide customers with the best solution that we can offer them that will meet or exceed their criteria. This might, for instance, result in the creation of a bundle consisting of products, services, or both. The emphasis is on delivery of real value that truly meets the customer's needs and wants efficiently and cost-effectively and doing so better than any other supplier to which the customer has access.

Implicit within the definition is that our product or service must be clearly differentiated from those of the competition. This demands a much deeper discovery process and the collection and assessment of a lot of customer and competitor data. Since each customer is different, our products and services will offer different advantages to each depending on context. As a result, we will charge a uniquely constructed price for each deal. Even if the sum charged ends up being the same, the underlying transaction will differ from situation to situation.

COMPARING VBP WITH CONVENTIONAL METHODS

In Chapters 3 and 4 we reviewed the advantages and disadvantages of cost-based and competition-based approaches to pricing. While there are some favorable aspects to those approaches, they all suffer from serious systemic flaws.

Table 6.1 compares conventional approaches to VBP across a number of dimensions. While VBP potentially can offer greater advantages to the user than conventional approaches, we need to use VBP carefully. It is not a panacea, and it should not be used in every situation. We certainly do not encourage rebuilding of price lists using VBP exclusively or indiscriminately.

Table 6.1   Comparison of Conventional and VBP Methods

	Competition-based	Cost-based	Value-based
Focus	Competitors' prices and specifications	Internal costs and their reduction	Delivery of measurable benefits to all parties to the relationship
Encourages	Pursuit of market share rather than profit	Formula-based approach that is applied by rote and without specific consideration	Cooperation, partnership, and deep customer knowledge
Customer relationships	Not well developed	Not well developed	Central to all transactions

Reward for innovation	Minimal or none	Minimal or none	High and sustainable returns if innovation leads to meaningful product or service differentiation
Selling methods	Transactional with emphasis on features and specifications	Transactional with emphasis on features and specifications	Consultative/ solution-based demanding a detailed understanding of a buyer's business context and value-adding processes
Inducement to buy	Discounting and deals	Discounting and deals	Demonstrable economic advantages at different places in the value chain
Organizational approach	Junior/middle management with significant discretion for salesperson	Junior/middle management with significant discretion for salesperson	Needs to be part of a company-wide initiative to build value into all parts of the business
Ease of calculation	Relatively quick and easy, but sometimes competitive prices are difficult to unearth, and judging the correct position may be unreliable	Quick and easy with most data available in-house	More complex because it requires detailed information about how the product or service affects the buyer's value chain economically and how it affects decision makers and users emotionally
Selling skills	Transactional but requires reasonable knowledge of competitors' prices and relative performance	Basic order taking and some transactional	Demands the highest level of development of selling skills and negotiation skills of a very high order, possibly leveraged by a team approach
Value capture	Limited or none for the vendor, with the customer enjoying excessive consumer surplus	Limited or none for the vendor, with the customer enjoying excessive consumer surplus	Complete or as well as our salespeople can negotiate based on an analysis of the client's value-adding processes and how we can enhance them

When should VBP be used?

- *New or enhanced products and services* where these offer significant improvements in two or more areas of the Value Triad (e.g., Alathon, introduced by DuPont as an alternative to polytetrafluoroethylene)[1]
- *Products incorporating novel technology* that offer dramatically improved performance or significantly reduced costs in use (e.g., Dyson's vacuum cleaner)
- *Products completely new to the world* with no viable technology alternatives (e.g., flexible fiber optic endoscopes)
- *Existing products and services being introduced into a new geography*, where they represent a major improvement in performance compared with incumbent methods in that geography (e.g., mobile phones in remote areas of India or Africa)
- *Where other companies in an industry are already using VBP* to price their products and services (e.g., accident and injury lawyers, logistics companies, and specialized consultancy services)
- *More complex transactions* requiring a customized approach based on clear understanding of the customer's situation and context (e.g., speciality chemicals suppliers and specialized management training)
- *Where we are able to meet a customer's needs through our ability to construct a unique package of products and services*, even within a highly competitive market (e.g., Virgin Mobile)

Where the customer is conditioned through custom or usage to expect high performance at unrealistically low prices, reeducation will be necessary. In some cases, this will be impossible, especially if the buyer is a price buyer and rejects or ignores all our efforts to demonstrate value. This is a very difficult challenge. It requires the buyer to acknowledge the value we bring, perhaps for the first time, within a context in which the buyer has previously possessed and has been willing to wield significant buying power. If the buyer seeks to dominate the relationship and is willing to apply raw buying power, there is virtually no scope for a VBP deal unless the problem owners can be engaged instead. Where the buyer is intransigent, the best approach is either to walk away or to recognize that VBP is not an option. In this case, the final price should be as close as possible to the highest price the customer is prepared to pay, and the product or service should be configured in such a way that the buyer receives only what she pays for.

Curiously, exactly the opposite seems to be happening in one industry. For as long as the profession has been in existence, it seems, lawyers have been charging by the hour for their services. Dissatisfaction with this approach to billing has been growing for many years because corporate clients find it difficult to correlate huge fees with measurable value. Recession has brought this to a head. Clients are now demanding clear demonstration of value and are requesting alternative billing arrangements. According to an executive from Crowell and Moring, a well-known international law firm,

> We align incentives with clients, a clear-cut shift from pricing hourly billing inputs. We no longer consider these arrangements as alternatives but as our primary fee arrangements. It gives us an advantage in the credit crunch and has led to a substantial increase in work.[2]

BUILDING A VALUE-BASED PRICE

The Value Triad is used to analyze the real value that we offer to our clients. This may be related to reducing customers' costs, to increasing a customer's productivity, to reducing her "hassle," or to improving her peace of mind. The first two elements of the Triad—revenue gains (RGs) and cost reductions (CRs)—generally are *relatively* easy to quantify. It is somewhat more difficult to put a rigorous economic value on emotional contribution (EC)—and even more difficult to defend it on objective evidence.

Typical Business-to-Business (B2B) Example

A company manufactures specialized adhesives (resins) for use in the automobile industry. Resins are used in gluing bodywork components during assembly. This adhesive is more durable than and more than

Table 6.2   Value Triad Analysis (from Vehicle Builder's Perspective)

	RGs	CRs	EC
Longer lasting, more durable joints	Fewer injuries, better productivity	Reduced warranty claims	Reduced hassle
Low volatile organic compound (VOC)/ toxic emissions	Lower absenteeism through workplace allergy-related sickness	Fewer claims, lower absenteeism, avoidance of health and safety (HSE) investigation	Peace of mind for managers
Wider range of operating temperatures	More choice of geographical markets with extremes of temperature.	Provides greater flexibility in manufacturing process design	

twice as strong as competitive materials, which make it a very attractive alternative to competitors' materials. The adhesive itself can be used effectively at a wider range of temperatures than competitive products. The resin is free of formaldehyde, which is toxic and unpleasant to work with, and has a much lower content of organic solvents, which are common resin components. These properties give rise to advantages both to the company incorporating these adhesives in its products and to its customers. Table 6.2 provides a Value Triad analysis of this situation.

From the point of view of the end user, the properties of the new adhesive enable him to use the vehicle in more extreme environmental conditions, but most important, "things don't fall off," necessitating an inconvenient and time-consuming visit to the workshop. Better adhesive properties even may eliminate catastrophic failures at speed.

The Role of Pricing within the Marketing Mix

Most managers are familiar with the concept of the *marketing mix*. This is a set of tools marketing people use to generate customer demand at the time of the transaction (e.g., the "four P's"—product, place, promotion, and price) or to build a strong customer relationship (e.g., the "seven P's"—i.e., the four P's plus people, process, and physical evidence). The mistake that is often made is to decide on the price upfront and then shoehorn the other mix elements to fit. This thinking is completely the wrong way around. We cannot possibly start to think about price until we are clear in our minds about the proposition we are offering to the customer; and we cannot be clear on that if we have not properly thought through our solution, the logistics of delivery, and how we will communicate the whole package.

Price is the last part of the mix that we should consider. To do so, we need to know

- The nature of the product or service required to resolve the customer's problem
- What it costs us to deliver it
- The economic, strategic, or emotional benefits that satisfactory delivery of a product or service creates for the customer

Until we know these things, we are not in any position to calculate the customer's total cost of ownership or assess the benefits she gains and how price fits into this. Price is often the first element of the mix to be considered, and this then dictates everything else. The thinking is generally much less than rigorous. When the mix is assembled in this way, selection of the product or service element is based on cost rather than on delivery of real value.

THE BUILDING BLOCKS OF VBP

In building up a value-based price, we focus entirely on the value our products and services offer to customers compared with some reference (usually a product or service that they are currently using or would choose if our solution were not available). The building blocks of a value-based price (Figure 6.1) include

- The price of a reference product or service (RP)
- The quantified net gains in revenue relative to the reference (net revenue gains, or NRG)
- The quantified net reductions in cost relative to the reference (net cost reduction, or NCR)
- Emotional contribution (EC), for example, greater peace of mind, risk reduction, reduced "hassle" and inconvenience, and so on

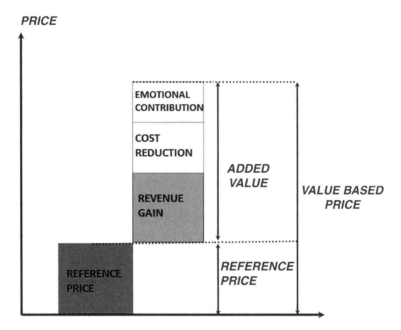

Figure 6.1   Building blocks of VBP.

Although difficult to quantify objectively, these factors can be immensely influential in the buying decision.

The formula for calculating a value-based price is

Maximum value-based price = reference price (RP) +
net revenue gain (NRG) + net cost reduction (NCR) +
emotional contribution (EC)

We need to know a lot about our customers' businesses to be able to assess how our product or service enhances revenue streams or helps to eliminate costs. Once we have captured this information and we are able to justify our calculations, it becomes easier to construct a target value-based price.

Unless the customer fully accepts and buys into our estimates, we are certain to be challenged on our calculations. In making this kind of calculation, we need to use the customer's own data as far as we possibly can. If such data are unavailable, perhaps because the client declines to provide them, we should use authoritative third-party sources. We use our own estimates only if there are no viable alternatives. If the customer then challenges our figures, we can at least ask him what figures *he* considers to be appropriate.

Let's now examine these building blocks a little more closely.

Reference Price

The price of the reference product is an essential component of the calculation. This is the price that the customer would pay for a product or service which he perceives to be similar to the one that we are offering—his *reference product*. If our product offers no added value compared with the reference product, then there is neither revenue gain nor cost reduction, and VBP is not a realistic pricing option.

The *reference price* is the price that the customer expects to pay (and is conditioned to pay) based on the price he paid on the last occasion he was in the market for a purchase of this nature. Industry practice may vary. For instance, the total price to the customer may include a bundled price consisting of the capital cost of the asset and the costs of a variety of accessories and components. Alternatively, the price may be broken down to show itemized price elements. In calculating our offer, and when we are attempting to estimate NCR and NRG, we need to know and understand, as clearly as possible, the details of any competing offer so that we are genuinely comparing our offer with the customer's real alternative. This means collecting sound factual information about the probable invoice price that the customer is likely to pay. In some cases, this information is readily available—the customer even may volunteer it, or it may be available with a little digging in public-domain sources, through competitive intelligence, from other customers, and from the competitor's own marketing communications.

Customers may not be willing to share this information with us and may expect us instead to make an offer based on our understanding of their situation. This is perfectly reasonable. However, it places us under greater pressure to think through our proposition fully and to identify where we think our proposition differs (positively or negatively) from other offers the customer may be considering.

In many cases, it will be quite straightforward to identify a realistic reference price. In two particular scenarios, however, establishing a reference price is rather more difficult—the completely new product and the very large, very infrequent purchase.

If our product is new to the market—perhaps even new to the world— there will be no real reference for us to use. In this case, the reference price will be based on an analysis of how the customer is currently solving the problem or dealing with the situation. This makes matters very difficult for the buyer because he does not have a realistic benchmark against which to compare our offer. Such measures may be manual in nature, and the customer does not in fact perceive any problem. (See, for example, the Aquarius case study at the end of this chapter.)

There are many examples of products or services that offer step changes in performance or were even completely new to the world when they were introduced. Typical examples of such innovations include flexible fiber optic endoscopes (for medical and industrial inspection or diagnosis), the smart phone, and fax machines.

Customers who more readily recognize the benefits of an innovative solution are those for whom existing approaches are inadequate or unsatisfactory. These customers have the greatest compelling need. They seek new approaches to solving problems that demand performance levels as yet unachievable by conventional methods.

Customers with highest-priority needs consist of those charged personally with solving some challenging business problem. These individuals have a compelling need and potentially will pay a price that is much greater than that other individuals elsewhere in the market would contemplate for an effective solution. The initial value proposition for these users recognizes this need, and prices are set in a manner that might seem high to the early majority and perhaps even insane to laggards and late majority customers. If we can demonstrate that our offer can solve an otherwise intractable problem, we have a bridgehead into the market, and a new market emerges as new users appear and new applications are developed.

Very large-scale value-pricing projects pose different problems. In such cases, the reference price is considerably more difficult to assess accurately. Some of the complicating factors we have encountered in consulting practice include the following:

Scale of the Project

Very large-scale capital projects are almost impossible to compare item by item, and any attempt to equate two even contemporary projects is fraught with difficulty. Therefore, reaching agreement on an appropriate reference price is a negotiation process in its own right.

Historical Prices

Purchases made many years ago will be based on different costs and quite different commercial contexts than today's purchases. It may be possible to apply some scaling factor such as the producer price index in an attempt to create comparable figures.

Current-Market-Context Factors

These also have a bearing, for example, the degree to which competitors' resources are committed and, as a result, whether there is a temporary surplus of demand over supply. In this case, the reference price will need to be updated to reflect the price that a competitor would quote today in order to make this new business attractive.

Fairness

Technology almost certainly will have moved on in all but the most conservative of industries. This means that today's costs are likely to be very different (lower) in the event of technology change. Allocating a very high reference price based on elderly and outdated technology practices will be unfair and invalid. Such prices also may be anticompetitive.

Net Revenue Gain (NRG)

The NRG is the aggregate of all incremental revenues that result from use of our product or service compared with the reference product. We should note here that we need to calculate *net* revenue gain. It is conceivable that in order to access greater revenue, we will need to change processes, procedures, or approaches. These actions create a temporary reduction in revenue. If the change is truly beneficial to our customer's business, this reduction will be minimal and transitory. For instance, introducing highly automated machines to replace manually operated equipment will involve closing down current operations, preparing the site for new equipment, staff training, and potentially writing off old plant with temporary loss of production and revenue. Such costs are substantial, and we look at these under net cost reduction. Revenues are also reduced as a result of the changes, but we are betting that the new machines will pay for all of this in due course through higher output and more predictable quality.

Net Cost Reduction (NCR)

NCR is the aggregate of all avoided fund outflows from the customer as a result of employing a product or service in her business. We need to measure *net* cost reduction. Not every element of a product or service will lead directly to a cost reduction. In order to access the overall cost reduction, the user may need to make additional investments to enable the full cost reductions to be realized, for example, when introducing new equipment (as in the preceding example) or when investing in new accounting software. This requires customers to move from an Excel-based approach, which their business may have been implementing successfully for many years, to a more sophisticated system. To access the full benefits of the new package, they need to change accounting procedures, train staff, procure consultancy to implement the system, accept an initially higher level of errors, and troubleshoot until the system is fully operational. There are significant upfront costs that, one hopes, the downstream cost reductions achieved will more than pay for. In understanding the economic impact of our products and services, we need to think through these issues fully.

In building a value-based price for the customer, we need to pinpoint the key costs and pain factors that exist, demonstrate how these can be managed, and quantify the savings.

Emotional Contribution (EC)

EC is inherently difficult to quantify objectively, as we saw in Chapter 5. While it may be possible to assert a particular economic worth to a given EC element, this must be a reasonable and believable figure. EC elements are particularly useful when used in face-to-face selling and the negotiation stages of a transaction.

The Negotiation Corridor

In VBP, there is often an element of negotiation (Figure 6.2). This comes about because the reference price, in the customer's mind, is much lower than the value-based price the seller offers her. This gap must be bridged, and it is bridged by the ability of the seller to convince the buyer of the economic attractiveness of the value-based offer. Unless there are compelling overriding reasons (e.g., urgency, managerial stress levels, political expediency, etc.), it is unlikely that the seller will achieve the maximum value-based price. In fact, the rational buyer would never accept this price, barring overarching EC elements, because the maximum value-based price is an *indifference* price—that is, there is no economic advantage to the buyer in making this choice. In fact, when we factor in the time value of money, the maximum value-based price is likely to be less attractive than the reference price.

The final negotiated price will lie somewhere in the corridor between the reference price and maximum value-based price. How high will depend on the strength of the arguments and the seller's advocacy skills, on the one hand, and the buyer's budget, her determination to achieve the best deal she can for her company, and her ability to use her sources of information as a counter to the seller's arguments, on the other. If the seller consistently fails to achieve a price higher than the reference price, then something has gone seriously wrong. Either the seller

Figure 6.2   The negotiation corridor.

does not have the skills, or the relevant facts (and this is his employer's failing) or the product genuinely does not offer any advantage.

Price negotiations have a tendency to polarize positions and points of view and to become contentious. Pricing is an emotive topic, and we should perhaps expect some push back. If we could avoid or reduce the need for negotiation, this would pay benefits in terms of reduced hassle and conflict between the parties and help us to achieve the win-win outcome everyone hopes for. This can be accomplished at least in a few cases where there is complete openness and cooperation between buyer and seller in reaching agreement on the work to be done and how the downstream benefits will be shared. Several case studies in Appendix B show how some companies have achieved this.

THE VBP WORKSHEET

The VBP worksheet enables us to capture all the relevant data to calculate a value-based price. It is the basis for a checklist to be used in client discussions (Table 6.3).

Table 6.3 Generic VBP Worksheet

Product/service	Our solution	
Scenario	Select this carefully—could be useful for life, a year, or some other unit that makes sense in the context	
Customer/client	Name of client and of contact person	
Date	Date on which calculations were made	
Value Triad elements	**Our solution**	**Comments**
Emotional contribution		Add up cash value of all intangibles if calculable. In practice, quantifying these is difficult or impossible, but we should capture them on this worksheet because they can be powerful persuaders in face-to-face negotiations.

Total emotional contribution (EC)		
Add: Revenue gains		Readily measured gains such as increased revenue, improved yield, etc.
Less: Revenue losses		Productivity losses from implementing our solution (e.g., cannibalization, scrapping of stock).
Net revenue gains (NRG)		**Net cash value of all benefits in the scenario.**
Add: Cost reductions		Ways in which our solution increases our customers' costs. These need to be quantified objectively and ideally independently.
Less: Cost increases		Ways in which our solution reduces our customers' costs. These need to be quantified objectively and ideally independently.
Net cost reductions (NCR)		**Net cash value of all cost savings.**
Total added value		EC + NRG + NCR
Unit reference price		Price of reference product, which could be a competitive item or a previous version of our product.
Maximum economic price		RP + EC + NRG + NCR
Minimum economic price		RP or cost based or competition-based price
Target price		Negotiable

There are a number of important points to highlight.

Scenario

This is the basis on which we estimate the total value delivered to the customer. It might be the total life of the product in normal use or a year of experience in delivering a service. We select the scenario that best enables us to calculate our value-based price objectively and believably, remembering that we need to be able to use it to persuade our customer of the validity of our case. The scenario must be one with which she can identify.

Quantified Value Triad Elements

We must try to capture these elements as comprehensively as we can because we shall be building up our price using these ideas. It is possible that our solution will have some disadvantages over that of the competition. We need to identify these and make a realistic calculation of their impact on the overall argument. If our solution has too many disadvantages compared with the reference product, VBP may not be the best option, and we should use an alternative pricing method—there is no differential advantage.

Our Solution

We identify here the economic advantages and disadvantages associated with our solution. We must categorize these comprehensively. If we miss something significant, especially if doing so works to our advantage, this certainly will be picked up and challenged by the customer and may erode the credibility not only of our argument but also of our whole solution.

Comments

Use this column to record how we reached the numbers in the worksheet—it is easy to forget—and to make necessary reference to original third-party sources of information. Also, we should not forget to make a note of the various EC items. These can be overlooked easily or even forgotten in the course of negotiation, and we would lose a potential advantage.

Maximum Economic Price

The *maximum economic price* is the maximum price we can justify on objective data. In reality, the customer may well be prepared to pay more because of the EC elements, but we cannot justify this on numbers alone. In a B2B situation, the decision maker may have to answer to others inside his organization for his selection—so we need to give him some powerful arguments.

Minimum Economic Price

The *minimum economic price* may be one of several things—the current (or time-adjusted) reference price of a competitor (which may be zero if the method is manual or very basic), our price to the customer for a previous product, or even the full-cost recovery price for our product. It does not need to be any of these. We can simply say that "*x* is what we want to achieve as a minimum for this sale." Whatever we choose, it must be a realistic reference price to the customer and an absolute negotiation backstop.

Case Study: Aquarius

Aquasystems was incorporated in 2002 to exploit a number of polymer technologies possessed by its founders. One of these technologies is the active ingredient in the Aquarius product.

Aquarius is a fabric bag that contains the active ingredient in pellet form. The bags can be made to any size and shape, but the typical configuration is 18 inches circular. The pellets absorb up to 10 times their own volume of water. Over a period of several weeks, this water is released, and the pellets dry out, returning to their original size. While in the swollen state, they retain structural integrity and permit easy circulation of air between them. This process can be repeated indefinitely with no deterioration in water absorption and release. A fully saturated 18-inch bag will release its charge of water uniformly over six to eight weeks depending on the humidity of its immediate environment, which, in turn, depends on external environmental factors. The material is unique—it can be manufactured only by Aquasystems—and is covered by international patents that have 20 years to run. Patent searches (by the U.K. Patent Office) and in-depth market research at the time revealed no similar technology in use anywhere in the world.

(Continued)

Interior landscapers (sometimes called *interiorscapers*) make a business of installing growing tropical plants in offices, homes, and public buildings. In any one building, there might be several hundred such plants. Usually, plants are rented, leased, or bought outright by the client. Almost always, part of the deal is a contract for maintenance of the plants. Plants are installed in planters (i.e., big pots or troughs) as part of the contact. They are then kept in good health by regular visits by technicians. Contracts run for three to five years. Rental/lease fees are between $3.30 and $6.60 per unit (i.e., per container) per week depending on size and type of plant and on the design of the container. Industry experts estimate that increasing the watering interval from two to four weeks would increase gross profitability to 67 percent; increasing the interval to six weeks would increase this to over 80 percent.

In general, a technician visits each plant once every two weeks. He will remove dead leaves, clean the surface of the soil, remove extraneous debris, feed and water the plant, and sometimes polish the leaves. The frequency of visits is determined by the watering cycle. During the summer, plants need to be watered more frequently. This commonly creates a problem for interior landscaping managers, who must try to schedule holiday cover. No competitive system at the time permitted a watering cycle of more than two weeks. The market is cynical about automatic watering systems. There have been many similar claims, but in general, they do not work very well, and most interiorscapers have gone back to manual watering methods.

In very small interior landscaping businesses, the owner/manager is also the technician. Such businesses tend to remain small family affairs because the owner has no time to spend developing the business or building a larger customer base. They are often barely profitable. Aquarius could break this cycle by improving productivity and releasing the owners to undertake more business development.

In repeated (comparative) trials, an 18-inch Aquarius system consistently provided enough water to sustain a typical plant in good health for six weeks without watering. In these trials, plant death from overwatering was eliminated. The technician time spent on each plant was halved.

The single largest cause of plant death is overwatering. This usually occurs because technicians err on the side of caution (i.e., give more water rather than less). Plant watering is seen as more of an art than a science, with every horticulturist having her own opinion about what any given plant requires. Strangely enough, most plants prefer to be too dry rather than too wet. Extremes of wet and dry (as well as cold or heat) can damage plants severely. The result is that wastage is anything from 15 to 25 percent over the course of a year, overwatering being responsible for about 80 percent of these cases. Plant replacement can cost as much as $165, with about $60 being the average cost (including repotting and reinstallation). Insurance premiums are becoming very expensive both because of plant replacement and because of the occasional carpet damage caused by water spills from broken planters. Interior landscaping contractors are expected to absorb these costs.

In general, technicians are unskilled and are paid at or about minimum wage—on average, around $9.00 per hour at the time. They work a 37.5-hour week with 27 days' holiday per annum (including statutory). Sickness absence and training account for another 8 days. Working efficiently, a technician can look after 25 sites per day depending on the density of the installations. Each site has an average of six plants. Cycle time currently is two weeks but varies considerably depending on whether the contracts are in urban, suburban, or rural locations, as well as on the logistics of each site (e.g., if water is readily available or has to be carried for a distance). A significant problem, particularly in cities, is the rate of parking costs and fines. One to two fines per week is not unusual, and parking wardens have little flexibility (or interest) in "turning a blind eye" to a trader.

Industry managers are concerned about operational costs—the industry is very labor-intensive, and personnel are often very poorly trained and motivated. Managers need to find a foolproof and cost-effective method of plant watering if margins are to be maintained. Clients are becoming more interested in artificial plants, which now look very lifelike and have virtually no maintenance costs. The market share taken by artificials is increasing steadily at the expense of live plants.

(Continued)

The general feeling in the industry is that if it were possible to find a reliable way of maintaining live plants, then the decline in demand would be reversed. There are many health and well-being arguments in favor of using live plants in the workplace. In trade association surveys, office workers have repeatedly expressed a preference for "real" plants. Even the National Aeronautics and Space Agency (NASA) in the United States has weighed in with arguments in favor of living plants because of the psychological effect on workers as well as their ability to "clean" the air (i.e., remove CO_2 and introduce oxygen through photosynthesis).

Aquarius offers managers two quite distinct options:

- Achieve greater revenue from the same or fewer technicians (i.e., doing more with the same staff), or
- Doing the same amount of work with fewer staff

Aquasystems' management needs to decide on the best way to price the product both to gain volume rapidly and to recoup product development and patenting costs.

Solution

There are at least two broad scenarios that can be considered in this case study—a business-development option (i.e., using the reduction in labor enabled by the technology to manage a higher workload) or a cost-reduction option (i.e., using increased technician effectiveness to reduce head count and related costs). The following solution reflects a business-development scenario using the 18-inch circular version of the product and assuming one technician-year (226 days).

Value Triad Analysis
(See Table 6.4.)

Table 6.4 Value Triad Analysis (from Equipment Operator's Perspective)

	RG	CR	EC
Extends duration between watering	Revenue per unit remains the same. Technician cycle doubled (BD option).	Or the company can half the number of technicians (cost reduction option).	For client, less hassle because technician is on site less frequently.

Plant health	Technology enables use of more exotic species at higher unit price.	Plant replacement needs are eliminated and cost savings are achieved.	Feel good factor because plants look healthier.
Elimination of consequential damage	May encourage greater use of live rather than artificial plants.	No liquid water in planter; therefore, no risk of spillage or damage to office fabric.	Peace of mind. Avoidance of hassle.
Technology drives process		Cheaper technicians and much less variability in potting process.	Easy to implement and manage—so again no hassle.

Productivity Gains

On the current 10-day cycle, technicians are able to handle 150 units (i.e., containers) per day. Aquarius permits them to visit less frequently and while on site to look after the leaves, soil, and container appearance in addition to watering the plant. Existing methods make this very difficult because technicians are always under serious time pressure on site. Thus Aquarius leads not only to better watered plants, but they are also healthier and more attractive, which enhances the client's workplace.

If the frequency of visits drops to once every 20 days, this effectively doubles the technician's capacity and therefore also her productivity. The company can sell an extra 1,500 units at 67 percent gross margin, resulting in added income of

$$\$2,478.30 \times 3 \times 52 \times 0.67 = \$259,031.92$$

Cost Savings

With 1,500 units, the present number of installations without Aquarius, there normally would be 20 percent plant loss on average, of which 80 percent is watering-related.

Total number of plants saved $= 0.2 \times 0.8 \times 1,500 = 240$

Cost of replacement averages $60 per plant

Total savings $= \$60 \times 240 = \$14,400$ (see Table 6.5)

(Continued)

Table 6.5 Application of VBP Worksheet to Aquarius

Product/service	Aquarius	
Scenario	Business-development option, 12 months, 18-inch circular version.	
Customer/client		
Date		
Value Triad elements	Our solution	Comments
Emotional contribution		• Less hassle for the client (and therefore for contractor) • Feel good factor because plants look healthier and therefore for contractor less anxiety about cost of replacement • Peace of mind through avoidance of damage • Easier to manage a standardized setup and operational process
Total emotional contribution (EC)		
Add: Revenue gains	$259,031.92	• Directly accruing through revenue gains on business-development option
Less: Revenue losses	0	
Net revenue gains (NRG)	$259,031	• Net cash value of all benefits in the scenario
Add: Cost reductions	$14,400	• Directly from avoided plant loss and replacement • May be reduction in parking fines because technicians are on site for a shorter period • Insurance premium increases avoided
Less: Cost increases		
Net cost reductions (NCR)	**$14,400**	• **Net cash value of all cost savings**
Total added value	$181.94/unit	• EC + NRG + NCR

Unit reference price	0	• Price of reference product that could be competitive item or previous version of our product
Maximum economic price	$181.94/unit	• RP + EC + NRG + NCR
Minimum economic price	Depends on unit cost*	• RP- or cost-based or competition-based price
Target price	$100	• Negotiable

*This is a real company with a real product. Unit-cost data are confidential, but for the purposes of this case, they can be assumed to be less that 10 percent of the sale price per unit. A cost-based price in this scenario would yield very unattractive margins.

CHAPTER 7

Review of Value-Based-Pricing Methods

Price is what you pay. Value is what you get.

—Warren Buffett

A *value-based price* is one that is designed and communicated such that all parties understand, recognize, and accept the distinctive worth of products and services purchased in the transaction and participate optimally in the gains created by their use.

VALUE-BASED-PRICING (VBP) METHOD CRITERIA

For the purposes of this book, and to support the preceding definition, a VBP method must be one that fulfills the following criteria.

Criterion 1

The pricing method can be described easily to the customer in straightforward language.

Pricing should be transparent to buyer and seller alike. Salespeople are at the front line in presenting and justifying price levels and strategies. If they do not understand your approach, then your customers are unlikely to either. In some cases, VBP calculations are best developed together with the customer, sometimes making use of computer-based models to walk the customer through any complexity (e.g., optional extras). In this way, the price architecture is seen clearly, and the salesperson is on hand to explain the value of each element. Industries where we have observed this approach in action include information technology (i.e., printers and copiers), medical devices, construction, and automotive component suppliers. The guiding principle is to keep the price structure as simple as possible and to be able to demonstrate confidently how it works. Sometimes prices evolve from an informed dialogue with a cooperative customer, and this is a very attractive method.

Criterion 2

The pricing method is based on the economic and emotional gains accruing to the customer.

A value-based price is constructed from the economic and emotional advantages accruing to the customer. Tangible elements are relatively easy to calculate. Intangibles are much less tractable because every customer is different. What one customer may think is a reasonable monetary value for peace of mind, another will reject out of hand. So we need to interact with the customer to find out what is important to him and use this as a basis of estimating the final price that will apply. A VBP method must permit us to understand and demonstrate how emotional and economic gains are used.

Criterion 3

The pricing method enables a fair apportionment of the gains to all parties.

As in most things in business, prices are negotiable. Through negotiation, parties bargain their way to a mutually acceptable outcome. In VBP, we want and try hard to engineer a beneficial win-win (or even win-win-win) outcome. This can be truly achieved only where supplier and buyer are prepared to work together and share information and their understanding of what *value* means to them. The definition of VBP requires that all parties *understand, recognize, and accept the distinctive worth* of the products or services involved in the transaction.

Criterion 4

The pricing method can be used in conjunction with non-VBP approaches

There is no reason for every part of the deal to be priced exclusively on value, although, of course, this is our ultimate aim. VBP is still relatively new in the experiences of many customers, and they may find it difficult or impossible to migrate wholesale to your new approach. If this is the case, then a hybrid pricing deal may be easier for them to understand and accept and easier for you to sell. Alternatively, you may have developed some clever new product, such as specialist software, that needs to work with existing components. The software itself generates exceptional returns for the customer but needs to work with conventional hardware. In a case such as this, price the software on value, but price the hardware in the normal way. Do not simply give away software (or, for that matter, any other valuable component) as an inducement to buy lower-margin hardware. Table 7.1 lists 10 pricing

Table 7.1 VBP Pricing Methods

Method	Also known as or closely related	All Criteria
Outside-in		☑
Contingency	Payment by results (PBR), performance-based	☑
Guaranteed		☑
Retrospective		☑
Premium	Prestige, skimming	☑
Shared gain	Shared savings, shared profit	☑
Manufactured unit		☑
Price bundling		☑
Versioning	Variant, product form	☑
Product line	Line pricing, bait pricing, self-selection	☑

methods that we believe *are* VBP methods because they meet all the criteria we have set.

REVIEW OF VBP METHODS

There are many methods of using VBP, each with specific advantages and disadvantages in a given application.

Outside-in[1]

In conventional VBP, we try to build up a price based on the Value Triad measurements of revenue gains and cost reductions. It takes time and effort to collect this information, and a lot of the time we are looking for objective sources of evidence that we think will be persuasive to the customer. Of course, we must do this, if only to satisfy ourselves that we really are offering differential value. But the fact remains that if the customer doesn't buy it for whatever reason, we have rather an uphill struggle to persuade her.

Outside-in pricing turns this idea on its head. In outside-in pricing, we ask the customer upfront how much she thinks our solution is worth. If you try this approach, ensure that you, your salespeople, and the customer all understand and recognize the detailed nature of the work proposed and how this affects the buyer's business and your own time and other resources. This is really crucial because if the customer doesn't understand your proposition, she will not place anything like its real value on it. Once you are comfortable with her understanding, ask the customer what *she* thinks the solution is actually worth to her! You may be surprised by the response. The customer may place a much higher price on this work than you had set as a target.

The downside, of course, is that the customer may price the work much lower than your VBP calculations indicate, and this is undoubtedly a risk. In this case, take it as the first marker in price negotiation. However, do recognize that there is pressure on the buyer not to look like a cheapskate or to run the risk of insulting you, particularly if there is already a solid and cordial relationship in place or if her relationship with your business is important to her.

Outside-in pricing does not absolve you of the responsibility of carrying out a thorough Value Triad assessment and the measurement of the important differential value you offer.

You can use outside-in pricing if you are uncertain of the totality of the value your product or service offers (although you should have a good idea through Value Triad analysis) and believe the customer is honest and trustworthy.

Contingency[2]

Contingency pricing is used in circumstances where the customer is unable or unwilling to take all the risk of an unsatisfactory outcome. Payment is contingent on the customer achieving a defined set of results. In the event of a satisfactory outcome, the seller's fee is significantly more than he would earn from a simple straightforward fee arrangement. The premium rewards him for the risk he has incurred. In the event of an unsatisfactory outcome, the buyer pays nothing. Shared-savings or shared-gains pricing is a special case of contingency pricing.

In contingency pricing, fees are based on the results achieved for the customer. In this approach to pricing, both buyer and seller need to be very clear on what results are to be achieved. This forms the basis of the contract. In this approach, achievement of any result demonstrably less than the agreed-on result attracts no payment. It is completely different from cost-based pricing because supplier's costs are not involved in the calculation and are the supplier's own concern. In a professional services context, for instance, a service provider needs to be confident that he can deliver the results promised. He cannot later expect the client to pay fees on a time basis if he gets it wrong. The risk in this approach is wholly on the side of the service provider. There is minimal downside for the client apart from, perhaps, lost time and some disappointment. In the event that the provider does deliver the results promised, the profits can be enormous, and both parties are completely satisfied with the deal.

A seller electing to adopt a contingency approach is well advised to understand fully all the risks before entering into such an arrangement and to have a solid and dependable track record in undertaking work of the kind offered. However, he also should recognize that if the project is selected cleverly, he stands to make a great deal of money.

Because of the risk inherent in such a contract, companies may choose to offer a combination of cost-based and contingency-based pricing propositions. For instance, the basic arrangement may be cost-based (e.g., hourly fees) plus a bonus for success. In order for this to be attractive to the customer, there typically would be some degree of discounting on the normal rates (i.e., reducing the customer's risk in the event of failure) so that the seller can participate in the upside advantages in the event of success. Examples include "no win, no fee" in legal services, construction contracts against deadlines (usually in conjunction with a conventionally priced core service), professional training services, and consultancy contracts.

Guaranteed[3]

This is a very high-risk pricing method for the vendor and is an extreme form of contingency. The key element of the arrangement is a cast-iron guarantee of a satisfactory outcome. The benefit to the buyer, of course, is that because a satisfactory outcome is assured, she can forget about it and concentrate on other matters. All the risk and responsibility lie with the vendor. You should only ever consider this approach if you are *absolutely* certain that you fully understand the nature of the engagement and have the skills, time, knowledge, and resources to tackle the task to a satisfactory conclusion. This is not a commitment to be entered into lightly! The peace of mind enjoyed by the customer should carry a sizable—even enormous—premium. An example is professional services, such as a planning consultancy, in which the seller understands fully all the issues; is familiar with contextual factors such as geography, decision makers, local politics, and so forth; and, importantly, has undertaken similar or identical assignments successfully in the past.

Retrospective[4]

Retrospective pricing is used when the eventual outcome cannot be fully predicted. The nature of the work may be such that there are numerous options emerging at different stages, and each option itself leads to further options downstream. The fee is agreed on at the end of the project once the outcome is known. This option might be adopted if the exact work plan cannot be defined properly in advance and changes as the project progresses. Again, this method places a lot of risk on the vendor and demands that appropriate metrics be identified in advance of work commencing. Two other risks to be aware of are the honesty and integrity of the client and what provisions can be made at the outset for stage payments or at least coverage of fixed costs and expenses. Once a final fee is agreed to, these costs then can be deducted from the contract price. Examples include contract research and development (R&D), litigation, major construction development projects, and anywhere in which the downstream benefits to the client are large or involve large sums of money.

Premium[5]

Premium pricing and skim pricing are sometimes confused with one another. In premium pricing we deliberately establish ourselves as the suppliers of the highest-priced product in the market segment(s) we are targeting. This premium price persists throughout the life cycle of the product and is a signature strategy in all the segments we address. A premium-pricing strategy will appeal to discerning customers or those with a compelling need and for whom price is a minor consideration. For instance, Sony has long maintained a policy of being "first or best" in every market it addresses. If a company boasts several products targeting different customers in the same segment, it typically will create a product range with top-end (premium-priced), midrange (average-priced), and lower-end (economy-priced) products. Accounting firms, for instance, will establish services at a very high premium price where the issue is of great importance to the customer (e.g., merger and acquisitions work), a midrange price for routine professional work (e.g., tax planning and investment), and low rates for commodity-type services (e.g., bookkeeping).

Shared Gain[6]

This is similar to contingency in that payment is made on the basis of a satisfactory outcome. The difference, however, is that both parties share the risk, and if successful, both parties share the gain, according to a predefined and agreed-on formula. The risk taken by the seller is that he might put in a great deal of effort and time only to achieve no savings or other gain for the client or that the gain is so small as not to be worth the effort. Indeed, his effort may result in a loss to the customer, and depending on the contract, he may even be expected to share in the loss to the same proportion. This could be a disastrous outcome and demonstrates the need for both tight contracts and the seller's confidence in his ability to deliver the service in the given context. A sensible clause for the seller to include in the contract is some provision to compensate him for the lost time and opportunity. Contracts are important, and both parties need to satisfy themselves that there are adequate remedies built into the agreement to cover unexpected outcomes, how performance is to be measured, how to resolve disagreements, and how exactly payment is linked to performance of the work. A mixed-fee cost based in the event of failure to achieve contingency outcome plus a performance bonus on achieving particular outcomes is a popular way of managing this situation. The bonus could be calculated on incremental value. Baseline estimates are essential in this form of pricing.

In this approach, the provider is able to influence the buyer's productivity or costs directly. Payment is by means of an agreed-on share of the calculated and mutually agreed-on profit surplus created. Fifty percent is a fairly typical fee rate. The costs savings are assessed and agreed on, with reference to the baseline, and the client pays 50 percent (or other agreed percentage) of the cost savings, revenue gains, or profit improvement. Consultants' profit levels can be very high, often many times the level that might have been achieved through a more traditional ("time and line" or straight fee) approach.

This type of pricing approach is also much easier to sell. In practice, the customer is asked to pay only a proportion of the cost savings she would not have been able to make on her own. The consultancy service costs her nothing—or at least, this is how it is presented by an astute salesperson. Examples include specialized consultancy (i.e., business process reengineering, tariff analysis, facilities management, etc.).

Example

This example demonstrates how price can be built up from the revenue gains and cost reductions achieved through clever application of technology to solving a customer problem.

Until the U.K. Bovine Spongiform Encephalopathy (BSE) crisis in the mid–1990s, pharmaceutical companies routinely used organically derived protein to catalyze the manufacture of very highly priced drugs. The ban on using animal-origin materials was enacted because of the fear that they contained prions, which were known to be precursors to Creutzfeldt-Jacob disease (CJD), the human form of BSE. As a result, manufacturers were obliged to find an alternative catalyst for their production processes. Although much less expensive alternatives were available in the form of purified inorganic salts, these also were much less effective and reduced the yield dramatically. A biotechnology company produced a chemically similar material from a biotechnology process rather than from animal origins. Although not as efficient as the now-proscribed animal proteins, it still worked extremely well and very much more effectively than the inorganic salt.

A pharmaceutical company wanted to purchase the material (on an exclusive agreement) and sought a budget price for the new material. The company's need was urgent because it was losing millions of dollars daily in reduced productivity from using the inferior product. The problem for the biotechnology company was how to calculate the price for its unique synthetic protein. Internal suggestions ranged from $35 per gram (the cost of the inorganic salt) to $175 on the basis that "our material is much better than the salt." There was little to go on in terms of reference pricing because this was a completely new approach, and the reference product (organically derived material) was no longer available.

Using a simplified VBP worksheet (Table 7.2), the following calculations were made. (Note that the real figures are disguised for reasons of client confidentiality.)

The scenario is one production run using a single fermentation vessel with a capacity of 10,000 liters. The yield from the inorganic salt method was 5,000 grams of drug. The total cost of the raw materials used in the fermenter was just under $20 million for a full charge,

(Continued)

not including the cost of the inorganic salt. The cost of the salt was $35 per gram, and for each fermentation, 3,000 grams were required, of which only a small proportion was economically recoverable (ignored in the calculation).

By comparison, the yield from the process catalyzed by the new protein was known from trials to be 9,100 grams of drug, which was much closer to the theoretical yield calculated by development chemists and approximating that of the earlier method. No major adjustment of the process was needed, apart from cleaning and recharging the fermentation vessels. For the purposes of this calculation, this is simply ignored. Furthermore, the yield required less downstream processing to refine into the final form. Only 1,000 grams of the synthetic protein were required. Current end-user price for the drug was $3,500 per gram. Although for the customer there was a lot of emotional contribution—reduction of hassle, reduction of anxiety, and peace of mind—these are again ignored.

Table 7.2   VBP Worksheet for Biotechnology Example

Value Triad elements	Our solution	Comments
Revenue gains	$14.35 million	Increased yield multiplied by end-user price: 4,100 × $3,500 = $14.35 million
Less: Revenue losses		None
Net revenue gains (NRG)	**$14.35 million**	**Net cash value of all benefits in the scenario**
Add: Cost reductions	0	None—no additional plant or other equipment or services was required; new material easily incorporated into current methods
Less: Cost increases	0	

Net cost reductions (NCR)	0	Net cash value of all cost savings
Total added value from 1,000 grams of protein	$14.35 million	EC + NRG + NCR
Unit reference price	$0.105 million	3,000 grams of salt at $35 per gram because this is required for a full load on fermenter.
Maximum economic price per full load (1,000 grams)	$14.445 million	RP + EC + NRG + NCR
Minimum economic price	$0.105 million	RP- or cost-based or competition-based price
Target price per 1,000 grams	$3.500 million	Negotiable target of $3.5 million per 1,000 grams or $3,500 per gram of material; this was the same as the end-user price for the produced drug (this arguably could be much higher, but the client was uncomfortable with the size of the numbers)

Manufactured Unit[7]

The majority of volume-manufactured products are priced either on a cost-plus or a competition basis. Mass-produced items typically may be marketed to several quite different market segments. Sometimes such segments have "walls" between them, for example, different country markets or even different application segments within given geographic markets. In such circumstances, it is relatively easy to create the *perception* of a different product through packaging, color schemes, branding, or some other mechanism. If this can be achieved and customers do not communicate with one another, then it may be possible to establish and maintain pricing differentials.

In a situation where a company mass markets a unique product to a variety of vertical markets, maintaining a price differential between those markets becomes rather more difficult. If a price variation in one market is discovered, customers in other markets will quickly seek the lower price for themselves. We discovered a situation just like this in the automation engineering sector. A company with a number of divisions each routinely purchased proximity sensors from the same supplier for quite different products targeted at different markets. Each division ordered essentially an identical component (only the part number and packaging differed), but prices varied by over 200 percent at the extremes in a single region. The situation was worse when different geographic markets were taken into account. The situation was not discovered until the purchaser started to implement an enterprise resource planning (ERP) system at the corporate level. Reverse engineering rapidly revealed that the components were identical, and pressure was brought to bear on the supplier to harmonize the prices or lose the business. We have encountered similar situation in chemicals, biotechnology, and information technology (IT).

The best way to handle this, provided that the item does have demonstrable uniqueness, is to establish a standard value-based price that is acceptable to all potential buyers. The standard value-based price is a weighted-average value-based price for the item across all target-market segments, the weighting depending on the anticipated demand from each segment at that price. Having established a standard value-based price, the task then becomes one of *value-based selling*, in which the salesperson creates a different value argument for each target subsegment. Figure 7.1 illustrates three different scenarios.

In all three scenarios, which are only illustrative (there will be many more), the price is the same. The relative importance of each of the four elements on which the price is based will differ from case to case. Consequently—and obviously—a one-size-fits-all approach cannot work. In conventional features and benefits (F&B) selling, the focus is on identifying one or more features that provide putative benefits to the customer. Seldom is there any real attempt to map this to economic value. When an F&B argument is offered, it tends to be vague and does not stand up to scrutiny if a savvy buyer chooses to perform a specification-by-specification comparison. When this approach fails,

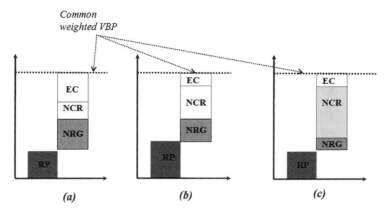

Figure 7.1   Value-based price for a mass-manufactured product.

as it does so often because no clear "what's in it for me" argument is presented, the seller's only approach is to discount, thereby destroying any possibility of demonstrating credibly superior value.

The approach advocated here, which also can and should be applied to conventionally priced products, deliberately focuses on Value Triad elements rather than on specification and seeks to map the product's performance to the customer's value chain *and* provide quantification in support rather than mere assertion. In reality, this is what good salespeople and well-organized companies have been doing for years because they, too, recognize the danger of specification comparisons.

In Figure 7.1*a*, emotional component (EC) is significantly more important to buyers in this segment than the other elements of the Value Triad. In crafting the value proposition, the seller will need to think through and assemble the arguments she can use to justify the price. This is probably the most difficult of the variants presented here because of the significance of EC elements to total customer value.

In Figure 7.1*b*, the reference price is higher than might have been used in the calculation of the weighted average value-based price. This might be a wonderful situation to face if the comparisons between our product and that of the reference demonstrate an economic argument that returns to the customer much more value than the weighted-average price. Of course, the reverse may be the case. The competitor with a higher reference price may be much more difficult to challenge because the customer value delivered is close to what we deliver. The same principle applies. If we have no differential value, we *cannot* make a differential-value argument—and we certainly cannot rationally defend a higher price. However, if there are other aspects of our total offer that do offer differential value, then we bring them into play. Whatever approach we adopt, we will not succeed unless we have a very good understanding of how our product compares with that of competitors and are able to make the differential arguments from a position of sound product knowledge and deep customer understanding.

In the segment represented by Figure 7.1*c*, NCR is considerably more important to customers than the other Value Triad elements. The customer wants to hear how the product will create sustainable cost advantages and will expect to see well-argued and well-documented evidence—perhaps from field trials and evaluations or case studies from other purchasers.

Bundling[8–12]

Bundling is the process of putting a package of products together to meet a customer's requirements as closely as possible. The supplier seeks to create as much demand as possible for his products and services while keeping costs under control. From his perspective, it is ideal if through bundling he can generate demand for both fast-moving products and more slowly moving items. The customer, of course, wants to get as much as she can for the money she is prepared to spend. From her perspective, it is preferable to secure all her requirements from a single source to minimize search time and cost and to optimize her prospects of obtaining a reasonable discount.

Bundling meets both parties' needs neatly. If the seller is able to provide most or all of a customer's requirements from his own product range, this is an efficient use of resources, especially if through this process he leaves as little money as possible on the table. An attractive bundle will stimulate demand because other customers perceive the advantages. The customer obtains more for the same money than she would be able to do by purchasing each of the items separately. The price of the total package is less, perhaps a lot less, than if she were to buy the individual components separately.

It is important to be aware that bundling is more than just putting together a collection of unconnected bits. We try to link these functionally as well as economically.

To make a bundling strategy work, the seller needs to have an excellent understanding of the needs/wants of a market segment, especially what products and services are important and valued and which are not, and the seller also needs to be able to estimate demand at different price levels.

Versioning

Versioning is used to provide a customized form of a product to appeal to different market segments. Versioning is ideally suited as a tool for pricing digital and information products, although it has applications in other markets. Hardware products (i.e., products for school student use, amateur do-it-yourselfers, and professional users), chemicals, and biotechnology reagent manufacturers all make use of versioning. Table 7.3 presents variations of the versioning approach adopted by different companies.

Versioning is a clever form of segmented pricing in which the segments have different but nonoverlapping needs. Textbooks are a great example of versioning. A book can be provided in hardback, paperback, and eventually, e-book format. They even might be reconfigured as practical workbooks and even Web sites, either expanding the market further or removing more consumer surplus.

Note that in Figure 7.2*a*, showing only a single version of the work, there is a lot of white space underneath the demand curve. This consumer surplus is money left on the table that could be captured with the correct strategy. Figure 7.2*b* demonstrates how much of the consumer surplus is captured by multiple versions of the work, each version appealing to different segments with differing price sensitivity.

Authors and publishers create book Web sites and companion materials such as worked cases and calculations, downloadable PowerPoint presentations, and even user groups. Take a look, for instance, at

Table 7.3   Versioning Variants

Versioning type	Objective	Example
Convenience	Restrict time, place, or length of access	Paid-for WiFi services in hotels and airports, e.g., SwissCom, BT Openzone
Comprehensiveness	Big premium for offering more in-depth detail	Online versions of Emerald management journals, newspapers, McKinseys (standard and premium), Worden TeleChart (silver, gold, and platinum)
Manipulation	Ability to store, duplicate, and print data	LexisNexis, online banking, Worden TeleChart online trading software
Community	Access to other users	Friends Reunited, Facebook, BeBo, LinkedIn, etc.
Annoyance	Ability to switch off a pop-up ad by paying a license fee	WinZip
Speed	Different versions of software running at different speeds	Mathematica
Data processing	Various additional data-processing facilities to appeal to different user levels	TaxCalc, MktgEng
User interface	Easy user interface for home/casual users or more complex interface for professional users	Adobe Premiere Elements and Adobe Premiere Elements Pro
Image resolution	Low-resolution thumbnails to assess image and large image to download	Getty Images—1 mb @ $120 up to 48 mb @ $600

Source: Based on Carl Shapiro and Hal Varian, "Versioning: The Smart Way to Sell Information," *Harvard Business Review*, November–December 1998.[13]

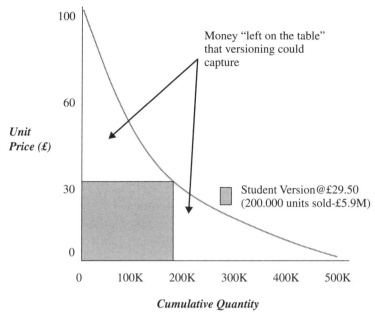

(a) Revenue from a single version

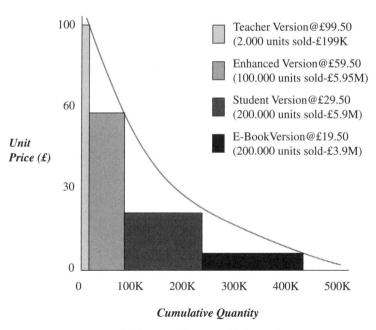

(b) Revenue from multiple versions

Figure 7.2 Versioning in books marketing.

www.mcgraw-hill.co.uk/textbooks/jobber and also at the Exploring Corporate Strategy Web site at www.pearsoned.co.uk.ees. Versioning has been applied to software, online databases, textbooks, journals and magazines, newspapers, and other information products.

Product Line[14-16]

Companies assemble product lines ranging from low-specification/low-price items to very high-specification/high-price items. To be effective, companies wishing to apply product-line pricing should have a complete portfolio of products and services that spans the range of customers' needs and budgets. By self-selecting, the buyer can position himself such that his purchase meets the majority of his needs. There are obvious tradeoffs to be made here, and the shrewd seller will provide options, possibly even bundles, at each major level in the product line that help the buyer to customize the purchase even more precisely to his own needs. Bait pricing is often used in conjunction with product-line pricing. The idea is to entice customers with a lower-priced item in the line and then encourage them to trade up by presenting attractive options within the line.

Many companies build and sell product *ranges* rather than individual products. For example, car companies (e.g., Ford, Vauxhall, GM, Chrysler, BMW, etc.) sell vehicles at different specifications and different prices to suit different segments. Figure 7.3 demonstrates a typical product-line structure. Each vehicle in the range is targeted at a specific segment, although within each segment there may be considerable variation of preferences. For instance, the Ka is focused on the young professional woman (arguably), the Fiesta on the young couple perhaps with their first child, the Focus on the typical family of two adults and two children (and possibly the business market), the Mondeo on the older family and certainly on the corporate market. Each model overlaps to a greater or lesser degree the succeeding or preceding model. This provides a natural upgrade (or downgrade) path. In Figure 7.3 we also have identified the number of variants of each model. The variants provide enormous flexibility to the buyer in terms of what she can secure on her budget. Interestingly, when General Motors introduced line pricing in 1921, the categories did not overlap.

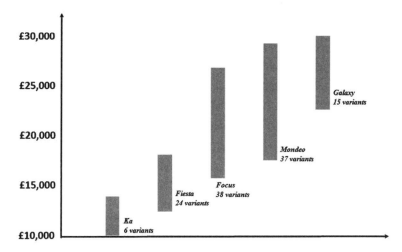

Figure 7.3   Ford car product line.

In product-line pricing, manufacturers recognize that their markets consist of many segments and that each segment has broad expectations from the product it purchases. If designed cleverly, each model in the range can meet the needs of more than one subsegment, thus broadening the appeal and also creating higher demand to achieve scale economies. For example, the Mondeo, with 37 variants in early 2011, can meet the needs of a number of different corporate users (i.e., middle managers, sales representatives, service engineer, taxis, etc.), as well as several consumer segments (e.g., older or larger family user, older driver who likes a bit of comfort, and so on). The trick is to design the model in such a way that the customer is willing to pay for the attributes she wants and is prepared to accept some functionality that she doesn't really need (i.e., paying a premium for her preferred functionality). A large number of variants makes it possible for the customer to self-select her precise choice horizontally within the specific model with relative ease. Several models, at least in the case of Ford prices, are positioned very closely to one another at each "node" to make the choice as easy as possible.

The pricing challenge is to establish a price level for each model that enables the customer to recognize real value to herself through the performance, specification, and styling of the vehicle while still being profitable for the manufacturer to produce.

Critical decisions that need to be made by the producer include

- Establishing the low-end product in the line and the prices, specifications, and variants to offer.
- Establishing the high-end product in the line and the prices, specifications, and variants to offer.
- Fitting in the other models in the range such that each maps efficiently to its target market while optimizing upgrade choices and variant selection.

Deciding on price differentials is tricky partly because collecting the data required is nontrivial. Assessing the interdependencies of costs and demand and the complementarities is important and necessitates psychological, accounting, and economic analyses.

The following are principles for setting price differentials within a product line:

- Each product must be priced correctly in relation to all other products in the line; any differences should be equivalent to perceived-value differences. The cost of providing these differences should be less than the marginal revenue gained from their sale. This gives the supplier some additional economic gain.
- The highest and lowest prices in the line provide reference points to other models. High and low ends should be priced so as to encourage the perceptions we want. Interestingly, the branded Ford range described earlier fits almost precisely into the £10,000 to £30,000 (about $16,500 to $50,000) corridor with only one model breaking through the top end.

An important question relates to how many models should be included in the range. This question can only be answered on the basis of segmentation analysis and comparisons with competition. At each level in the line, segments targeted should offer broadly similar characteristics, especially in terms of price elasticity of demand. However, it should be recognized that depending on price levels and specification, some customers will want to trade up (we want this!), and some will trade down (we *don't* want this!). The way to get around this is to ensure that the higher-level product has some feature perceived as very valuable and attractive to the customer but at a very affordable and less than expected additional price compared with the next-lower option. The price differential should be seen as *less* than the extra value gained by going up-market. This gives the buyer some EC gain.

Product line pricing is very pervasive. Typical examples include hotel rooms, car rentals, new car purchases, the Argos catalogue, software packages, and so on in B2C segments and workstation computers, medical devices, power tools, and car tires in B2B segments.

CHAPTER 8

Building the Value Proposition

I bet your mother knows where the money is, and what you did to get it!

—*Psycho* (1960)

The *value proposition* (VP) concept made its appearance in the mid–1980s. Until then, we didn't have value propositions as such, and certainly no one told us about them when we were young salesmen. We did have other approaches, though. We used to call them—and still do—*elevator pitches, key phrases, opening benefit statements*, and *key messages*, and many people still use these approaches. They tend to focus on a features- and benefits-driven statement of customer outcome. As a result, they are not value propositions in the fullest sense of the term, but when they are used, they "kind of" work. In an unsophisticated way, they communicate why the customer should consider using us. Many of these approaches are now inaccurately called value propositions, but as we will see, there is much more to a well-crafted value proposition.

The most important thing we need to understand about today's VP is that it is a concise summary statement of why the buyer should choose our product or service in preference to that of a competitor. It must be able to answer the question, "Why should I select your product or service rather than your competitor's, and what additional value will I enjoy as a result?" This needs to be articulated convincingly and compellingly. This means that it must focus on the real needs and pain points of the buying organization and offer a believable and practical solution to that organization. A VP statement needs to use understandable and unambiguous language that is meaningful to the customer and the individuals who make up the customer's buying decision-making team. It must be provable in the sense that it is based on some visible and demonstrable element of uniqueness your company possesses (and, of course, ideally that your competitor does not possess or at least not to the degree that your company does).

In order to put the VP into clear context, let's set the scene with a charming little story: Once upon a time, a father went shopping for a pony to buy for his daughter. After looking at dozens of little horses, the man and his daughter narrowed the choices down to two ponies. They seemed identical in every respect. Even the prices were the same. Unable to make up their minds, they decided to take a second look at both ponies.

The first farmer, eager to make the sale, talked on and on about how gentle, how smart, and how cute his pony was. A classic features- and benefits-style approach. The father thanked him and went on his way. The second farmer's approach was completely different. Instead of bragging about his product, he simply said, "Look mister, I'm so sure your little girl is going to love this pony, here's what I suggest. Give me a check, and I'll hold it for 30 days. I'll bring the pony, a bridle and saddle, and 30 days of hay to your house. If your daughter decides to keep the pony, let me know at the end of the month, and I'll cash the check. Otherwise, I'll give you back your check, pick up the pony, and even clean up where he's been."

Who made the sale? The one who reemphasized the benefits? Or the one who made the decision easier by making the purchase and the delivery easy, gave extra support (i.e., the delivery, bridle, saddle, and hay), and made the whole transaction risk-free? The second farmer offered both father and daughter a compelling overall value proposition and not surprisingly secured the business.

In both cases, the product, the pony, and the price were the same. What was different about the second approach was the focus on the overall customer experience.

DEFINING THE VALUE PROPOSITION

At its simplest, the VP is a statement of the real values—tangible and intangible—that we promise to our customer. If it is persuasive enough and resonates sufficiently with the customer's important needs and pain points, we hope she will decide to buy our product or experience our service in preference to that of any competitor. What the customer actually experiences should be the same as or better than she was promised. *Our* VP is *our* promise to *our* customers. A meaningful promise is one that engenders the expectation of material improvement in the customer's situation. To build longer-term business relationships, improvements need to be documented and measured.

So what is a value proposition?

> A value proposition is a clear statement of the tangible and intangible results a customer gets from using your products or services that clearly differentiates your offer from those of competitors.

The definition links a number of important ideas:

- The supplier's demonstrably superior capabilities, which enable the delivery of...
- Tangible and intangible benefits, building...
- Confidence that these benefits will be delivered and will...
- Result in material improvements in the buyer's situation—cost reduction, revenue enhancement, or emotional contribution, the key elements of the Value Triad.

Let's return to the pony story. The first pony seller thought that a clear statement of the benefits and advantages of his pony would be

Table 8.1 Pony Decision Table

	Seller 1	Seller 2
What the daughter wanted		
A loving friend	✓	✓
Fun	✓	✓
Something to love and care for	✓	✓
An opportunity to try	✕	✓
What the father wanted		
A happy daughter	✓	✓
Joy at seeing her excitement	✓	✓
Minimum hassle	✕	✓
Low-risk transaction	✕	✓

enough to "swing the deal." In fact, he was merely redefining his promise. The second pony seller delivered the promise and all its components in a manner that was compelling to the father and his young daughter. Why was the second seller's proposition so compelling? To understand this, we need to examine both the needs and wants of the buyers (the father and his young daughter) and how the second offer interacted more effectively with these needs (see Table 8.1).

In specification terms, the "product" offered by each seller was identical. Whichever pony was purchased, there is no doubt that the emotional needs of both father and daughter would have been met perfectly. If both sellers had offered exactly the same deal, the decision almost certainly would have been settled on purchase price, on the likeability of the seller, or on some other nonproduct aspect of the transaction. In this simple example, the value is almost exclusively emotional contribution. In B2B scenarios the value can come from anywhere within the Value Triad—revenue gain (RG), cost reduction (CR), and emotional contribution (EC).

Seller 2's strategy was brilliant. He understood that in a competitive marketplace, something more than product was required. He could, for instance, have offered riding lessons, a discount on horseshoes, a branded saddle, and so on. Instead, he realized that the most important determinant of this sale was to engineer matters such that the daughter would fall hopelessly in love with the pony. So he differentiated not the product, in this case, the pony, but his overall service package. More than that, he differentiated it in areas that were of particular importance to the buyers. Once this happened, there was no possibility that a loving father would send the pony back. So the problem simplifies into one of how do you make the promise real? And the solution is obvious: Make the deal persuasive and clear to the direct beneficiary(ies) of the purchase while simultaneously compelling to the principal decision maker by eliminating all risk and hassle from the transaction.

The pony story is a simple but powerful example of building a compelling VP based on a detailed understanding of the things that are important to the customer. Good salespeople seem to be able to do this almost instinctively. Generally, though, it's a result of great questioning, great listening, and the ability to see things from the customer's perspective[1].

PAIN AND PLEASURE POINTS

In complex commercial transactions, the selling company usually has a portfolio of products and services that can be assembled to deliver real customer value. Not all of the portfolio, of course, can or should be used at any one time. However, a subset of these products and services may be appropriate. But which subset?

To answer this, we need to understand, deeply, the value-adding processes critical to our customer's success. Satisfaction of the needs relating to the value-adding processes will bring pleasure to the customer's management team. Failure to manage deficiencies in these areas will cause the management team further pain and dissatisfaction.

The idea of *pain points* is used regularly by IBM, among others, when searching for opportunities to improve their customers' business performance and to help pinpoint where their offer can have an immediate, measurable impact. Table 8.2 gives some examples of possible pain points across various areas of a business.

Table 8.2   Pain Points

Potential problem area	What can go wrong	Consequence (pain points)
Inventory	Too much stock Too little stock	Too much working capital locked up in slow-moving stocks Not enough stocks to meet production schedules.
Sales, general and administrative costs	Expenses too high Expenses out of control	Inefficiency, perhaps also symptom of management weakness or incorrect staffing levels
Accounts receivable	Taking too long to get paid Poor credit control	Cash-flow and liquidity problems
Accounts payable	Taking too long to pay creditors Poor cash flow	Interruption of operations Conflict in business relationships Loss of preferential terms Suppliers threaten to stop Bad supply-chain relations
Fixed assets	Production bottlenecks Quality problems Catastrophic equipment failure	Delay to customer orders and deliveries Customer reject received goods Urgent repair or expensive unplanned capital expenditure
Revenue	Checks don't clear Wrong amount Invoice errors	Liquidity reduced and lack of working capital Time wasted to resolve problems
Cost of goods sold	Manufacturing costs soar	Immediate impact on profitability and perhaps also cash flow
Sales	Longer sales cycle Increasing discount levels	Cost of sales increasing Individual customer profitability declining

The list is not intended to be comprehensive but is simply an indication of the sorts of issues that may be important in different areas of a business. When we find viable solutions to one or more of these pain points and package and present them effectively, they become an attractive proposition. If, furthermore, our offer is a superior overall package or is perceived by the buyer as being so, this will become the buyer's preferred solution and will move our relationship with him nearer to real sustainability.

Figure 8.1 looks at how various solutions might map to a customer's needs and issues (pain points). These are represented within circle *A*. The importance of the sales team and background research in establishing this accurately cannot be overstated. A real understanding of the customer and her needs and issues is the foundation of any VP and, subsequently, the sale. Anything else, and it becomes little more than guesswork. Some authorities describe these as *profitable points of difference.*[2]

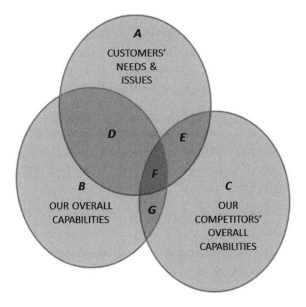

SOLUTIONS MAP

Figure 8.1 The solutions map.

Circle B represents our overall capabilities. Our job is to understand the customer's issues in detail and then overlay our solutions on them. The more of the customer's circle we can cover, the better. Clearly, there are likely to be some things that we can do that do not overlap with a particular customer's requirements. At this point, we also may consider creating tailored solutions to meet the specific needs of individual customers.

Circle C represents the capabilities of our competitor(s) (among which could well be the customer's own internal capabilities). Logically, there are likely to be some things that we can do for the customer that our competitors cannot do or do as effectively. These are shown as segment D. Equally, there are likely to be things that the competitor can do that we cannot, at least not as well. These constitute segment E.

Segment F identifies the things that the customer values that both we and our competitor can do, whereas segment G identifies the things that we can both do that the customer does not require.

Within this map, our target is clearly to cover more of circle A than our competitors can do and to communicate our capability to do so compellingly through a powerful and persuasive VP. Failing to communicate the package effectively means that the customer has to determine what she thinks your VP is for herself. This is clearly fraught with danger and runs the risk of a customer either failing to appreciate fully just how valuably differentiated your solution might be or making assumptions that turn out to be incorrect. Either way, you lose out.

As yet we do not have a real VP. This emerges from the coming together of our initial understanding of the customer's likely requirements gained from our background research, in-depth discussions with the customer, and discussion and analysis of all the intelligence with our colleagues in sales, marketing, and product management. During these discussions, we test the assumptions we made initially, constantly refining our understanding of the customer's real needs and issues.

We also need to recognize that in a significant purchase decision, it is virtually certain that more than one individual is involved. The VP must offer something meaningful to each member of the team who has influence over the ultimate purchase decision. We use a simple tool to collate this information.

THE VALUE PROPOSITION WORKSHEET

The *VP worksheet* is designed to help you formulate, from the very start of the sales process, considered approaches that are based on structured and robust thinking (Figure 8.2). Before you even get to the first customer meeting, you should complete a VP worksheet. The worksheet then should be updated constantly as new information becomes available so that you can really firm up your understanding of the key issues and develop and justify your propositions. It is often sensible to save your VP worksheets as you develop them so that you have a record of how your thinking has changed over the life of the sale.

KEY ISSUES FACING THE BUSINESS Potential impacts	HOW CAN WE HELP? What potential solutions can we offer?	BENEFITS How does our solution improve CR,RG,EC	EVIDENCE TO SUPPORT THE PROPOSITION How can we demonstrate validity of our proposition?

Figure 8.2 VP worksheet.

Key Customer Issues Facing the Business and Potential Impacts

Initially, this is the column in which to literally "brain dump" your ideas as to what these issues are likely to be. This should be done on the basis of assessing available research and intelligence. It also might help to identify potential information gaps that need to be filled. As the sale progresses and your understanding of the customer develops, you will be able to clarify and confirm the information you have in this column. This information will include issues that the company must resolve (which are the drivers for the company looking for external solutions). Ultimately, this is information that we will have collected from value-chain analysis; strengths, weaknesses, opportunities, and threats (SWOT) analysis; benchmarking; competitor intelligence; market research; customer meetings; and any and every other source we can identify. Potentially, it is possible to have a whole range of issues, and inevitably, some will be more important than others. In developing the VP, we want to focus on the critical issues, demonstrating how we can differentiate ourselves while addressing those issues.

How Can We Help?

A detailed understanding of the customer's needs and issues, as well as priorities, allows us to begin to identify how we believe that we can help the customer in terms of the products and services we have available or could develop. At this point, the need for an accurate understanding of the customer's key issues becomes evident. Without it, our ability to come up with the right solutions is impaired—perhaps disastrously.

Potential Benefits

What will be the impact of our solution, if adopted, on our customer's business? One of the key concepts in basic selling is that "Customers buy benefits." They do not buy what a product or service is; they buy what it can do for them in the situation in which they find themselves. We need to broaden consideration to such matters as superior strategic position, market-share growth, and market expansion. This column, therefore, is all about running through each of the products and services that you believe might fill a customer need and asking yourself what benefits the customer would enjoy as result of them. Within the context of value, however, we need to determine what specific value our solution potentially delivers across the Value Triad and what net benefits the customer would enjoy from dealing with us rather than with our competitors.

Evidence to Support the Proposition

Being naturally cautious people, many potential customers are likely to demand evidence that demonstrates your capability to back up your claims. Prepare these demonstrations in advance of any meetings you may have so that you look and come across as fully prepared. Ideally, use examples that are close to the potential customer's areas of understanding and expertise, and wherever possible, put numbers on them. Almost all VPs that we see say that they can save the customer money—you need to demonstrate how much and how. But you also need to look much more widely than this, ensuring that you cover both RG and EC elements.

The VP worksheet can be a primary source of thinking in creating and developing your VP for the customer. At its heart, however, should be your company's overall VP—the statement it makes to its potential customers about what it does. To see where it should fit, we shall examine the VP hierarchy (Figure 8.3). We say *should* fit because in reality, the VP is frequently an afterthought generated by sales and/or marketing once the product/service solution has been designed and delivered. In reality a business's corporate VP should be a central part of its overall business strategy.

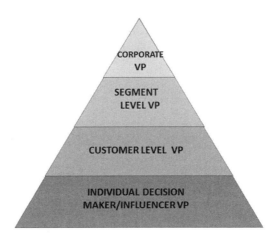

Figure 8.3 The VP hierarchy.

YOUR CORPORATE VP

This is the overarching VP that your business communicates to its total potential market. Even if it exists, which it frequently does not, it is often unclear to the very people who are charged with the task of communicating it. As a simple check, just ask your colleagues in different areas of the business if they are clear on what the corporate VP is. Expect thunderous silence! In an ideal world, however, the corporate VP, effectively communicated to the target market, is what has created the sales opportunity in the first place.

Segment-Level VP

If the business has segmented its marketplace, it should have developed a VP that is tailored to the needs of each segment. At its core will be the corporate VP, adapted to the segment.

Customer-Level VP

The VP is tailored further to the needs of individual businesses within the segment. Again, at its core will be the corporate VP, but now it is targeted at the specific needs of a specific business within one of the target segments. Every business has unique problems and opportunities. Some companies may be focused on fast growth, some may be perfectly content to play in commodity land, one or two may have brilliant technology to exploit, one may be close to receivership, and one may be floating leaderless without a chief executive officer (CEO). All are different, and you need to be able to identify their issues so that you can adapt your VP to demonstrate that you understand them and have ways of addressing them.

Individual Decision Maker/Influencer VP

Finally, on the basis that it is individuals who make decisions, the VP should be tailored further in conversations to the needs of the individual decision makers and influencers. The needs of the chief financial officer (CFO) will be different from those of the chief operations officer (COO), those of the CEO, and so on. To tailor your VP and your solutions so that they meet the needs of individuals, you need to find out how each of them sees things. "What does a good project outcome look like from your point of view?" "How do you see the situation from where you sit?" And so on.

SEGMENTATION, TARGETING, POSITIONING (STP) AND THE VP

As we have seen, few areas of the business demand closer cooperation among sales, marketing, and product management than in creating and delivering the VP. Marketing executives spend much of their time developing marketing strategies and plans. Marketing strategy emerges from the careful and creative application of three tools—segmentation, targeting, and positioning. It is well beyond the scope of this book to delve into these topics in detail, and there are many excellent works that cover this ground quite comprehensively. These processes are summarized in Figure 8.4 so that you can understand clearly the crucial link between market positioning and the VP.

While the first three tools are *predominantly* marketing activities, to be really effective, the creation of a VP must be a joint sales, marketing, and product-management activity. In technology-based firms, it is also very valuable to include scientific and engineering people to gain the widest possible perspective on the issues.

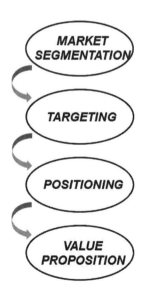

MARKET SEGMENTATION

Market segmentation is a process, usually undertaken by marketing management, of considering all possible users of our product or service. In segmentation we decide on clear groupings of potential customers who have certain common characteristics that enable them to be addressed using a specific marketing mix strategy.

TARGETING

Segmentation may reveal many potentially viable market segments. However, the resources of most businesses are finite and a choice usually needs to be made about which subset of these segments will best repay marketing and selling efforts

POSITIONING

Having selected a target segment, we need to identify the relevant competitors in each case, and the basis on which they are competing. We seek to position our offer in a different manner to the competition but emphasising differentiated advantages of relevance to each segment.

VALUE PROPOSITION

The final step in the process is the creation of a series of value propositions. Each VP will be based on the differentiated advantage embedded in the positioning statement, but will be adjusted to highlight a specific package of advantages relevant to each particular customer

Figure 8.4 STP and the VP.

SOME APPRAISAL TOOLS

There are many robust approaches to diagnosing strategic capability, including value-chain analysis, benchmarking, and SWOT analysis. We can apply the same tools to building a VP.[2]

Value-Chain Analysis

Value-chain analysis refers to all the activities, from receipt of raw materials to postsales support, that together create and increase the value of a product. Value-chain analysis is an important tool for evaluating a company's competitive advantage. We are searching for those parts of our company that give us a potential competitive advantage in our dealings *with this customer.*[3]

Competitive Benchmarking

No value proposition should be developed in isolation; it has to include an analysis and appreciation of competitor capabilities. What do you need to know about your competitors? Everything! One way of then using this information is in comparing or benchmarking your capabilities against those of key competitors.[4]

Strengths, Weaknesses, Opportunities, and Threats (SWOT) Analysis

This immensely useful and extremely well known tool for strategic analysis helps us to link information about the external business environment directly to our own business and to see where important connections can influence our business-development strategies. It is important that internal data are collected as objectively as possible because we use this as the rock on which to build strategy going forward. If the input data are flawed, so also will be the strategy. This can lead to important factors (good and bad) being overlooked because the manager is too close to the situation. The internal analysis generates strength and weakness data, which are used to populate one half of the SWOT matrix.

The external analysis tries to identify short-, medium-, and long-term factors that are relevant to the business and which are likely to give rise to opportunities or threats. It is worth emphasizing that these are external to our business and therefore not subject to our managerial control. They are givens and represent the external business reality around which we need to work. In analyzing the outcome of the SWOT analysis, it is important that a systematic matching process is applied in which each entry in the matrix is matched with every other entry on the opposite side. In this way, strengths are matched with opportunities to help identify high-priority business issues to help build the business. Weaknesses are matched with threats in order to identify and characterize the vulnerabilities of the business to external competitive challenge.[5,6]

Customer Research

While we can apply all the analytical processes just described, the most important determinant of the buyer's acceptance of our VP is his perceptions of our offer compared with the competition. The best way to collect this information is through some form of market research, perhaps through a multiclient study. Such studies can help us to develop insights into how we are perceived, attribute by attribute, compared with other suppliers. In some cases, for example, consumer products, such information already may have been collected and be available in reports in the public domain, for instance, on price comparison, Web sites or product-comparison Web sites (e.g., Consumer Report, Buyer's Lab, Compare the Market.com, and Which?).

The B2B situation is rather more difficult than the B2C situation because in most cases there will be many fewer potential customers, and in any case, comparative data may not be readily available in the public domain. In these circumstances, the company will need to make a choice between securing this information through formal market research or merely relying on the market feedback and industry/customer knowledge of the people who are closest to the customer—the sales team. This is a difficult choice to make and is very important because the decision will dictate the validity and effectiveness of the VP we develop.

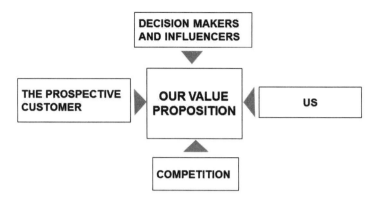

Figure 8.5   Assembling the VP.

STRUCTURING THE VP

In our considerations of the buying organization, we must assess the overall needs of the business with a view to understanding the problems and pain points it is facing both as a corporate entity and as working individuals. The Value Triad, which we introduced in Chapter 1, can inform our thinking about both the organization and its people.

The Prospective Customer

This is about understanding our prospective customers in detail. How do they generate value for themselves and for their customers? What does their value chain look like? Do we know? What are the needs and issues they are trying to address? At an organizational level, we are focusing our attention on revenue gains and cost reductions (an organization may have emotional needs, but they are difficult to identify). Therefore, at an organizational level, issues such as market-share expansion, increased turnover, improved productivity, lower labor costs, fuel economy, and so on are vital and, in principle, measurable. This area is driven by the quality of our background research and the capability of those involved in the sale to get below the surface and really understand the things that are truly important to customers at a business level. This should be clearly identified on the VP worksheet.

Decision Makers and Influencers

Businesses don't make decisions. People do. If the first stage is about understanding the business as a business, this stage is about understanding the people as people. What are their business issues, and what are their personal issues and aspirations? This information can only be collected during careful discovery interviews and with the application of good questioning skills. There is a great temptation, particularly among sales and marketing teams in highly technical businesses, to accord low priority to—or even completely ignore—the emotional contribution elements and to rely exclusively on the uniqueness of the technology. This temptation really must be resisted. In a commoditized market these might be the only differentiators available to you.

The Competition

In our considerations of the supply side of this model, we are searching not only for important attributes of our offer that will interest the customer but also in particular for attributes that distinguish us from and cannot be copied by our competition. If we have not taken the competition fully into account in our thinking, we are in serious trouble. Managers need to have a meaningful reference point against which to compare alternative offers. Buyers are thinking about the competitive offers even if we are not. And if we do not also think about the competition, then we are courting disaster.

Us

Our objective is to identify clearly those areas where we can offer or create a meaningful differentiation that really matters to our customers —one that we can articulate in a compelling and persuasive way through our VP. It is important that we have a real understanding of our own capabilities and of our own business strategy. This will ensure that we don't end up pursuing opportunities that fall outside of our own overall VP. In assessing our own capabilities, we really need to be able to answer four key questions. These are central to our ability to build a VP.

- How does what we do create value for our customers? *Advantage*
- What are we really good at—at least as good as the competition? *Parity*
- Where are we less good than the competition? *Realism*
- Where do we really excel? *Potential differentiation*

It should be clear that we need to answer these questions *from the perspective of our customers.* Unless we can do this, the ideas we come up with, while perhaps attractive to us, may have little or no relevance to our customers.

There is a risk that the VP can end up as a long, rambling statement. This is not the intention. Ideally, your VP should encapsulate for your customers, succinctly and concisely, the reasons why they should choose you rather than a competitor. At best, it should be no more than two or three sentences that are effective and persuasive. To be effective, it needs to answer three questions and pass the VP reality check.

The Key Questions

1. How does what you offer address the key issues and meet the customers' value drivers?
2. How does it help to differentiate your offer against competitors?
3. Why should your customers choose you rather than a competitor?

The VP Reality Check

1. If you gave your VP to a competitor, could the competitor use it? In other words, if by simply replacing your name with theirs the VP is still valid, you have failed to come up with one that *differentiates* your offering—it fails to answer the question "Why you?"
2. Has it targeted the customers' key priorities? Go back to the VP worksheet and check the "Key Issues" column. Are they addressed effectively?
3. Can you deliver? This is a strange question, I know, but you wouldn't be the first business to win work and then wonder how on earth you were going to deliver.

Case Study: Workhorses A/S

Workhorses, Ltd., is a small Danish company specializing in metal-constructed gymnasium equipment for the corporate and institutional market. The company has been in operation for about four years and has built up a 5 percent share of the U.K. market. Company turnover is €9.5 million, 85 percent of which is in the sales of Maxigym, the company's flagship multigym product. Maxigym is used by a number of large European companies that are interested in the product to maintain the physical fitness of their employees, usually sedentary managerial and office workers. The market is becoming saturated, and the company needs to expand its operations. Apart from selling equipment, Workhorses also specializes in health and fitness and through its highly qualified team of fitness instructors, sports medicine specialists, and dieticians can offer a comprehensive advisory service to users. This is seen as unique in the market and is offered as part of the product. One of the user companies, Mensa, Ltd., is very impressed with the equipment (a prototype the company acquired two years ago) and has made great advances in the health of its employees. Mensa worked with Workhorses to develop a fitness program incorporating equipment use and counseling as a package. This work was reported recently in an article in a human resources journal. This article discussed the use of in-house gymnasium equipment and the positive effect this has had on the morale and fitness of workers.

Inter-Corp, PLC, is a multinational company headquartered in Boston, Massachusetts. The seller is visiting the personnel manager at Inter Corps offices in Brussels. This facility employs 1,500 workers in attractive office accommodations. Inter-Corp is considering installing a gymnasium and offering additional health and lifestyle counseling services in Brussels and is speaking to several other possible suppliers of both gymnasium equipment and counseling services. Following a spate of recent injuries among women returning to work after a number of years raising their families and, particularly worrying, heart and blood pressure illnesses among middle and senior management, the human resources director has been instructed to "get the workforce fit."

(Continued)

Workhorses' Marketing Department has come up with some interesting information about Inter-Corp and about local competition. Inter-Corp employs 1,560 people at the local facility. Of this total, 850 are women employed largely in assembly and subassembly positions, and 600 men are employed in direct manufacturing activity. Of the 110 office, managerial, and clerical personnel, 50 men and 24 women are in senior or managerial positions. Medical research has shown that men are two times more likely to have serious stress-related illnesses than women, especially among managerial personnel.

Recent accounts have shown that Inter-Corp is unprofitable, including the Brussels operation. Press reports, confirmed by "intelligence," suggest a high level of stress in the company, and the company has been criticized in several newspapers for its stress levels.

What Is the Workhorses VP for This Company?

How would this change for different functional managers in the company? See Table 8.3.

Table 8.3   VP Worksheet

Key customer issues	How can we help?	Benefits	Evidence
Inter Corp is unprofitable	Comprehensive range of fitness equipment	Contribute to improved productivity (RG)	Journal and magazine articles
Stress-related illness and absenteeism among senior staff	Team of health/fitness professionals	Reduce/eliminate fitness-related absenteeism (CR) Lower human resources costs of recruitment and training (CR)	Visit to Mensa to examine its results
High injury levels among female staff	Creation of customized programs for staff	Enhance employees "feel good" factor (EC)	Ongoing monitoring of staff sickness levels
Company morale	Advisory service for management	Improved public relations image (EC) Opportunity for networking between staff and managers (EC)	Mensa

Improvement of public image	Bundled packages to suit specific groups	Contribute to reductions in injury and reductions in health insurance premiums (CR)	Journal and magazine articles, Mensa
Could lose key skills through early retirements	Individual advisory/ diagnostics for key managers	Human resources director looks good to her peer group, which could lead to more business for Workhorses (EC)	
Healthier business environment	Advice to canteen/restaurant for healthy menus	Better and more attractive meals (EC) Contribute to overall employee health (EC)	

Workhorses' VP "Elevator Pitch"

Workhorses has a convincing and demonstrable track record in improving the productivity of companies like InterCorp through delivery of unique and customized packages of equipment, programs, and counseling designed to improve employee health, morale, and fitness.

Detailed Support Statements

- Our consultants will work with your management team and your people to identify the main issues that can be resolved by a managed fitness program.
- We will design regimens of exercise and activity for specific groups of employees or even for individuals geared to enhancing fitness and reducing stress.
- We will recommend, install and maintain all the equipment required to implement the recommended fitness program.
- Our specialist, highly skilled staff will train your people in the correct use of all equipment and services provided.
- We will monitor all program participants on a monthly basis, making changes to their schedules as necessary and providing detailed feedback of results to management to show staff sickness levels and improving health.

CHAPTER 9

Value-Based Selling

The definition of salesmanship is the gentle art of letting the customer have it your way.
—Ray Kroc, The Founder of McDonalds
(October 5, 1902–January 14, 1984)

In implementing value-based pricing (VBP)—which is our focus—the sales function is utterly vital. This means that other managers need to recognize this. VBP compels salespeople—and their organizations—to adopt a value-based approach to selling and indeed to business in general. In an increasingly team-based approach to complex sales, *everyone* is involved in the sales process, whatever their job title.

There are so many different approaches to selling that it is sometimes difficult to keep track of them all. However, a brief review of the many approaches tends to highlight three key activities that form the core of any effective sales approach:

1. Understand the customer's needs/requirements/issues.
2. Show how your solution can address those needs/requirements/ issues.
3. Gain commitment and agreement to the next steps necessary.

All other activities, such as targeting the right potential customers, validating opportunities, gaining access, building rapport, networking, gaining information, identifying the decision makers and influencers, establishing how the decision will be made, differentiating your solution, writing proposals, making presentations, and so on are designed to ensure that the three core activities can be accomplished successfully.

So what makes value-based selling different? By its very nature, it is a consultative approach. It's the focus that is different. As its name suggests, the focus is not on products, features, and benefits, important as these are. The focus is on value and value delivered. This means that we need to understand exactly what it is that the customer does value and then consider how well our solution delivers that value when compared with competitive solutions.

This leads us to our definition:

> *Value-based selling* is an approach to selling that aims to quantify the value that your solution delivers to a customer in economic terms, highlighting your advantages when compared with competing products or services.

In order to do this, we need to do a number of things:

1. Understand the things that our customers consider to be valuable. Remember, value is defined by the customer, not by us.
2. Understand how we can leverage our capabilities to deliver the value the customer requires and differentiate our solution from that of our competitors.
3. Understand our competitors in detail. These are the people we are up against.
4. Be able to quantify our value and capture it in our price.
5. Be able to communicate that value effectively in a way that is powerful and persuasive.

Everything we have discussed up to this point has led up to the development of the value-based price. As Figure 9.1 suggests, now we have to sell it. We have to convince the customer that our solution to the problem/opportunity comes at a price that is worth paying given

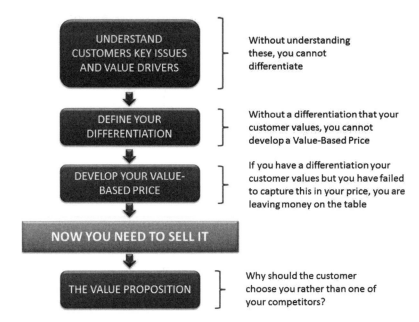

Figure 9.1 VBS process.

the value that it delivers. The success of VBP depends on an organization's ability to understand fully the needs, issues, and value drivers of the customer and then to communicate effectively how they can be addressed. The need for a highly skilled, well-trained sales team is paramount.

In simple terms, the task can be broken down into four primary steps:

Information. This is the information gathering that is necessary to provide a solid basis for the development of a differentiated solution, a powerful value proposition (VP), and a justifiable value-based price.

Differentiation. This is the process of assessing how you can construct a solution that delivers more of the value the customer is looking for than competitor solutions.

Calculation. This is not just the value-based price, but also the quantifiable value that your solution offers the customer in terms of net revenue gain and/or net cost reduction plus the intangible value of the emotional contribution.

Communication. No matter how good your solution is or how much money you can help your customer to make or save, if you fail to communicate it effectively, you will fail. In other words, you might have the best solution, but you failed to convince the customer.

UNDERSTANDING THE CUSTOMERS' KEY ISSUES AND VALUE DRIVERS

The initial role of the seller is not selling—it is information gathering. In the same way, the initial role of the buyer is not buying. It is identifying and crystallizing her own needs and requirements and investigating the various options she might have to help her address her needs and issues. Trying to sell to buyers who are not ready to buy is one of the most frequent and fundamental mistakes of many salespeople. This doesn't mean that salespeople can't be proactive. But it does mean that sellers should spend a great deal more time getting to understand their customers, how they do business, and what their issues are than they do talking about their own products and services. The process is summarized in Figure 9.2. This is an iterative process and is designed to be a *conversation—not* an interrogation, when you are asking questions, and *not* just a presentation, when you are presenting and demonstrating.

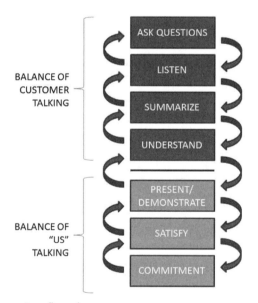

Figure 9.2   Discussion flowchart.

But even before the conversation with customers starts, you need to undertake some background research. We've already seen that sellers can begin the process of understanding customer value through the quality of the questions they ask. Customers perceive people as competent not so much because of what they say but through the quality of the questions they ask and how carefully they listen to the answers. Background research will allow pertinent questions to be framed. To help in doing this, the VP worksheet is a key tool.

However, this does assume that you are dealing with customers who are prepared to engage in *value conversations*. This is a key point. You cannot sell value to people who are simply not interested in value. This introduces a number of issues.

If the only conversation you are having with an organization is with procurement, you shouldn't be surprised that the only conversation the procurement team wants to have is about price. This is what procurement people are paid to do. Value is not their driver—price is. Frequently, the procurement team does not make the purchase decision at all. That is made elsewhere in the organization, and the procurement team is then tasked with getting the best terms and conditions. To do this, the team makes the simplifying assumption that everything is a commodity—indistinguishable from competitors other than by price. This gives poorly trained and supported salespeople real problems because the only variable they can manipulate is price. The implication of this is that you need to be talking to the people in the organization who really do care about value and can see how you can contribute to organizational goals. Figure 9.3 demonstrates this.

The bottom left-hand corner is all about price-driven buying. This is where the primary competition is based on price rather than value. In a situation such as this, it is important to strip out any peripheral costs wherever possible in order to generate an acceptable margin. Your relationship with the customer will be (or should be) purely transactional, and any extras demanded by the customer should be charged for. In other words, if the customer is only prepared to pay the baseline price, the baseline product should be all that's delivered.

Unfortunately, all too frequently, salespeople are ill prepared to deal with price pressure and reduce prices in the face of it. The fear of losing business is a real one. However, the real danger is in retaining or winning

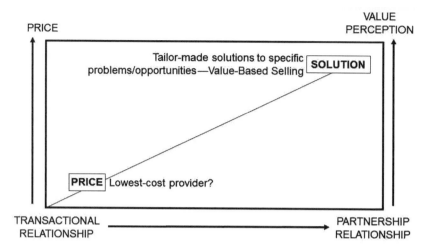

Figure 9.3   Strategic choices.

business on the basis of price while still providing all the services and support that higher-price buyers enjoy. This is a recipe for disaster—your margins are decimated at the lower end because you are providing a five-star service for a one-star price. And if your higher-price customers find out, as they will, they will either demand their own price reductions or leave.

There is nothing inherently wrong with doing business with price-driven buyers as long as they get what they pay for and nothing more. The risk is always that as soon as someone is less expensive than you are, then the business goes. The trick therefore is to try to limit your dependence on these customers. This can be difficult because they often represent, numerically, a significant proportion of your revenues (and cover a significant proportion of your fixed costs). If you can, you should try to move away from selling to price-driven buyers toward selling to value- and relationship-driven buyers. With luck, you might even be able to convert price buyers to value-driven buyers if you can find the right product or service.

Clearly, the further up the line one goes, the higher are the prices. But then the value delivered should also be much greater. As you progress up this line, the nature of the individual decision maker changes from one obsessed with price to one driven by compelling need and the pursuit of real value. The top of the line requires a partnership relationship with the customer if a tailored solution is to be developed and delivered. This is a crucial element of value-based selling and value-based pricing.

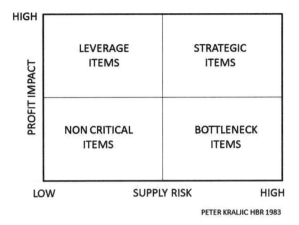

Figure 9.4 Product purchasing classification matrix.

If your customers will not talk to you, in-depth, about their issues and the things that are important to them, then your ability to create and deliver a differentiated value is severely limited. Whether a customer is prepared to enter into this sort of business relationship with you will depend to a great degree on the level of importance the customer attaches to your company, the products and services you provide, and the ability of your salespeople to establish and build personal relationships with key members of the decision-making unit. Some customers will vigorously resist any attempt to establish such relationships, and for them, a value-based selling approach is almost certainly a waste of time and effort.

The product purchasing classification matrix, shown in Figure 9.4, was developed by Peter Kraljic around 1983 to help purchasers maximize supply security and reduce costs by making the most of their purchasing power. There are four item classifications.

Strategic items (high profit impact, high supply risk). These items deserve the most attention because of their degree of importance to the customer. Any supplier in this segment is key to the customer who will want to work closely with the supplier to develop effective solutions.

Leverage items (high profit impact, low supply risk). The chances are that there are a number of alternative sources of supply, so supply risk is small. This allows the customer to exert his full purchasing power, substituting products or suppliers and placing high-volume orders to get the best prices.

Bottleneck items (low profit impact, high supply risk). In this segment are products that do not have a huge impact on profitability but do have a supply risk. In this situation, it is possible that there are only a limited number of suppliers. This makes the customer potentially vulnerable, so he'll be constantly looking for ways to control suppliers and seek out alternative sources of supply.

Noncritical items (low profit impact, low supply risk). In this segment, there are many suppliers of a low-risk product or service. The objective is to reduce transaction costs and all other costs associated with ordering and stocking the product.

The question is, "Where does the customer put you on his matrix?" If you can never get to see the customer despite the fact that you consider him to be a key customer for you, you might not be a key supplier for him. This is an important consideration because it will, or should, have an impact on the decisions you make about the levels of contact and service you want to supply and how you wish to develop your overall customer strategy. Targeting customers in the upper-right segment is where most value is likely to be, but most businesses are a mix of customer types. The key is to ensure that they are treated appropriately. Realistically, if you provide noncritical items, you are likely to be seen very much as a commodity supplier and treated as such. Remember, you can only talk value to people who really care about value—and that means value on their terms, not yours.

THE VALUE-BASED-SELLING PROCESS

So what does the value-based-selling process look like? At some point or another, most examples appear to have some or all of the following in place.

Targeting/Validating the Customer

Realistically, a business cannot pursue every single opportunity that comes its way (although we have worked with some that have tried and have spread their resources so thinly as a result that their potential success has been compromised). So decide what your ideal customer looks like, and target customers that appear to have those characteristics. Then validate each opportunity before you start investing time, money, and effort into it. This is where background research is important.

Key Tool: The VP Worksheet

The value of the VP worksheet is its simplicity. Despite this, or perhaps because of it, it is immensely powerful in helping to develop a detailed understanding of the customer and to create solutions and frame the sales argument. It is important to remember that this is a dynamic tool. You should start completing it the moment an opportunity arises. Column 1 is particularly important at this early stage. Obviously, at this point, your estimate of the customers' key issues will be exactly that—an estimate. The questions you ask should be formed around your educated assumption of the key issues and designed to begin the process of firming up your understanding of what is and what is not important. At this stage, this is far more important than telling the customer about all the things you could do.

Remember that this is the information-gathering stage of the process. It doesn't stop you, though, from considering the types of products or services you could provide that would address the customer's key issues (column 2). At this point, you also should be thinking about the potential benefits of your solution to the customer (column 3), how this can be demonstrated, and how it can be proven (column 4). As the sale progresses and the key issues begin to firm up and can be prioritized. So also will your understanding of how you can help most effectively and what the benefits will be to the customer.

Gaining Access/Building Rapport/Networking

How you gain initial access to the customers with whom you would like to do business is a subject of ongoing debate. There are so many options, and it will very much depend on the nature of your business. We have seen lots of approaches work and lots fail. Approaches that work in one situation might bomb in others. Some such approaches include personalized letters to key people followed up with a phone call, a straight cold call, meetings at networking events or professional seminars, direct mail, "advertorials," and so on. Generally, the key is to adopt a targeted rather than a scattergun approach. We tend to prefer a personal letter followed by a phone call over cold calls because that works for us. Ideally, though, nothing beats a warm recommendation from someone who is respected by your target customer. The purpose, whichever route is taken, is to begin the process of developing a relationship. Remember, though, that most people won't be ready to buy just because you've taken the trouble to contact them. They may well be perfectly happy with the current situation. Your job is to develop the relationship between their business and yours so that when an opportunity does arise, you are well positioned to take advantage of it.

Gaining Information

The VP worksheet is a key information-gathering tool. Used in conjunction with your customer relationship management (CRM) system or whatever other information tools you have, it provides an important focus. Within a sale, it helps you to see the issues and develop solutions. At the early stages of the relationship, it helps to structure your thinking and begin to uncover potential opportunities. The key skill at this point in the sale is great questioning and great listening. No matter how well you understand the value-based-sales sales process, if you aren't great at both these fundamental skills, gaining quality information will be difficult.

We also have found that while technical people find it relatively easy to ask technical questions (objective data—revenue gains and cost reductions), they find it much more difficult to ask more subjective questions (emotional contribution). This is often more important than it may appear at first. Our fundamental premise remains—businesses don't make decisions; people do—and for as long as that remains true, the need to understand people and the things that are important to them personally is important. Just because you have the best-looking proposal on paper does not mean you will get the business.

Identify the Key Players and the Decision-Making Process

Complex and/or important buying decisions generally are made by more than one individual. As a result, it is vital that all the key players are identified and contacted by the appropriate people on your team. Much has been written by others about buying roles, decision makers, and decision influencers, and it is not our intention to pursue this in detail here. Suffice it to say that it is hugely important in complex, multiplayer sales situations to identify and contact all the key people. It is equally important to understand how the decision will be made. The only way to find this out is by asking, and you should ask not just one member of the buying team but each of them or at least as many as possible. In this way, you are likely to arrive at a more practical view of how the decision is really going to be made.

Differentiating Your Solution

The key word here is *solution*. Increasingly, products appear similar. Customers have plenty of time and opportunity to compare products, and it is unlikely that they would talk with you if they didn't feel that your product could do what they wanted done, at least in broad terms. Therefore, while the search for product differentiation is an ongoing one, the real value and differentiation increasingly are to be found in the overall solution you deliver—the product and everything that goes with it. In looking for your differentiation, don't just think product—think total solution. So it is important to recognize that you are delivering more than just a product or service but a total package—a value bundle.

However, in order to differentiate your solution in ways the customer values, you also need to understand the people you are up against—the competition. There is no way a differentiated VP can be developed without a full understanding of the capabilities of the competition. Therefore, the questions at this stage are

- How can we address the customer's key issues and priorities effectively given our capabilities?
- How effectively can our competitors address the customer's key issues?
- How can we differentiate our product/service/overall solution against that of the competition in ways customers will value?
- How can we demonstrate this differentiation and value?

In order to be able to identify whether you have a differentiation that the customer will value, you need to understand how your offering compares with that of your competitors.

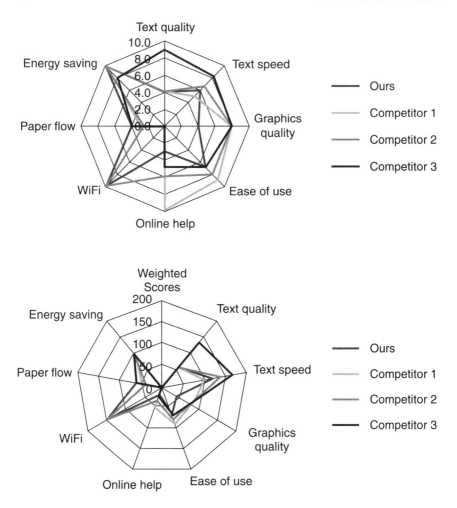

Figure 9.5 Competitor capability analysis office printer suppliers.

Key Tool: Competitor Capability Analysis

This tool, shown in Figure 9.5, is more focused and allows you to analyze the comparative capabilities of your company and the competition (which may include your customer's in-house solution). Having taken the key issues from the VP worksheet and your conversations with the customer, these are listed and *weighted* in terms of their importance to the customer. (Note that in this example, only functional, tangible criteria have been selected. This is not to imply that emotional contribution elements are unimportant. Far from it. However, they are more difficult to evaluate and score in a dispassionate way—hence their exclusion at this point.) The task then is to identify the relative capabilities of the various potential solution providers against each of the selection criteria. To be able to do this effectively, it is vital that you know everything possible about your competitors and their capabilities. If you don't, you will find it difficult to compare your solution with theirs and thus develop a winning differentiation.

Assuming that there are things that you can do to improve your perceived performance, you need to look at ways to eliminate or reduce the impact of areas of your performance that are not as good as those of your competitors while maximizing the impact of your strengths. Ultimately, you need to be able to demonstrate that your overall package delivers greater value than the solutions provided by your competitors. This will include all three elements of the Value Triad—not just your ability to help your customers reduce their costs or increase their revenues. You also need to consider the impact of the more subjective judgments—the emotional contributions of factors such as relationship, trust, and risk. Despite the fact that on paper a competitor might appear to have the best overall solution, she may be a completely new supplier that the customer has no experience or significant relationship with and that the customer considers risky. What kind of an impact is this likely to have on the customer's decision?

Writing Proposals/Making Presentations

Except in some formal bid situations, where communication with the client is strictly controlled, it is assumed that you have been in constant contact with the prospective customer throughout the bid process. During these meetings, you will have been constantly updating your understanding of their issues, both as a business and as individuals, and checking out the suitability of your proposed solutions and the benefits and value they potentially could deliver. It is possible that at some point a written proposal and/or a more formal presentation will be required. Either way, this is the point at which your focus is on communicating your solution and your value. A key tool for this is the VP.

What is the VP from the seller's perspective? Simply, it is a statement that summarizes for customers the reasons why they should choose you rather than a competitor. If you have ever had to make a sales presentation to the board or buying committee of a key client, you'll recognize this scenario. You and your team arrive and are made welcome (generally); you set yourselves up, make yourselves comfortable, and begin. At the end of your presentation, you ask if there are any questions. Questions are asked, and then, just before you leave, one of the people on the client side turns to you and says something like, "Thanks very much for your time this morning. Now, before you go, would you please sum up for us why you believe that we should choose your company?" Do you

- Look at each other and gulp nervously?
- Make something up on the spur of the moment and hope that it works?
- Hit them with your VP?

Ideally, the VP should be the key vehicle that carries your argument to the customer. When you first stand up to talk to the customer, after thanking him for the opportunity and introducing him to your team, you should hit him with your VP. At the end of your presentation, when you pull the threads together and summarize, you should hit him again with your VP. Finally, at the end of the question-and-answer session, whether he asks you to remind him why he should choose your company or not, you should hit him once more with your VP. It should be in your proposal document and constantly in your mind as the flag behind which your supporting arguments are developed. It needs to be good. It should answer three important questions.

How Does What You Offer Address the Key Issues and Meet The Customer's Value Drivers?

To be able to answer this question, you need to know what the key issues and value drivers are. Understanding the customer's issues also should allow us to calculate by how much you can improve the customer's situation—either by reducing costs or by enhancing revenues. This would allow you to make positive statements in the VP, such as "Our ability to reduce lead times by four weeks will deliver additional revenues to your company of $3.5 million in the first year."

How Does It Help to Differentiate Your Offer versus That of Your Competitors?

This is key. Understanding the customer's requirements is clearly vital, but the question then is how can you differentiate your solution and the value that you can deliver against your competitors? To be able to do so, you need to understand your competitors' capabilities in detail so that you can compare your solution with their probable solution. You need to be able to identify possible weaknesses that you may have so that you can plan to minimize their impact, and you need to understand your strengths—the things that you are really, really good at—so that you can maximize their impact. So how are your competitors likely to be able to enhance your customers' revenues, reduce their costs, or deliver a valuable emotional contribution? The strength of your differentiation will be an important factor. It should allow you to say such things as, "Our unique project-management approach shortens lead times and provides a complete turnkey solution, significantly reducing the risk of delayed deadlines and cost overruns."

Why Should the Customer Choose You Rather Than One of Your Competitors?

From the first two questions, you need to be able to develop a statement that

- Demonstrates your superior capabilities, which enable delivery of …
- Tangible and intangible benefits, building …
- Confidence that these benefits will be delivered, which …
- Results in material improvements in the buyer's situation—cost reductions, revenue enhancement, and/or emotional contribution—the key elements of the Value Triad.

Putting everything together, you could have a VP on the lines of

Our unique and proven project-management approach shortens lead times and provides a complete turnkey solution, significantly reducing the risk of delayed deadlines and cost overruns. As a result, our lead time will be four weeks less than scheduled, delivering additional revenues to you of $3.5 million in the first year.

The VP also has to pass what we call the *VP reality check*. Namely,

1. If you gave your VP to a competitor, could she use it? If all a competitor had to do was to remove your name from the VP and put hers on, then it has clearly failed to differentiate your offering.
2. Has it targeted the customer's key priorities? This means the customer's *key* priorities, not all of them. It means the ones that really matter.
3. Can you deliver it? Winning business is one thing; being able to deliver the promise of your VP is another. Your long-term credibility is based on your ability to do so consistently. This provides further evidence of your capabilities and stronger VPs in the future.

Delivering the Promise

The final step in the sales process is implementation of the solution and delivery of the promise. It is important at this stage to measure the quantitative impact the solution actually has compared with the promise. This demonstrates your integrity to the customer and provides you with useful references for future sales (assuming that all goes well, of course).

Ongoing Account Management

While *delivering the promise* may be the end of this sale, it should be the start of the ongoing relationship with the customer and further sales opportunities in the future—each handled in the same, structured way.

DEALING WITH PRICE OBJECTIONS

When the price is an objection, value is the solution. One of the main reasons salespeople feel trapped by the price objection is that *they don't know how to quantify value*. The only tool they have is price, and they manipulate this to deliver a discount. Using the tools you now have, you should be able to deal with price with more confidence. All too frequently salespeople believe that discounting the price will speed the sales process. All it really does is undermine your value offering and commoditize the solution.

The other fear, of course, is that not lowering the price will result in loss of the business. Winning business on price and making little or no money as a result is not a sustainable strategy unless you are or aim to be a lowest-cost producer. In such a case, volume and cost management are king and queen! VBP and value-based selling are not about lowest price. They are about differentiated value. Remember—you cannot sell value to people who are not interested in it. For those who *are* interested in value, you need to have a detailed understanding of the value they are looking for and have a way of demonstrating that you can deliver more of the value they want than competitors.

Perhaps a story will help to pull the VBS threads together. This story concerns a small winery in northern New York State. The owners started growing grapes there after the end of World War II, and this story took place some time in the 1950s. At that point, the winery was not known for producing very good wines; in fact, its wines were considered to be quite poor. This particular winery owner, however, was very ambitious, and he wanted to grow his business. So he came up with a strategy of targeting some of the best known, most prestigious restaurants in New York City. He calculated that if he could get one or two of them to stock his wine, he could use these as a reference to persuade other customers to buy his wine and hence grow his business.

So he identified a couple of these well-regarded restaurants, and he called on their wine managers. There was one restaurant in particular that he spent a tremendous amount of time and effort on. He brought samples of his wine and did everything he could think of to convince the wine manager to take his wines. He went there regularly for lunch and for dinner. Over about six months, he tried everything. Nothing seemed to work. Anyway, after six months of no success, he decided that he either needed to give up or change his approach. He wasn't willing to give up because he was convinced that his overall strategy was a good one, but it was clear that his tactics weren't working. He then discovered that the owner of the restaurant would take his lunch after the restaurant's lunchtime service at the end of the bar.

One day he walked in at the end of lunch service, and he introduced himself to the owner of the restaurant and asked for a couple of minutes of his time. As you can imagine, the restaurant owner wasn't too happy to have his lunch interrupted, but he was polite and agreed. The winery owner told the restaurant owner that he ran a small winery in New York State, told him a little about his wines, and asked him, "Would you, please, buy my wines?"

The restaurant owner looked at the winery owner in utter amazement and said no, he would not buy his wines because they tasted terrible. The winery owner replied, "I agree. However, I have spoken to a number of your waiters who tell me that they have been asked by some of your customers for my wine. Indeed, I estimate that if you do buy my wine, your restaurant will make another $200 a week in profit. So I ask you again, would you please buy my wines?"

The restaurant owner thought about that and said, "Okay. We'll give them a try." The rest is history. The winery owner shipped the restaurant five or six cases of his best wines, and the patrons ordered the wines. He used this restaurant as the reference he had always wanted to persuade other customers to buy his wines, and today he is the owner of one of the largest and most highly regarded wineries in New York State.

So what's the point of this story? In order to understand that, we need to answer three questions.

Question 1:

What did he end up selling?

The answer, of course, is the profit. He didn't sell the wine to the restaurant owner, he sold the $200 a week profit. If, when the restaurant owner told him his wines tasted terrible, he'd defended his wine and told him other people thought it tasted great, would he have sold the wine? No chance. *So sell the value not the product.*

Question 2:

Why did his earlier tactics fail?

To answer this, we need to think about why the wine manager constantly turned him down. The wine manager was employed to select fine wines. What would have happened to him if the restaurant owner had lost confidence in his ability to select good wines? He could have found himself out of a job. So, in a roundabout way, the winery owner was asking the wine manager to risk losing his job—not a risk he was prepared to take! So what was the benefit to the wine manager of buying the wine? Nothing—in fact, it was a high-risk decision for him. The only real benefit in buying the wine was the extra $200 of profit, and that went to the restaurant owner. If you looked at the organization chart for the restaurant, the wine manager was the right person to sell wine to. He would have been the decision maker when it came to the selection of fine wines. However, he wasn't the right person to sell the value to, and in this case, that was the person who benefited from the $200 profit. *So sell your value to the person/people who will benefit from it.*

Question 3:

Why did the restaurant owner finally take the risk of buying the wine?

Because he could see the value, and the value was quantified. More than that, it was the sort of value that the owner wanted—extra profit. And where did the information come from? It came from his own waiters and his own customers. It wouldn't have been nearly as persuasive if the winery owner had said, "There's a restaurant down the road that makes $200 a week extra profit selling my wines." It would have had some impact, but not nearly as much. *So quantify the value in the customer's terms.*

To reiterate, there are three golden rules of value selling:

* Sell the value, not the product.
* Sell your value to the person/people who will benefit from it.
* Quantify the value in the customer's terms.

And you have to do all three—two out of three might not be bad in the song. In value selling, it will get you nowhere. Selling the product but not its value gets you nowhere. Selling the value to the wrong person gets you nowhere. Failing to quantify your value in terms your customer understands gets you nowhere. If you succeed in all three, then you are *really* selling value!

CHAPTER 10

Building a Value-Based-Pricing Strategy

Top management says, "It's just pricing. What do you need more resources for? It's just a case of changing the arithmetic. Isn't it?"
—Global Pricing Manager, Specialty Chemicals

For a value-based-pricing (VBP) strategy to be successful, it is essential that everyone along the value-adding chain in your company is committed to creating real customers. There needs to be a company-wide focus on customer value creation, as well as the processes necessary for the introduction and successful implementation of a VBP strategy. This focus must be more than mere lip service, which in itself is a form of mild resistance to change. Everyone involved must believe deeply in and support company initiatives to create real value for the customer. This is a real leadership challenge. Top and senior management must be actively engaged and supportive and be seen to be driving it. It cannot be delegated down to the ranks. This simply will not work, and if this is your intention, you may as well not bother and continue to use cost- or competition-based approaches, with all their flaws.

OUR RESEARCH

We approached over 100 companies that we knew had either implemented VBP or were considering doing so. These companies included some that had sent delegates to our VBP training events, supplemented by companies that we believed for various reasons were likely to have implemented VBP or at least were considering it seriously. The spread of our initial contacts included automotive suppliers, automotive manufacturers, energy consultants, logistics companies, biotechnology, legal services, engineering, mobile telecommunications, chemicals, medical devices, telecom network providers, power-generation companies, and travel consultants.

Pricing is emotive, politically sensitive, and strategically significant. Many of the companies we approached declined to offer a full case study for one or more of the preceding reasons but were happy to share some of their experiences on a confidential basis. Their observations and comments completely supported what was shared in the full case discussions. In the event, we selected eight of the companies we interviewed. The selection of cases was driven by our need to provide a spread of industries as well as companies at different stages in the VBP journey—some just starting, some trying for the second time, and others being a lot further on. While the specific contexts and sectors are widely different (all from B2B), surprisingly consistent messages emerged from those interviews and are summarized in this chapter. They provide a great deal of practical guidance for any executive seeking to make VBP a reality in her organization. The case summaries are included in Appendix B.

THE KEY MESSAGES

We distinguished six factors of VBP implementation that we encountered consistently in the interviews—change drivers, dissatisfaction with current pricing methods, customer value, changes required, apprehension, and implementation. These differed quite markedly among those starting off on the journey (or who had walked some of the road previously) and those who had implemented VBP successfully. Table 10.1 summarizes the key issues under each heading.

Table 10.1 Key Issues in Implementing VBP

Key Factor	Issues for Attention
Change drivers	• Improvements in revenue and margin • Shorter product and technology life cycles • Dissatisfaction with quality of the business
Current methods	• Pricing structure and decisions • Value capture • Selling methodology • Discounting discipline • Contract selection
Customer value	• Customer dialogue • Creating effective solutions • Value measurement • Value proposition
Changes required	• Move to solution selling • Salesperson recruitment and training • Client selection • Migration to value-led culture • Interactive price setting
Apprehension	• Explanation of what VBP is and is not • Encourage informed buy-in from all parties • Demonstrate how a value-based approach can enhance selling effectiveness • Move from intuitive to intelligent selling • Encourage value dialogues inside the business
Implementation	• Active sponsorship by top management • Establish ownership and accountability • Recognize the journey • Work through open-minded staff members • Select products and services amenable to a value approach • Segment markets on value • Engage channel partners

Change Drivers

Managements need to be aware of the need for change and must be able to explain the need to all involved in a way that will secure their commitment. This is a leadership task.

There was relatively little difference between the motivations of companies electing to adopt a VBP approach. The most important determinant appeared to be a clearly defined need for the company to achieve better results in terms of both headline revenue and margin. Indeed, perceived margin erosion in traditional, largely commoditized sectors appeared to be central to this type of initiative and also drove searches for cost reduction. When the drive came from business leaders or business owners, this stimulated all kinds of activity. However, this failed if there was no real plan to implement a VBP strategy.

Linked to this was the realization that as product and technology life cycles were getting shorter and the pace of innovation increasing, businesses would have much less time to achieve returns on investment than before. A product that might last 10 years in the market, say, 10 years ago, is today rapidly being made obsolete by newer versions driven either by new technology or by regulatory pressures (e.g., fuel and CO_2 emissions policies). Without serious attention to pricing and costing, this shorter life cycle would prevent acceptable returns. VBP is known to generate superior returns.

Conviction that companies could—and should—be doing better also was a driver. Managers often were dissatisfied with their organizations' results and were searching for innovative ways of capturing more and better business. There was widespread discontent at apparently interminable and increasingly contentious price negotiations and frustration that customers seemed not to really recognize the worth of what they were being offered. For some, the tipping point had arrived when they discovered that salespeople, confronted with disappearing margins and unable to make an argument based on value, were giving away "for free" high-value services to secure uneconomical deals.

Current Methods

Companies at the start of their journey usually make the obvious adjustments to the business that normally would lead to business improvements. If these do not yield the hoped-for results, VBP may be the approach to adopt.

In a number of the companies whose managers we interviewed, pricing methods were unstructured, with little or no discipline in place. Sometimes pricing decisions were delegated wholesale to salespeople. This led to a confused and confusing price structure and inconsistent and arbitrary pricing decisions. This was recognized, and most companies had started to put in place price-information databases and review processes. Others were undertaking surveys and other enquiries to assess how their products and services were perceived by customers.

When prices are linked to costs, as in the case of cost plus, a reduction in costs per unit is almost instantly matched with a reduction in price. While the margin may remain constant in percentage terms, the cash value inevitably drops, and the business is worse off. Price reduction offers only temporary respite to the salespeople, who often are savaged by aggressive buyers. Indeed, a willingness to grant a discount on demand leads to further and increasingly outrageous demands for more of the same.

Many companies in our sample implemented cost-based pricing. Cost-based pricing leads to obsessive focus on cost cutting. To maximize margins, companies' production engineers go into overdrive and make heroic—and often technically brilliant—efforts to cut costs. This is how companies always have tried to improve margins, and cost reduction is built into these companies' DNA. Managers are often very comfortable with this approach because they understand it and it is familiar, even though they may not like it. We describe these approaches as cost-based-pricing *hygiene factors*. These are certainly necessary but for VBP work undoubtedly not sufficient. To change these attitudes requires equally heroic efforts. Even after making these efforts, these companies are unable to capture all the value available because they lack the pricing discipline and infrastructure necessary. More successful companies deliberately searched for ways of moving away from cost-based pricing methods, usually by assembling bundled solutions in which detailed cost data were not used in price calculations or by otherwise changing the nature of the offer.

A cost-based pricing environment frequently leads to an order-taking mentality, overfocus on product specification, and underfocus on customer value. The consequence, of course, is that the salesperson has no ammunition to fight back against discount demands and in order to win the deal feels that he must offer the discount. This certainly was the behavior observed among some of the companies in our sample. Even if the salespeople had been fully briefed on the customer value impact, it is highly unlikely that it would have made much difference—80 percent of salespeople are order takers and lack the skills or motivation to fight back. This was acknowledged without prompting in virtually every case. By contrast, more successful companies made more use of team selling, in which technical specialists rather than salespeople would prepare and present the proposition. Functional experts would work through the propositions in detail directly with clients, explaining the value being created at each point and ensuring that customers really understood what was on offer and its economic impact on their businesses. Such discussions were rich in data, in that data collected during earlier discovery discussions, background research, and previous contracts were shared openly with client decision makers. This approach fosters an environment of trust in which customers are encouraged to share their own information and is the foundation of a long-term relationship. When salespeople were involved in this, companies spent a lot of time and effort ensuring, first, that they had the right salespeople and, second, that they really understood and bought fully into the value-based-selling process and were competent in the use and presentation of data.

Important pricing decisions frequently are delegated to the sales team, in one case permitting salespeople to discount to whatever level it took to win the work. There were no criteria in place regarding what discounts could be offered or their magnitude, management being content with letting salespeople use their discretion based on experience and gut feel. An unintended consequence of this, and a potentially dangerous one, is that it can lead to discriminatory pricing—charging different prices for different customers for essentially the same product without clear justification. Once prices were implemented, often companies did not monitor their effectiveness in winning work or the profit levels of each contract because there were no metrics in place to monitor pricing effectiveness to either vendor or buyer. This also makes it difficult to identify and repeat successful and effective pricing practices.

The more successful companies focused on the quality of the deals they pursued, preferring to select contracts with high profitability rather than high revenue. They were willing to walk away if the deal offered was unacceptable. Every one of the more successful companies insisted on working with the problem owner and would refuse to deal with the buying agent. This refusal stemmed from the insight that buyers are more likely to focus on irrelevant factors such as lowest upfront price, whereas problem owners were more concerned with reliability and robustness of the solution, how quality would be managed, and whom to contact in case of problems. The problem owner is likely to be in place for a longer period than the buyer and has personal reputation riding on the solution. Such executives can repent at leisure.

Customer Value

A consistent and unifying theme running through this book is the concept of customer value. Not surprisingly, companies implementing VBP successfully had taken careful steps to characterize fully— qualitatively and quantitatively—what really mattered to customers. Companies on the journey were at different stages in this process and may not even have started on this process until the cost-based pricing hygiene factors had been dealt with.[1]

Arguably the biggest challenge facing companies at the beginning of their journey was to identify the competitive advantage (or advantages) that were to form their vehicle for VBP. This is a rather scary and quite subtle consequence of a cost-based approach. Intense focus on specification and functionality of products, coupled with a search for a competitive advantage, leads almost inevitably to technological development of some aspect of the specification the *seller* considers to be important. Companies have a good microscope but are using it to look at the wrong thing. If and when a differentiation is found, it is almost certain to be product-based. As time goes on, this becomes harder and harder to do regardless of how much money is spent. Focusing exclusively on product innovation, and spending all their effort and development funds on this, prevents companies from looking in the right direction—namely, understanding what value the customer is looking for. Therefore, we often hear managers saying that they don't understand what customers want. They have never really tried to find out in an insightful and disciplined manner. The truth of the matter is that a conventional approach to product innovation will lead to clever products containing the latest technology; a customer-focused approach will yield insights into customers' problems and issues that need a *solution*—not a product. Companies progress rapidly when they ask, "How can we use all our products, knowledge, and technologies to solve customers' problems." This is exactly what the successful companies have done and are doing. The VBP journey is in large part a journey from seller's product to buyer's solution.

If we do not know our real differentiation or we do not know where in the customer's value chain this should be targeted, then, of course, it will be very difficult or even impossible to quantify the value we offer. We will not be able to describe or measure success in the customer's terms. We will not be able to craft a really effective value proposition. And we will be unable to create a quantified argument unless we are very fortunate and hit on just the right thing by chance. However, successful companies deliberately engage in dialogues with customers over a period of time that enable both parties to get closer to an understanding of each other's needs, pain points, and aspirations.[2] This is in fact part of their pricing and commercial process. This kind of dialogue leads naturally to a customized solution that then can be linked to customers' (and suppliers') value chains and a *consensus in idem* that forms the basis of a subsequent contract.

In order to get closer to isolating the true value they can offer to customers, a number of companies in the sample adopted one or more objective quantitative tools or qualitative instruments. Internal data (which may be widely distributed across information systems in the company[3]) and external data are both appropriate for study and review. Quantitative tools include discrete-choice modeling, conjoint analysis, an analytical hierarchy process, net promoter score, and Pareto analysis.[4] They also include conducting controlled field tests in which a company's products are compared with those of competitors in a practical customer application. Qualitative tools include face-to-face discussions with customers in focus groups or executive interviews or debriefing of customer-facing staff (i.e., sales, service, and applications people) to try to discern insights. The most successful companies use all three of these methods. The data from these studies are used in developing economic arguments. Companies that do not use at least some of these measures are flying blind. Used effectively, data collected and insights generated in these ways, particularly with customer support and involvement, are difficult to challenge rationally. Therefore, good data can help to avoid the need for potentially damaging and contentious price negotiations. In fact, by selecting the right metrics—those which the customer uses to assess economic impact—it becomes possible to link price structures to measurable outcomes. Even in the same customer segment, you should expect that some customers will have a much higher value for your product or service than others.[5] All the companies that had implemented VBP effectively found very little pushback and little need for price negotiation. It was all part of the ongoing conversation with their customers.

Need for Change

No business is ever going to embark on a VBP journey—or any other strategic change initiative—unless it perceives the need for change. Every company we interviewed expressed dissatisfaction with existing methods and described, in greater or lesser detail, their change objectives. For the most part, these emerged from recognition of weaknesses in their current approaches and that the customer value they delivered could be improved.

In every case—across all respondents—there was full acknowledgment that an effective approach would demand a more or less radical approach to sales and selling. In every case, respondents' products and services incorporated a medium to high level of technology or professional know-how. Most had recruited to their sales teams individuals with high graduate-level—and often postgraduate-level—qualifications. Chemical and biotechnology companies, for example, recruited, often direct from the laboratory, individuals with master's degrees or even doctorates. The level of technical understanding, accordingly, was very high. However, it was this very fact that reinforced and perpetuated the specification selling and product technology development phenomenon that we encountered so often both in this series of interviews and in our training work across the globe. It's also what makes the job of the buying agent so easy when confronted with such a salesperson. All the buyer needs to do is challenge the salesperson that her product is no different from the competitor's product. As a scientist, she cannot refute this fact. Benzene or phenol sold by Bayer, BASF, or Hexion is chemically identical. The issue is not the product—it is the total offer that matters. Delivery, technical support, laboratory tests, assays, and so on are all seen through the lens of helping to sell the (more or less commoditized) product and not as value-adding elements in their own right. This is where the problem lies. Sellers often consider themselves to be scientists first and salespeople (a long way) second. While sellers can understand the arguments about the total offer, their training and education take them back inexorably to discussions of product technology. Since they are selling on the basis of product specification, they can do nothing else but cave in when a buyer demands a discount on the basis that the product in question is a commodity. This is demoralizing for this kind of salesperson because she can see no way out.

In fact, there are things that companies can do, and those further on the journey have made the changes necessary.

The first point was to ensure that they had the right type of salesperson. And often the seller was not a salesperson at all but one or a group of functional or technical specialists. In one case, the company had gotten rid of its salespeople. In another, salespeople were used to create the opportunity for a team of professionals to follow up on and make the pitch. This is quite a long way from the conventional selling model and rather closer to the concept of key account management.

The second thing—and this was strongly exhibited by successful implementers of VBP—was that they selected their clients very carefully. They typically would not chase after price buyers but would go for companies with which they could establish a dialogue and thereafter develop a relationship with the business problem owner.

The third point was to make the difficult transition from a product technology–led culture to a customer value–led culture. This is a rate-determining step and cannot be hurried. Attitudes take time and perseverance to change.

The fourth point was that the VBP calculation can be quite complex and very difficult for any salesperson, however talented, to be able to carry out while face to face with the customer. Nevertheless, customers often are looking for at least a ballpark figure at some point during the sales interview. Some of the companies further along the journey have created software tools that can be used interactively with customers in developing a value-based price. This will not work in every case, of course, but if the calculation is relatively straightforward and involves a relatively small number of variables, it is worth trying to create such a tool.

Apprehension

Implementation of a VBP strategy usually involves changes—often quite significant ones—to prices. Resistance to price changes will come from those who need to make changes in their methodology.

These typically might include product managers (who may support or resist depending on their function), accountants and information technology (IT) specialists (who may have to create new systems), and applications engineers (whose job might suddenly become more complex).[6] General management also may be apprehensive that significant price increases are not matched by competitors. This exposes the company (and possibly themselves personally) to criticism and possibly even ridicule if they have to make embarrassing climb downs or difficult explanations.

Most respondents said that the biggest source of opposition came from salespeople. The reason for the opposition was the general perception that VBP inevitably would lead to price increases that they would have to sell, making their job even harder in an already difficult economic situation. The sales team issue is quite complex but enormously important.

One chief executive officer (CEO) insisted (with strong reinforcement from the product-management group) that salespeople just "needed to try harder." This failed miserably and generated all kinds of overt and covert resistance, as well as seriously damaging the morale of the sales team. In this case, there was no strategy in place. The whole initiative costs a huge amount of money (value-based-selling training for the sales team and developing value arguments and marketing collateral). Salespeople felt themselves to be seriously under pressure. Sales team managers, who were not fully bought into the whole initiative, ended up giving lip service to the changes and did the job at best half-heartedly. Training failed because the arguments presented did not persuade the team at *both* intellectual and emotional levels. Lack of manager commitment meant that the necessary coaching did not take place, and performance reverted pretty quickly to previous levels.

Price setting is often part of the function of salespeople. In circumstances in which there is little support to salespeople from elsewhere in the business, the only tool they *can* apply is discounting. Customers get to know this and put pressure on salespeople to discount on demand. By taking away pricing flexibility, their job becomes so much more difficult, and they end up alienating their customers. Salespeople perceive VBP as imposing across-the-board price increases and resist on that basis.

Management can help salespeople to buy into the process by demonstrating how value arguments actually can make their job easier. One company "on the journey" was making great efforts to bring the sales team on board. In this case, management had lost control of pricing, and there was a laissez-faire approach that led to all kinds of arbitrary and intuitive pricing decisions, no quality control, and potentially hazardous price discrimination. Management wanted to move pricing out of the intuitive landscape and into more of an intelligence-driven discipline that also used pricing to drive better top- and bottom-line performance. Pricing metrics were being developed to track effectiveness but also to incentivize salespeople.

Companies that implement VBP successfully spend a great deal of time working on and refining the whole value proposition, making sure that it is relevant from the perspective of different customer decision makers. Once the arguments have been refined and tested, such companies proceed to the creation of suitable collateral—brochures, data sheets, Web pages, case studies, and testimonials. Wise companies engage the support and cooperation of salespeople as well as product managers and marketing communication (marcom) specialists to ensure that the materials are fit for the purpose. Without this full engagement, the very people who need to use these tools—salespeople —may refuse to do so. Salespeople, perhaps more than any other single group in the company, need to understand fully and buy into—viscerally—the value arguments. If they do not, they will not make the arguments compellingly in front of customers—or even at all. When deals are lost, it will be invariably on price and not because the arguments were poorly presented, the proposition was wrong, or for any other reason.

Implementation

Top management must be active owners and sponsors of the whole VBP initiative. They alone can ensure that the right resources are put in place and that different functional groups in the business will support and facilitate the process.

It was clear from our interviews that those companies in which VBP was introduced successfully had active backing and championing from top management.[7,8] Top management can help by removing obstacles and by making time, funds, and expertise available. Top management also can help by recognizing that VBP is a journey and will deliver good results in time.[9] Expectations of top managers need to be handled carefully or what will happen is that they will look for too much too soon and perhaps even sabotage their own initiative. Another thing to look out for is trumpeting the new VBP approach to the market. This will lead to pushback by customers. It is far better to slowly and quietly slip it into company strategy over time. Perhaps the most important thing that management can do is to make it clear to everyone in the company that this is a serious initiative and is vital to the long-term survival and prosperity of the business.

While top management needs to endorse and support the transition to VBP, managers also need to put in place clear and definitive ownership of the activity. Successful companies make it very clear who actually "owns" the program and give that individual clear status in the company hierarchy.[10,11] One major international chemical company has evolved a 30-person pricing-management team. This team, under the leadership of the global pricing manager, takes responsibility for improving and developing pricing methodologies and ensuring that these methodologies are implemented homogeneously across the company.

All the companies that had implemented VBP successfully commented that it was a long-term change-management process and could take three to five years depending on the starting point. Even after 14 years, one company still was discovering ways of doing it better. The principal reason for the extended time period was that effective VBP demanded a culture change, especially if the prevailing culture was product- or technology-driven and the pricing methods cost-based. Such cultures are very difficult to change. Careful packaging of the message is essential. For instance, several respondents commented that quantification is essential if we are trying to convince scientific, engineering, and financial people. When the numbers tell a story that backs up the "softer" marketing arguments and the more esoteric strategic arguments, it is much easier to get buy-in. Indeed, presenting pricing as a scientific discipline rather than an art form will help to legitimize any initiative.[12] Change programs need to have a strategy and to be driven by board-level champions. Without this, programs will become mired in the status quo and will grind to a halt.

The sales organization must be engaged in the pricing process. Recognizing that as many as 80 percent of the salespeople are neutral or opposed to VBP creates an issue for top management. These people have real knowledge of customers and markets, and even though they may not be performing at the top of their game, they are still, nevertheless, bringing in the business.

So how do we bring about change? If it is genuinely lack of effort, a short, sharp shock *may* bring about a change in behavior. This can be risky. A better approach is to recognize that there are probably already a few salespeople who *do* understand this type of approach and even may be applying it already with success. The implementation strategy would be to work through them, developing and testing the new approaches and, when successful, making their successes visible and rewarding them publicly. This approach would bring on board those who are neutral and in this way gradually spread the adoption through the sales organization. Once the concept has been proved with respected individuals in the sales organization, the approach can be rolled out carefully to the rest of the sales organization and then, if appropriate, to other regions.

There is a temptation to migrate all the value-added products into the VBP price list. Arbitrarily raising prices of a number of products will incur strong resistance from customers. If prices are raised without offering any additional value, customers will see no justification in the price changes but instead view them as a blatant attempt to gouge them on price. One company in our sample attempted to do this and seriously damaged its business, losing several important accounts to competitors.[13]

Successful implementers are careful how they segment their markets. Not every customer is appropriate for a VBP approach. If a customer can see no incremental value in your offer compared with his next best alternative, there is no basis for pricing on value to this customer. The reality may be that he does not need the enhanced capabilities of your product or service and genuinely requires only the basic product. In such a case, give him just that. Do not offer anything more than the basics he is prepared to pay for. He genuinely may be budget-constrained, in which case your earlier discovery process will have elicited this. Alternatively, it may be a price buyer's ploy to get more for less. Select your deals and your accounts before applying VBP. There is no need to apply it to every customer and to every product. To do so, in fact, would be extremely foolish. Some companies in our sample applied a Pareto approach to segmenting the top 15 to 20 customers and deals and used this as the basis for selecting accounts suitable for a VBP approach.

The final point is to recognize that channel partners in many markets are an essential part of the value delivery process and should be included in the pricing arithmetic. Many of the companies in our sample, as well as many companies in our general pricing consulting experience, work through channel partners. If the channel genuinely adds value, pricing managers must give due consideration to how the benefits are split among themselves, the channel, and the end user.

Problems in measuring value, communicating value, market segmentation, and top-management support all have been identified as roadblocks to the effective implementation of VBP.[14] To these we would add recognizing the drivers for change, realizing that change is possible for the company, and being willing to make the efforts necessary to realign to identified customer value.[15]

Figure 10.1 presents a framework for implementing VBP. This framework was based on the research described in this chapter and consists of six principal elements (The six R's shown in Table 10.2).

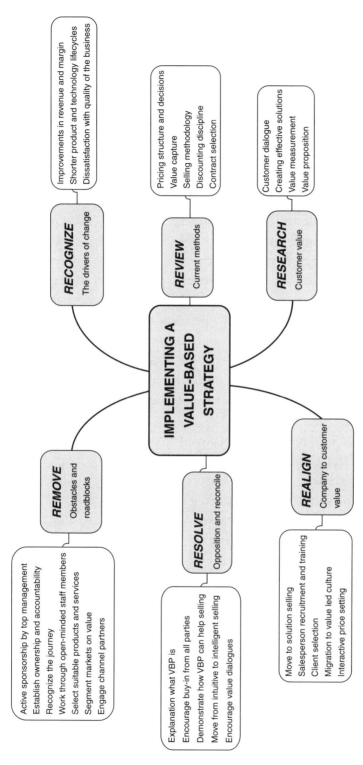

Figure 10.1 VBP implementation framework.

Table 10.2 Framework for Implementation

Recognize that change is necessary and why	There can be all sorts of drivers, but unless they are compelling to the management of the company and the need for change is clearly recognized, any subsequent attempt to implement a VBP approach at best will be flawed and probably will fail. If it is your or your management's judgment that no change is necessary, then just forget about it—at least in this company.
Review current methods	VBP is a strategic initiative—not just a case of tinkering with the pricing numbers. The review must go beyond price setting to examine the readiness of your company to embark on this journey. It might be wise to delay the start until the hygiene factors are in place, there is discipline and process in pricing processes, and sales teams have embarked on and are having some successes with value-based selling. You might want to make some low-risk experiments with VBP to satisfy yourself that the approach is valid and does deliver better results. But resist wholesale implementation.
Research and characterize customer value	This does not need to be undertaken "across the board" of all your customers. A sample of the most appropriate customers and products/services is a good starting point. Start small, and get some early successes in building up your understanding of what really matters to your most important customers and how your products or services map into this or not, as the case may be. After all, what do you have to lose. Use Pareto analysis or some other appropriate method, and make use of value-measurement tools across all the elements of the Value Triad.
Realign your company with customer value	This step and the next one are the rate-determining steps and will demand perseverance, leadership, and determination. The more traditional the business and the more deeply embedded it is in cost-based approaches, the longer it will take. In contrast, a new company starting up will be in a much better position to apply the principles from the outset. Whatever the current status of your business, give yourself plenty of time to make the big changes necessary. A multidivisional corporation may experiment with VBP—and you may be that experiment. Resist the pressure to short-circuit the process in the quest for fast successes. This potentially will cripple the process and make it take longer.

(Continued)

Table 10.2   *(Continued)*

Resolve opposition and reconcile genuine dissenters	VBP is a big change in your company, and there will be many people who, for their own reasons, will want to impede its introduction. You will need to be able to distinguish luddite obstructionism from genuine apprehension. Work with those who catch the vision, and infect them with your enthusiasm to make this whole venture work. Use all the tools of persuasion and advocacy at your command, and do not be afraid to build a team (virtual, if necessary) throughout the whole organization. Keep executive champions fully in the loop, and use them fully. Publicize successes inside the company.
Remove the obstacles and road blocks	As the change process gathers momentum and more people come on board, roadblocks will start to fall down. At this stage, when all the other bits of the process are in place, build a project plan.[16] Instead of a whiz-bang launch, just gradually move your business over to VBP when opportunities present— for example, new products, new markets, new technologies, and so on.

CHAPTER 11

Contemporary Pricing Issues

Any business can buy incremental unit sales at a negative profit margin, but it's simpler to stand on the corner handing out $20 bills until you go broke.

—Anonymous

Pricing decisions must be made within the context of ever-changing circumstances. The severe economic downturn is but one of them, but commoditization, discounting, price wars, competition, government pressures, and a host of other dangers are always present. We could write a whole book on any one of these (and some people have). Business generally takes place in choppy waters.

COMMODITIZATION

Commoditization is one of the biggest challenges facing business today. Certainly the effects on business can be significant. As a result of commoditization, a business is likely to suffer reduced profitability, reduced margins, weakened relationships with customers, loss of control over pricing, loss of customer loyalty, reduced funding for innovation, and the encouragement to focus on cost reduction rather than value creation.

So what is commoditization? It is the process by which a product comes to be seen as being of uniform quality and value. When a product becomes indistinguishable from others like it and customers buy on price alone, then it is a commodity. You may believe that you are delivering a high-value product or service, but if your customers cannot identify or understand the value, then there *is* no value from your customer's point of view. The one thing customers can understand is price, and in the absence of any other perceived differentiation, this is what they will use as their key selection criterion. This then leaves you with a product or service that is completely undifferentiated in the customer's eyes except for price, even though you know that it has excellent and important qualities. This gives clever buyers an excellent strategy: repeatedly deny the relevance of any differentiation so that all that is left for the seller to bargain with is price. Or walk away. The result of this is increasingly downward pressure on prices and the subsequent erosion of margins and profitability. Notwithstanding this, such perceptions may be quite erroneous and have come about from our inability or failure to present the offer in a compelling manner and demonstrate the real value that this differentiation has conferred. Quite literally, the customer has no idea of the worth of what he has just purchased.

Commoditization is nothing new. There is an argument that the process started in the United States in the early seventies as product availability and competition grew and the major grocery chains started to develop their own label offerings. According to figures supplied to *The Times* (Verdict Research, August 2009), private labels in the United Kingdom now account for in excess of 40 percent of grocery sales, with prices that are, on average, 22 percent cheaper than the branded equivalent. The tentacles of commoditization now can be seen almost everywhere and particularly in technology. The Sony Walkman was a premium-priced, highly desirable, and highly valued item when it was introduced. Since then, the market has been flooded with "me too" products, and prices have tumbled as a result. Other examples include digital cameras and mobile phones generally, and now even Apple's iPhone is under threat as truly competitive products start to reach the marketplace from such major and intimidating competitors as Samsung, HTC, Motorola, RIM, and Sony Ericsson. This truly is premature commoditization.

It also seems that the pace of commoditization is not going to slacken. Indeed, as a result of globalization and the increasing power and importance of BRIC (Brazil, Russia, India, China) economies, particularly those of China and India at the time of this writing, the process is almost certain to escalate.

So how does it happen?

In attempting to differentiate their offerings, some manufacturers pursue innovation to the extent that it outpaces customer needs. Customers then become confused because the increased complexity of the solution makes it difficult for them to make informed decisions. In this situation, it is easier for them to fall back on price as the key differentiator. When this happens, the pursuit of innovation as a valuable source of differentiation results in commoditization of the solution. This is horrible! In fact, *confusion marketing*, as this approach is called, has become a strategy. Make it impossible to compare products on a like-for-like basis by presenting a bewildering array of options and price packages. Customers just give up trying, frustrated with the complexity of the task, and either stay with their existing supplier or move to the one whose brand they trust most. This can be seen in the laptop marketplace, where manufacturers have increased specifications to such an extent that they exceed the needs of customers, and the significance and relevance of any different features are unclear and usually presented in incomprehensible language. Instead of prices rising to reflect the improved performance, they actually have fallen, and the market is becoming increasingly commoditized as a result.

In such a situation, it would appear that customers are once again using price as the primary differentiator simply because they don't fully comprehend or appreciate the apparent improvements in technical specification and performance. In an era of increasing complexity, customers need help in understanding their options and in making the most appropriate purchase decision. In its own way, this may provide a differentiation. We have certainly come across companies that failed to communicate their offerings adequately, and as a result, their customers failed to appreciate the value that they potentially could provide.

In difficult markets, this is a significant problem. It points to the fact that there are two key activities that need to be undertaken. One is *creating* the differentiation; the other is the *effective communication* of that differentiation and the value that it can deliver to individual customers. Value perception and the creative management of value perception are central issues in communicating pricing decisions.

It is clear, then, that the process of commoditization would *appear* to be almost inevitable. However, while the process may appear to be inevitable, it does not necessarily have to apply to your products and services. Commoditization occurs when customers can see no differentiation between your products and similar alternatives. Remember, we define *differentiation* not simply as being different but as being different in ways that are valuable to the customer.

So what can we do?

Accept commoditization as something of an inevitability in today's competitive marketplace, and redesign the business model accordingly. In this case, the strategic direction of the business needs to focus on cost reductions in order to become the lowest-cost producer and adopt a high-volume, low-margin business model. Business relationships with customers become increasingly transactional as contact costs are stripped out. The focus is on optimizing profitability by maximizing volumes at lowest cost and increasing market share. This also may mean migrating to markets in which low-cost competition—and low prices— is prevalent. In reality, this means moving to markets populated by low-cost/low-price competitors and price buyers. In any case, it may not be possible to change your business model quickly enough. If your company's ethos is to be a high-quality premium-priced supplier, this is unlikely to work.[1]

Refuse to accept the inevitable, and focus on differentiation through customer knowledge and value delivery. Business relationships have got to be close and meaningful with key customers. This will allow you to identify and design solutions to their key issues and pain points that differentiate your offerings from those of competitors and that deliver value to the customer. The focus is on optimizing profitability through maximizing perceived value delivery and capturing a proportion of this in your pricing. This demands an innovative approach and an assertive search for true differentiation.

A logical starting point is to understand your customer's current perception of the value that you and your company provide. This will give you a benchmark from which to begin. It also might provide an insight into either how much more you need to understand about your customers or the extent to which you are failing to communicate the value that you already potentially can deliver. In Chapter 2 we looked at a number of routes to differentiation. The starting point for all the approaches is to have a detailed knowledge and understanding of the customer's situation and requirements. Without differentiation, commoditization of your products and services is just a matter of time. But there is hope. Richard D'Aveni[2] believes that commoditization isn't necessarily inevitable, provided that the three *commoditization traps* are understood and action is taken in anticipation of any of these traps arising.

Deterioration

In this scenario, products or services face competition from lower-priced, lower-specification competitors that on the face of it seem to offer an acceptable alternative value proposition. In today's difficult market conditions, where price is truly an issue for many people, many are downtrading to lower-priced substitute products. These may not offer all the things customers are familiar with from their premium-priced preference, but they are prepared (or are compelled) to compromise.

Proliferation

Once upon a time, there was an iPhone. Now there are a raft of products all competing for a share of iPhone's space. Some of these are even more sophisticated, some less, but all are intent on stealing some of iPhone's market share. As a result, the market is becoming increasingly fragmented and intensely competitive.

Escalation

Laptop computers, mobile phones, digital cameras, photocopiers, and any other products are on an almost continuous treadmill of product innovation and improvement. However, rather than leading to higher prices for the delivery of improved performance, prices, if anything, have continued to fall. Early unique value propositions very rapidly become entry-level essentials in a technological battleground. However, as we saw earlier, this doesn't always guarantee success. Simplicity may be a route to differentiation in an increasingly complex environment.

In order to anticipate effectively any of these issues, it's important to look closely not just at competitors but also at customers to understand how their behaviors and aspirations may be changing. Understanding market trends becomes a key element in anticipating and responding to the threat of commoditization.

The power of buyers to manipulate the minds of salespeople is well illustrated in one B2B market. We were working with a major company in the automotive components market. The company had sent about 25 of its global and key account managers to our standard VBP course. As we opened up the session on commoditization, we asked the question, "Are your products specialty or commodity items?" We fully expected a robust assertion of "Specialty," given that the company in question enjoyed a market share of 56 percent of the global market. To a person, they answered "Commodity." We were taken aback by this answer. We explained the basics of commoditization, in particular, that in a commoditized market, your share is likely to be $100/n$ percent, where n is the number of competitors. In this market, there were four competitors. Consequently, if the market was indeed commoditized, as these delegates vigorously asserted, their share would have been around 25 percent, and certainly not 56 percent. We had to explore this. This company's product was indeed a highly specified and sophisticated product, but it unusually lasted much longer and was easier to install. Yet the delegates would not be shaken on their view that the product was indeed a commodity. Why? Their customers told them so. We took about half a day to get the delegates to see sense, and even then, only about a third of them really "got it." They had been thoroughly brainwashed—or hoodwinked—by their clever customers.

DISCOUNTING ON DEMAND

We seldom see more lunatic behavior displayed by otherwise rational and intelligent managers than we encounter in the discounting "space." Discounting on demand seems to be built into the DNA of many businesses and is almost the first strategy that under-pressure salespeople turn to when challenged on price.

Discounting in and of itself is not a bad thing. It is the very life blood of sectors such as product distribution, logistics, and retail. *Trade* discounts are given to channel partners in exchange for the work they are doing to capture and support end users. The more value channel partners offer, the greater is the trade discount you should consider offering. *Quantity* discounts are given in exchange for a clear customer commitment to purchase specific volumes at specific times. Because you can schedule the production of the product or the delivery of the service considerably in advance and as a result possibly also purchase materials or other resources in volume on attractive terms, this should reduce your costs. Some of these savings you can pass on as a volume discount either at the time of payment or at the end of a trading period. *Promotional* discounts are offered as inducements to purchase at the point of sale (buy one, get one free deals) or to try out a new product. These are generally of very short duration and are essentially tactical in nature. Finally, *cash* discounts are offered when the customer offers to pay in cash on or before delivery of the purchase. The discount is justified on the basis of reduced risk (cash in hand is a great incentive) or avoidance of expensive bank financing of the supplier's costs.

Do bear in mind that for a dominant undertaking in the market, discounting deals could be interpreted as anticompetitive. See Appendix A for examples of where discounts have been interpreted in this way by European courts.

Discounting becomes pernicious when, in the absence of any other available tactic, it becomes the sole means of winning business. Under the implied pressure of losing the deal to a cheaper competitor, a company gives in almost without a fight to what is perceived as superior buyer power. This win-lose situation leads to chronic erosion of profit, brand damage, and ill will from the perspective of the seller. From the perspective of the buyer, it is not really a sustainable long-term strategy. From an overall market perspective, discounting, if practiced by a majority of participants, leads to downward spirals in prices and margins and to chronic commoditization. All this makes it even harder for those choosing to remain in the market to assert their value. Disciplined businesses will encourage their salespeople to *walk* away rather than *give* away.

There are three basic questions we should consider when being asked for a discount:

- Why should I give you a discount?
- How much of a discount are you asking for?
- In return for what?

Find out what commitments the customer is willing to make in exchange for some concession on your part. This is basic negotiation. *Never* give away a concession without extracting one in return. You are sending a very strong message that your company is willing to cave in to pressure. Such concessions may be higher volumes, preferred supplier status, and so on. Get these in writing. Verbal agreements are instantly forgettable (at least by the buyer) and thus very deniable. Whatever you do, if you anticipate that your salespeople are going to be pressed for discounts, build the discounts in, and state very clearly the "line in the sand" that must not be crossed. This simple piece of discounting discipline can help you to avoid the lunacy of discounting on demand.

Unplanned discounting can have a quite catastrophic effect of profitability. Take a close look at Table 11.1.

Table 11.1   Effect on Sales Volume of Price Discount

Discount %	Gross Margin, %					
	5	10	15	20	25	30
1	25.0	11.1	7.1	5.3	4.2	3.4
2	66.7	25.0	15.4	11.1	8.7	7.1
3	150.0	42.9	25.0	17.6	13.6	11.1
4	400.0	66.7	36.4	25.0	19.0	15.4
5		100.0	50.0	33.3	25.0	20.0
10			200.0	100.0	66.7	100.0
15				300.0	150.0	100.0
20					400.0	200.0
25						500.0

Let's say that a company sells a product at the price of $100 and a gross margin (contribution) of 20 percent. The salesperson, Varsha, is pressured to offer a discount and on previous occasions has agreed to 5 percent. She does the same again this time around. She knows that she has got to get deals—her sales manager has told her so—and *this* is a deal. She offers 5 percent, and the client buys 100 units, which was his original plan. Varsha did not even ask for purchase of any additional units, and he smiles quietly to himself. He has just made a nice windfall profit. He would have been willing to pay $100 or more per unit. But why should he if, just by asking nicely, he can get 5 percent off? The 5 percent discount on demand allows Varsha to sell the item at $95 per unit, and instead of making $20 gross margin, she now has made $15 for each and every unit sold. The original total cash profit would have been $20 × 100 = $2,000. But now, after agreeing to the discount, her margin is only $15 × 100 = $1,500. To achieve the original cash profit of $2,000, she now has to sell 33.3 percent more units. But at least she has a chance of doing so, and there is at least still *some* profit in the deal. The buyer thinks "maybe next time I can ask for even more."

If the gross margin is a lot tighter (as one typically would encounter in a very competitive market)—let's say 5 percent—competition is likely to be intense, and sellers are under pressure to keep volumes high. A 4 percent discount would mean that the company would be required to sell 400 percent more—that is, five times as many units just to get to the budgeted cash margin. Maybe the company was selling a commodity product, and price really was the issue. In such a market, the smart move would be to build in enough margin not to look to the customer to be completely out of the ball park and then to make the customer fight for the discount through negotiation. The customer will want to do that. And who knows, you might just get lucky. On the other hand, your product might be offered in a commodity market but have some valuable benefits that differentiate it from the other offers. Giving away a discount is completely the wrong thing to do. In this situation, you should fight back with every argument at your disposal. The Value Triad should be used here to identify the value elements available either to help you to charge more or to prevent unreasonable demands for discounts.

Table 11.2   Effect on Sales Volume of a Price Increase

Gross Margin, %						
Increases, %	5	10	15	20	25	30
1	16.7	9.1	6.3	4.8	3.8	3.2
2	28.6	16.7	11.8	9.1	7.4	6.3
3	37.5	23.1	16.7	13.0	10.7	9.1
4	44.4	28.6	21.1	16.7	13.8	11.8
5	50.0	33.3	25.0	20.0	16.7	14.3
10	66.7	50.0	40.0	33.3	28.6	25.0
15	75.0	60.0	50.0	42.9	37.5	33.3
20	80.0	66.7	57.1	50.0	44.4	40.0
25	83.3	71.4	62.5	55.6	50.0	45.5
30	85.7	75.0	66.7	60.0	54.5	50.0

In Table 11.1, the dark-shaded cells indicate that these combinations of gross margin and discount can never achieve a profitable outcome. Now let's look at a different scenario in Table 11.2. This scenario is identical to the preceding one except that in this table we have calculated the impact of a price increase.

Let's say that in this scenario Varsha realizes that there is a shortage of supply of the item her customer needs. The planned gross margin per unit is still 20 percent, but Varsha is able to persuade her customer that she needs to charge $105 per unit rather than the customary $100. Her gross margin has just moved to 23.8 percent, and at this margin, she needs to take an order for only 80 units, 20 percent fewer in fact. The customer, however, might be just a little bit upset by this and will remember this transaction next time around.

In a shortage situation, we can achieve temporary price increases of this nature. Inevitably, on some future occasion, the swings would become roundabouts, and we would be back to the scenario of Table 11.1.

If Varsha had done her homework properly, she may have discovered, using the Value Triad, that there are a few additional aspects of her product offer that are attractive to the customer and that he could not find elsewhere. By focusing on these attractive and unique differences and using value-based-selling techniques to present the arguments to the customer, many more deals (not all, by any means) could be closed at higher prices. There are additional unexpected gains from this strategy. If this or another customer were willing to purchase an additional 20 units, Varsha's profit would have soared from $2,000 to $2,500—25 percent more. A good outcome. If the whole company adopted value-based selling successfully and condemned discounting on demand forever to the recycle bin, then the surplus capacity released could be put to good effect by producing more of the same or other high-value-added products, further enhancing the company's profitability.

PRICE WARS

In difficult economic conditions, price wars are an almost inevitable by-product. As sales weaken and competitors reduce prices to stimulate demand, the temptation to follow suit is almost irresistible. However, the temptation to respond to a competitor's aggressive price move with one of your own is not necessarily the best or only way forward. The obvious impacts are

- Declining margins
- Declining profits
- Quality perception—Does reduced price mean reduced quality?
- Potential for commoditization

There are a number of things that should be considered before engaging in a price-driven campaign.[3]

Price Sensitivity of the Market?

An analysis of your marketplace might suggest that there is no need to price aggressively. On the other hand, you may operate in a market that is highly price elastic by nature. This inevitably will drive your overall strategic direction. In the latter case, the pursuit of ongoing cost reductions may make you review your entire go-to-market approach and critically evaluate your value chain at every level.

Cost Cutting to Protect Margin

How well placed is your company to do this? Most businesses have gone through serious bouts of cost cutting already, and there is very little, if any, fat left. Cutting costs further at this point runs the risk of cutting capability and entering a vicious circle within which you can no longer afford to do the very things that customers need done or perform them to a less than acceptable standard.

Product Modification

If you have to get involved, can you modify your product to reflect the price reduction? If customers want to pay less, then they should get less. The danger is that if they don't, they get used to the new price point, and when the opportunity comes to raise prices, once more it will prove difficult. The new lower price point will be considered to be the norm.

Deep Pockets

Just how well placed are you to withstand a prolonged period of aggressive pricing? In other words, can you afford it? It is fruitless entering a battle you cannot win or at the very least survive. Difficult as it might appear, there is a need to investigate options other than simply price.

Product/Brand Perception

Will a lower price point damage the brand/quality perception and, if so, how badly? This is an important consideration. The biggest danger in reducing price in response to competitive activity is that value perceptions reduce with it, and price is seen increasingly as the differentiator—the road to commoditization. Could you introduce an "economy" version (sometimes these are called *fighter brands*) to protect the value of the established brand? U.K. supermarkets have done just this with Tesco's introduction of a "value" range and Waitrose's "essentials" range. These are positioned as cheaper alternatives to their normal own-brand or private-label offerings. (Note that use of the term *value* to describe Tesco's value range runs the risk of customers equating value with cheap. This is not the case. From the customer value line, we know that value is possible at any price point provided that it is balanced in the customer's mind with compensating benefits.)

Competitors

Just how well placed are competitors to withstand a long period of reduced prices? In all of this, we must recognize that this is happening within the context of a competitive marketplace. Our competitors are likely to be feeling similar pressures to our own. Accurately predicting how they might respond and how vulnerable they might be is helpful. Perhaps an aggressive pricing approach by you is something to which they could not afford to respond and is one way of driving a competitor from the market. (Aggressive pricing may be illegal in some jurisdictions, though.)

Competitor Response

How will your competitors react? It seems logical to assume that if I reduce my price in a bid to build volume and/or build market share, then competitors will react to this. If they do so by reducing their price to mine, all I have succeeded in doing is reducing the profitability of the market for everyone. If I respond by reducing my price further, a price war is under way.

Customer Sensitivity to Reduced Quality

What about the customer? The assumption in all of this is that price is the primary decision driver for the customer. Certainly price is going to be important—even more so in tough times. But what about quality, performance, availability, innovation, and so on. How important are they?

One of the problems is that price reductions are seen as easy to implement, quick to do, and reversible. While the first two might be true, the last is generally a good deal more difficult to achieve, as we have seen. Pricing too low just causes people to expect lower prices rather than focusing on fair pricing for the value provided. As we write, a champagne price war has broken out in U.K. supermarkets with prices plummeting. While the impact on volume has seen sales increase dramatically initially, what damage is this doing to the whole essence of champagne and its exclusive, quality image?

COMPETITION AND HYPERCOMPETITION

Throughout this book, competition has been identified as a key driver of our prices. We do not set our prices in isolation but rather within the context of the market as a whole. No matter what additional value in use we can demonstrate to the customer, customers still will see our solution and will evaluate it within the context of the market they know and the prices with which they are familiar. This isn't just a current problem but a historical and ongoing one. Competitors come in all shapes and sizes and from all sorts of directions. We should know the following:

Number of competitors. Just how many are we up against, and have we identified them all? If I'm in town and want something to eat, the competitor to the sandwich bar that I might use is the local pub, the hotel, going home and making my own, not eating anything for lunch, or buying a chocolate bar and a Coke! (Note here that eating nothing is also a competitor.)

Nature of the competition. Are we up against global players with huge resources or local suppliers with limited budgets but other possible benefits? Understanding the strengths and weaknesses of each is important in determining our actions.

Copy-cat competitors. How do we deal with imitators, people who simply copy what we've done and do it more cheaply?

Innovators. What can we do about companies that are wildly innovative, always pushing the boundaries?

Value builders or value grabbers. Are our competitors out to develop a reputation based on quality and value building or based on price and value reduction?

The implication is that we must understand our competitors in considerable detail. For most businesses, this will mean having a formalized way of collating competitor information. This can range from something fairly simple right up to sophisticated competitor intelligence (CI) systems. One of our clients maintains a large and complex database tracking every major project within its industry globally. It captures a range of information, such as what the time frames are for tender submission, contract signing, project completion, who was pitching for the business, who won, and at what price. It puts the company in a great position when it starts to look at putting together its own project submissions. Not only does the company have a good idea of the sorts of prices similar projects were won at, but it also can take a view as to how busy competitors are and what their current production capacities/shop loading might be as a result.

One thing is for sure, there's always someone who wants your customer's business. The more attractive the business you have, the more likely it is that other people will want it. Our job is simply to ensure that our overall value proposition to the customer remains relevant, persuasive, and effective. To do this, we need constantly to evaluate our competitors, both generically within the marketplace and specifically for each individual major sale with which we are involved. We also need to be constantly talking with our customers and staying abreast of their ever-changing needs and requirements.

Table 11.3 Competitor Analysis

Key Attributes	Us	Competitor 1	Competitor 2	Competitor 3	Competitor 4
Quality					
Service capability					
Service costs					
Logistics					
Payment terms					
Order/ delivery times					
Reputation/ brand					

Table 11.3 is an easy-to-use, simple tool for analyzing competitor versus our capabilities across a number of key selection criteria. For a market analysis, the criteria will be those most generally selected by buyers within that market segment. For an individual sale. it will be the criteria specifically identified by the appropriate buyer(s). If your solution has few benefits when compared with that of competitors, then this probably will need to be reflected in the price. If you have a number of significant strengths, then that, equally, should be reflected in a higher price. Customers' reactions to various competitive solutions can be ascertained through market research or simply by discussing their views with them. In reality, either way, competitor analysis should be a combination of both objective measurements and subjective analysis. However it is conducted, it is vitally important. All too frequently businesses invest heavily in creating competitive points of difference that end up being exactly that—points of difference rather than points of true differentiation (different is being different; differentiation is being different in ways that the customer really values).[4] The key is in understanding customer needs in detail and in depth and in recognizing how your solution can affect their business and their ability to do better business with their customers that is true value.

The term *hypercompetition*[5] was coined by Richard D'Aveni of The Tuck Business School. He considered hypercompetition to be a key feature of the new economy. Not only is there more competition, there is also tougher and smarter competition. The core idea was that competitive advantages were becoming unsustainable because of globalization and technological disruption. His view is that, if anything, this speed of change has accelerated, and he describes the current situation as "hypercompetition on steroids."

Together with his colleague L. G. Thomas, he describes hypercompetition as "an environment characterized by intense and rapid competitive moves, in which competitors must move quickly to build new advantages and, simultaneously, erode the advantages of their rivals." If they fail to do so, the likely end result is the commoditization of their products and services. The end result of that is reduced margins and reduced profitability.

The impact of this is that competitive advantages must be constantly re invented given how short-lived they are potentially likely to be. Doing so means truly understanding the things customers value and recognizing that value is in a constant state of flux. Knowledge then becomes an important factor, and the ability of the organization to respond to changing circumstances quickly and effectively becomes the competitive advantage.

Legal Issues in Pricing in the European Union

The price which society pays for the law of competition, like the price it pays for cheap comforts and luxuries, is great; but the advantages of this law are also greater still than its cost, for it is to this law that we owe our wonderful material development, which brings improved conditions in its train. But, whether the law be benign or not, we must say of it: it is here; we cannot evade it; no substitutes for it have been found; and while the law may be sometimes hard for the individual, it is best for the race, because it ensures the survival of the fittest in every department.
—Andrew Carnegie (November 25, 1835 – August 11, 1919)

European Union competition law applies to all undertakings that conduct some kind of commercial activity. In European parlance, *undertaking* is used to denote a business organization established for economic gain. Undertakings need not be profit-making. For example, those engaged in providing statutory health care are not caught by EU competition law because they are pursuing a social objective. Two or more companies that are linked together through common ownership may, for the purposes of this law, be considered as a single economic entity. Most developed countries will have some form of competition legislation that applies to companies within their borders. Legal decisions are having greater and greater impact on companies' commercial policies. In particular, and increasingly, the European Commission is taking greater interest in companies' pricing decisions, and several high-profile cases have been reported in recent months. Pricing executives must gain some understanding of what drives these decisions and be sure that they do not inadvertently place themselves or their companies at risk because of unwise decisions.

The reader should realize—and this we must stress—that this appendix in no way substitutes for professional advice from an appropriately qualified legal professional. The whole field of competition law is complex and constantly changing as new cases emerge and decisions are taken. If ever there is a question about the legality of a pricing decision, this must be referred to legal counsel before finalizing.

ARTICLE 102 TFEU: CONTROL OF DOMINANCE

Article 102 TFEU (Treaty for the Functioning of the European Union) is designed to control the activities of enterprises that have "market power." Article 102 TFEU seeks to control companies that have developed a powerful market position such that if they chose to do so, they could behave as monopolies. This would have serious impacts on the normal operations of a market. Any undertaking that is able, on its own, to affect normal economic behavior is described as having a dominant position. Article 102 TFEU offers an indicative list of conduct that is likely to abuse a dominant situation[1]:

1. Imposing directly or indirectly purchase or selling prices or imposing other unfair trading conditions
2. Limiting manufacturing output to the detriment of consumers
3. Restricting market or technical development to the detriment of consumers
4. Behaving in a discriminating manner by applying different trading conditions to identical transactions with other parties

5. Insisting that contracts are subject to conditions not directly related to the transaction in question

This list is indicative only, and particular situations may be interpreted quite widely if they are thought likely to impede trade between member states.

The two principal forms of abusive behavior include exploitative abuse and exclusionary abuse. *Exploitative abuse* occurs when an undertaking acts as a virtual monopolist and maximizes its profits by imposing unacceptable output restrictions or unreasonably high (or low) price levels. *Exclusionary abuse* occurs when an undertaking, in order to protect its market power, discourages or actively prevents new entrants from coming into the market. This closes the market to effective competition. Only an undertaking in a dominant position in the market has the power to engage in abusive behavior of this nature. If smaller undertakings were to engage in such behavior, rational consumers would switch to alternative suppliers.

WHAT IS A DOMINANT POSITION?

The European Court of Justice (ECJ) importantly defined in the very important landmark *United Brands* judgment a dominant position as one that relates to

> ... a position of economic strength enjoyed by an undertaking which enables it to prevent effective competition in being maintained on the relevant market by giving it the power to behave to an appreciable extent independently of its competitors, customers, and ultimately of its consumers ... in general a dominant position derives from a combination of several factors which, taken separately, are not necessarily determinative.

In order to establish dominance, three factors need to be examined:

1. How the market is defined (the relevant market concept)
2. How the undertaking's market strength is defined
3. The barriers to entry that apply within the market

Table A.1   Determinants of Dominance

Dominant Issue	Description	Case
Relevant markets—how to define markets in which an undertaking is dominant		*Continental Can vs Commission* (1973)
Cross-elasticity	Ability of consumer to switch supplier	
Physical features	Product specifications, features, and characteristics	*United Brands*
Price	Competitive pricing levels	
Intended use	Application of product in different markets	*Michelin I* (1983)
Potential suppliers	Ability of potential suppliers to switch into subject market	*Continental Can*
Geographic markets	Homogeneity of market characteristics	*United Brands*
Time frame	Seasonality	*United Brands*
Barriers to entry	Wide range of actions that dominant supplier can take to impede market entry of competitor	

Table A.1 lists the principal factors that are investigated to determine the existence of dominance, together with indicative cases where each factor was important in a legal ruling.

Relevant Markets

A dominant undertaking may apply market power in three distinct areas:

1. The product/service market
2. The geographic market
3. The period of time during which the market is active

Definition of the relevant market is of first importance in assessing abuse of dominance because only once this has been done properly can the precise nature of the physical characteristics and performance of competing products be assessed adequately. For individual products to be part of a market, they need to be "individualized" not only by their application but also by the way in which they are manufactured, which makes them particularly suitable for the purpose. To assist in defining markets, the European Commission issued a very detailed notice explaining the process in-depth.[2] Two key elements of dominance relate to *market power* and *market share.*

Market Power

In order to gauge the market power of a given undertaking, we must define the other products in the market that are competing with those of the undertaking under examination. This assessment should identify the undertaking's position in regard to potential or actual competitors. If the market is defined in too narrow a manner, with very few competitive products, it is more likely that the undertaking will be seen to be dominant. If the market is defined too loosely, then a dominant undertaking may escape the net. The court has established the principle of interchangeability as a test of dominance. This test measures the ease with which customers can switch from one supplier to another in the event of a price increase. If purchasers would move to an alternative product when faced with, say, a 5 to 10 percent price increase, then the undertaking's product and other products to which the customer has access would be deemed to be in the same market. If a given undertaking produces all substitute products available to the customer, there would be no competition, and the undertaking would be described as a *hypothetical monopolist.* In order to demonstrate product or service dominance, the commission requires to collect solid factual support from many sources.

Market Share

This alone does not constitute dominance but is evidence of the undertaking's power in the market. Its ability to maintain stable, high market share over a prolonged period of time is further evidence of dominance. Consequently, barriers to entry are strategically very important to the undertaking. Such barriers would have the effect of maintaining market share at a higher level and discouraging new entrants. Indeed, this is the intention of many competitive strategies. On the other hand, if market shares have varied significantly over a period, then this is evidence that healthy competition does exist. A market share of 50 percent is considered to be very large. Companies with such a share will be presumed to be dominant. A market share of between 30 and 50 percent also may indicate market strength, but here it is important to assess the shares of other large competitors in the same market. If, for instance, the company owns 40 percent market share and all other competitors have much smaller shares, then this company will be presumed to have market strength. Very large shares do not always indicate dominance. However, if dominance is established, then very high market share may lead to that undertaking becoming *superdominant* and requiring even greater care in its dealings with consumers and competitors. Given that most countries aim for the ideal of perfect competition, a company with very high market share is already distorting that ideal. A superdominant company is expected to act responsibly and not to disrupt the competitive process further. In order for an undertaking to be considered dominant, it must be in a position to defend its high market share.

Cross-Elasticity of Demand

If consumers move to a substitute product in response to a relatively small price increase, cross-elasticity of demand is high. If it takes a large price increase for demand to switch, then cross-elasticity is low. This means that consumers have no viable alternatives even with a significant price increase, and the undertaking's position is dominant.

Physical Features

If products are substantially similar in specification and performance, consumers are more likely to perceive them as interchangeable. It is possible for a given product to possess features that place it in different markets. Minor differences in products may alter the way in which they are seen to compete in a given market. Marketing efforts are often employed to create real or perceived differentiations, either through highlighting specific applications or by designing value-adding accessories and service offers.

Price

Prices of competing products may determine whether these products are part of the same market. For example, the price of a personal computer (PC) and the price of a mainframe computer are completely different even though both products are used to carry out complex calculations. There is no way that a PC could be considered as part of the market for mainframe computers.

Intended Use

A product may have applications in quite different markets even though the products are physically identical. In *Michelin I*, the company provided car tires both to original manufacturers and to the aftermarket. There are in fact two cases involving Michelin that appear in the literature—referred to as *Michelin I* and *Michelin II*. In the former case, manufacturers order tires in bulk and fit them to vehicles during production. In the latter case, tires are purchased as required in much smaller volumes and fitted during repairs and routine servicing. These are quite different markets.

Potential Suppliers

Noncompeting manufacturers (i.e., manufacturers producing products that do not currently compete with the product under consideration) may be perceived to be part of the same market if the supplier can switch manufacturing to produce similar products without significant additional cost. The existence of a potential competitor has the effect of increasing competitive pressure on the undertaking. In the *Continental Can* case, suppliers of cans for other purposes could readily switch applications and enter Continental Can's markets. They were not required actually to do so. The existence of potential competitive entrants was the relevant issue in the case.

Geographic Market

Not every geographic market within the community is identical. There may be physical, legal, technical, commercial, or other reasons why different markets have different competitive characteristics. This means that in some cases competition is unlikely or impossible and in other markets highly probable. An assessment of market power can take place only under circumstances where competition is likely to occur. This requires the commission to undertake sufficient market analysis to reach a decision in any given case. The commission will, if necessary, secure independent market, economic, and technical studies that then become a matter of public record. Such information can be highly sensitive and of great commercial value to competitors. Concern about disclosure of sensitive commercial data may lead undertakings to accept the EU's decision, even if they reject its validity, rather than raising a challenge through appeal.

Time Frame

Seasonality may have an impact on competition.

Barriers to Entry

This is a very important concept in strategic management and is part of the analysis that business strategists carry out in assessing the strategic position of a company. Porter's Five Forces model is a key tool in analyzing the competitive threat posed to companies by new entrants into the market. Porter's model assesses barriers to entry, substitute technologies, the respective powers of buyers and sellers, and the competitive situation existing in the market at a given point in time.

An important part of the strategic response to this challenge is to erect real or perceived barriers to entry. There is much debate around this subject. For example, a barrier to entry may be the extensive experience of an incumbent supplier who has worked hard to establish a strong competitive position in the market. A barrier to entry ultimately comes down to cost. If the cost to get into a market is higher for a new entrant than that originally experienced by a company already operating in the market, any barriers to entry erected by dominant incumbents may be judged as unfair. The existence of no or low entry barriers means that it is relatively easy for newcomers to enter the market and gain some traction. This clearly poses a challenge to incumbent organizations.

It is clearly in the interest of incumbents to create real or perceived barriers to entry. Incumbents can adopt one or more of a number of approaches to creating barriers to entry. These are summarized in Table A.2, together with case references illustrating each type of barrier.

Table A.2 Barriers to Entry

Type of Barrier	Description	Case Reference
Legal provisions	Statutory or regulatory powers granted by national laws; for example, intellectual property or government licensing can create monopoly positions that can be protected through national courts.	*Hilti AG v Commission* (1991) *Tetra-Pak v Commission* (1990)
Technological advantage	Possession of existing technology or access to future technology.	*Hoffmann la Roche v Commission* (1979)
Financial resources	A major undertaking with access to extensive funding may use that funding to defend against new entrants. This makes it difficult for much smaller businesses, especially small to medium enterprises (SMEs).	*Continental Can v Commission* (1973) *United Brands Continental BV v Commission* (1978)
Economies of scale	If a major undertaking has achieved significant experience curve advantages or economies of scale, this can prevent a new undertaking with much less experience from competing effectively.	*British Plaster Board/British Gypsum v Commission* (1978)
Vertical integration	If an undertaking is able to control upstream supply chain and downstream production and distribution, then it exerts a major control over the way products enter the market (vertical integration).	*United Brands Continental BV v Commission* (1978)
Product differentiation	Product differentiation, including branding, can create a barrier to entry. Consumers perceive the incumbent product to have major advantages not shared by the new entrant. Such advantages may be real or perceived. The issue here is the degree of real interchangeability between competitive products.	*United Brands Continental BV v Commission* (1978)
Conduct	If a company historically reacts extremely vigorously to a new entrant and exercises superior market power to prevent or discourage entry, such conduct may be abusive (1978).	*AKZO Chemie BV v Commission*

ANTICOMPETITIVE PRICING BEHAVIOR

This section summarizes exploitative and exclusionary pricing practices. The main categories of anticompetitive pricing include

1. Excessive pricing
2. Fair terms and conditions
3. Status quo (sometimes called the *quiet life*)
4. Discounting and rebating
5. Predatory pricing

Excessive Pricing

A dominant undertaking may choose to apply virtual monopoly power in charging very high prices in the knowledge that there is no effective competition to modify its pricing behavior. This strategy will enable it to achieve maximum profits. Its behavior may involve restricting productive output or reinforcing a perception of uniqueness and scarcity and raising prices accordingly. This is exploitative because customers have no option but to purchase at these inflated price levels.

It is difficult to ascertain what is and what is not an excessive price. One approach is to assess the degree to which the prices reflect the economic value of the goods to the user. There is little or no guidance on how economic value should be calculated. This issue has been addressed several times in case reports. Another approach is to try to identify a reference price by constructing a hypothetical competitive market. This is in fact very difficult to do, and again, no clear guidance is given by the Commission on how this calculation should be carried out.

Different approaches have been adopted to assessing the degree of excessiveness in pricing. One approach is to assess prices for similar articles in other European markets and identify whether a given price is truly excessive. The trouble with this approach is that no two markets have identical competitive characteristics, and therefore, such comparisons may be inappropriate. Variations in tax law, physical distribution, nature of selling, contracts, geography, climate, consumer behavior, marketing strategy, and many other factors, alone or in combination, may bring about conditions in which price levels genuinely need to be different but in which there is no hint of exploitative behavior.

The second approach is to apply a cost-based method to pricing. This approach is also unsatisfactory because some costs may be of a temporary nature or difficult to allocate correctly. This leaves considerable uncertainty in the use of costs in generating a price for the purposes of assessing exploitative pricing behavior.

There is a view that direct legal interference in market pricing decisions is wrong. Those who hold this viewpoint argue that the market itself should be left to control prices in line with normal supply and demand. If achievable prices are high, this will attract new competition and thus increase competitive intensity in the market. Provided that there are no unfair barriers to entry, new competition should be left to moderate the behavior of incumbent companies. If prices are lower, the issue simply does not arise because consumers are not being disadvantaged. It is interesting that there have been few decisions by the Commission on excessive pricing. Part of the reason for this may be the difficulty of collecting relevant cost and price information or coming to a robust and consistently applicable view of how exploitative pricing can be defined and diagnosed.

Fair Terms and Conditions

If unfair conditions imposed by a dominant undertaking restrict the freedom to act of customers, suppliers, and associates, then this is an abuse. Such abuses can be exploitive, exclusionary, or both. The majority seem to be exclusionary in nature.

The Quiet Life

If an undertaking is sufficiently dominant, it will have no incentive to increase operational or economic efficiency (*economic efficiency* denotes the allocation of resources in the best interests of consumers). Therefore, an undertaking that refuses to update operating methods to better and more efficient methods, even though such methods are readily available, may be viewed as exploitative because delivery of the associated product and service costs much more than a more modern approach.

Discounting and Rebating

Discounts can be used to tie customers to particular suppliers. They also can be used in the normal run of business to encourage a purchaser to buy one company's products rather than those of another. Indeed, customers often demand discounts aggressively in a deliberate ploy to encourage sellers to bid for their business. This is normal buying behavior in many industries. Another form of discounting is the *annual loyalty rebate*. Rather than offer individual discounts based on transaction value, the seller offers the buyer a discount based on total annual purchases. From the supplier's point of view, the objective is to encourage customers to remain loyal over an accounting period (perhaps 6 to 12 months). In exchange for their loyalty, buyers receive an agreed-on percentage discount in the form of a rebate based on the total sales value purchased during the preceding period and paid at the end of the period. Such a rebate may be based on a particular range of products that the seller is seeking to promote or may be aggregated across all products that the customer buys. If the customer chooses to move from one supplier to another during that period, no loyalty rebate would be made. Many companies apply discounts and rebates with the express objective of securing continued customer loyalty. In nondominant businesses, this is normal day-to-day business practice.

Discounting and rebating may, under Article 102 TFEU, be abusive if employed by a dominant supplier. A dominant supplier in general has much greater financial and other resources than a smaller competitor. The use of these resources in offering greater discounts than could be offered by smaller competitors amounts to an abuse of a dominant position and is exclusionary in that it will prevent smaller competitors from achieving market penetration and thus will limit consumer choice. Rebates ensure that customers are tied in for a period of time, as defined by the conditions of the rebate. There are different manifestations of discounting behavior applied by dominant undertakings. For instance, if discounts are tied to the achievement of specific sales targets, and a channel partner, perhaps a distributor or retailer, achieves these targets, that customer is rewarded with a very significant discount. When the volume of purchases is very high and the level of rebate very significant, this will encourage distributors to sell only the products of the dominant supplier. This is exclusionary if such arrangements are made on a case-by-case basis (and hence also discriminatory) rather than by applying a standard approach to all distributors. Discounts may be out of all proportion to the level of sales achieved. This is clearly an attempt to prevent other undertakings from achieving market share.

Not all rebates and discounts are abusive. If a company achieves cost reductions as a result of economy-of-scale savings or through better supply-chain management, or in some other way, and these cost savings are passed on proportionately to its customers, this is not abusive. However, all such discounts must be equally available to all customers and based demonstrably on evidence of cost reduction. Decisions in this area are both complex and contentious because of the complicated nature of pricing. In modern competitive markets, it is also important to realize that if discounting by a dominant undertaking is for the express purpose of inducing loyalty, it does not need to be shown that there *were* anticompetitive effects. The fact that the seller has implemented a policy for this reason is sufficient.

Predatory Pricing

In Chapter 4 we examined the idea of predatory pricing as a form of competitive pricing. You will recall that in predatory pricing, a seller that enjoys a significant cost advantage is able to manipulate market prices so that it can render the market uneconomical for competitors. The seller's unit costs of production (or of service delivery) are so low because of its cumulative experience that it still can make acceptable profit at prices that are much lower than average. When the seller deliberately drops prices to a level that is lower than the competitor's marginal cost of production, competitors have few options and may be forced to withdraw or face enormous losses. If the seller initiating this price-reduction strategy is dominant, then this is clear abuse of market power. A dominant player may be able to sustain its losses for a prolonged period because of its economic strength. Indeed, its unit costs may be such that it makes no losses at all.

The ECJ, in trying to decide whether such behavior is predatory and abusive, established a formula that can be applied in such circumstances:

1. If prices are below the average variable cost, then predatory pricing is presumed.
2. If prices lie between average variable costs and average total costs, then pricing is predatory only if it can be demonstrated that this was an attempt to limit competition.

The test itself relies on an investigator's ability to identify and allocate appropriate costs. This is difficult to do in a manner that is universally acceptable. There is also the issue of prices changing rapidly, for instance, in chemicals, agricultural products, or a huge range of raw materials and agricultural produce, to list a few, which renders precise cost identification impractical. Availability and seasonality may affect costs and prices significantly. Demonstrating that behavior was deliberately predatory would demand access to individuals and documents within the target company. Such access may be very difficult or impossible to achieve in practice.

Tying and Leverage

This idea can best be illustrated by a hypothetical example. Suppliers of photocopiers have long established a pricing method based on charging on a *per click* basis. Every time the user presses the "Copy" button, the number of copies is recorded and charged to the customer's account. In a straightforward equipment-supply contract, the supplier provides the equipment but also may offer associated service and consumables but does not compel the customer to use either. A different form of contract that became popular in the middle to late 1980s tied suppliers of paper, toner, and other consumables to the initial contract. In such a case, customers had no choice but to obtain their consumables from the supplier of the original equipment. This is an example of tie-in where the supplier sought to exercise influence over purchases of items outside the photocopier industry. If the supplier was dominant in the photocopying industry, then this attempt to extend influence into a completely different market could be judged as abusive. Such a deal might appear attractive to some customers but does in fact limit their freedom to source supplies from other suppliers offering better prices. This also would prevent competitive suppliers from supplying consumables to "tied" photocopier customers, thus restricting market access to competitors and limiting consumer choice.

A popular value-based pricing methodology, *bundling* (which we discussed in Chapter 7), involves linking two or more products or services together and pricing them as a package. For example, a supplier of fixed-line telephone services also may offer to supply broadband, television, mobile telephony, and other services. This is potentially very profitable for the selling organization and also may be attractive to the consumer. The bundling process effectively limits the customers' free choice by compelling them to accept the options provided within the bundle. If all aspects of the bundle are supplied by one organization (and only as a bundle but not separately), and if that organization has market power, such bundling may be viewed as anticompetitive and abusive. The implication for pricing managers is to study carefully the details of any intended bundle to ensure that there is no risk of being accused of abusive practices.

PRICE DISCRIMINATION

Before exploring how value-based pricing (VBP) fits in with all this, it is worth reviewing a few ideas around price discrimination. Although not specifically defined within EU law, *price discrimination* nevertheless is a term used widely in business and by economists. Price discrimination has been described as "a practice involving the sale of the same product to different customers at different prices, even though the cost of the sale is the same to each of them."[4]

Figure A.1 looks at the four alternatives arising from the "similar/dissimilar prices for similar/dissimilar products" issue. What emerges from this set of combinations is that the discriminatory combinations are similar prices for dissimilar transactions and dissimilar prices for similar transactions. Competitive undertakings applying similar pricing approaches are likely to come to fairly similar prices, and hence price lists from competitors will tend to offer similar products at similar prices and may publish them on their price lists. Dissimilar prices for

	SIMILAR PRICES	DISSIMILAR PRICES
SIMILAR TRANSACTIONS	TRANSACTIONS BASED CONVENTIONAL PRICING METHODS (COST-, COMPETITION-, AND MARKET-BASED)	CHALLENGEABLE UNDER ARTICLE 82(C)
DISSIMILAR TRANSACTIONS	CHALLENGEABLE UNDER ARTICLE 82(C)	UNIQUE, HIGHLY CUSTOMIZED TRANSACTIONS BASED ON VALUE-BASED PRICING

Figure A.1   Prices and transactions.

dissimilar transactions may be a useful way of looking at VBP trans-actions—every deal is different. It also shows that VBP cannot be described accurately as discriminatory. It probably would be unreliable to rely entirely on this categorization. Managers need to be certain—to avoid the accusation of price discrimination—that there is a sufficiently detailed *audit trail* in assessing both the prices and the nature of the transactions and that in any given case it will be possible to demon-strate real differences.

The term *price discrimination* generally is reserved for practices in which different customers are treated differently by a company in terms of pricing and other trading conditions. It is only when applied by dom-inant undertakings that it becomes subject to scrutiny under Article 102 TFEU(c). In fact, price discrimination is applied routinely by under-takings of all sizes and within all geographies and usually is a perfectly acceptable way of doing business. In some cases, such practices may be disadvantageous to individual parties and may be illegal under national legislation (e.g., Trade Descriptions Act, Unfair Contract Terms Act, Supply of Goods Act, and so on in the United Kingdom) irrespective of dominance. Nevertheless, principles of *caveat emptor* (let the buyer beware) and *caveat vendor* (let the seller beware) still apply. A party to a disadvantageous transaction can hardly complain if no laws have been breached, the outcome of the transaction can reasonably be foreseen, and the party simply has been foolish.

The objective of price discrimination is to capture as much as possible of the available consumer surplus. There are three broad categories of price discrimination:

First-degree price discrimination. This occurs when a firm is able to charge each customer the maximum he is willing to pay. This requires a great deal of information about the customer. Some economists argue that this scenario is unlikely to be observed in real markets.

Second-degree price discrimination. This occurs when the price paid by a customer varies with the volume purchased. Volume discounts and rebates fall into this category—the more of a firm's product that a customer buys, the lower the price per unit that he pays, usually according to some formula agreed on in advance. Two- or multiple-part tariffs in utilities contracts are very popular and pervasive and can be quite ingenious in their construction. At a European conference for mobile telephone operators in early 2008, one speaker estimated that there were at that time in excess of 15,000 separate tariffs in operation in Europe. Tariffs usually entail a baseline (frequently calculated to cover the fixed costs per user) that all customers pay irrespective of usage and a volume-dependent price. This favors heavier users but discriminates against very light users. It also has the effect of encouraging all subscribers to consume more of the service.

Third-degree price discrimination. This occurs when a company charges customers a price based on their price sensitivity—that is, very price-sensitive customers are charged the least, and price-insensitive customers are charged most (Ramsey pricing).

Price discrimination practices include discounting and rebating, tying, bundling, and selective price cuts. Such practices are routine in modern business and (probably) contribute positively to the well-being of both buyers and sellers.

VBP AND EU COMPETITION LAW

In Chapter 6, we defined VBP as a price "designed and communicated such that all parties to a given transaction understand, recognize, and accept the distinctive worth of products and services purchased in the transaction and participate optimally in the gains created by their use." Several important points arise from this definition when we examine it through the lens of competition law, price discrimination, and the various cases described herein.

Capturing a Fair Share of the Consumer Surplus Created

As we have described in detail, conventional pricing methods such as cost- and competition-based pricing usually fail to capture a fair share of the consumer surplus that arises in a business transaction, with the result that the customer may gain disproportionately, the vendor lose disproportionately, and commercial relationships between the parties become uncomfortably strained, if not irreparably damaged. The reason for this, more often than not, is that the seller has not clearly enough understood what that value actually is. Her emphasis has been to secure the sale through the discounting mechanism, and she is encouraged to do so by the buyer. There is generally a systematic failure among vendors to identify and articulate value *from the customer's perspective.* This is a very pervasive error, and consequently, in a great many transactions, consumer value is neither identified nor articulated in the sales negotiation. The result is that customers not only have gained a serious consumer surplus, but they also do not even realize it. The objective of VBP is to deliver to the customer and encourage him to recognize superior value and in the process for the seller to capture a fair share of the benefit created in the transaction.

There Are No Losers

In VBP, the objective expressly is *not* to maximize profit at the expense of the customer or other trading partners. This would not be sustainable. Quite the reverse, in fact. When implemented correctly, VBP should lead to the clear identification and quantification wherever possible of the benefits accruing to the buying party and to any channel partners involved in the transaction and contributing to the value-delivery process. Companies implement a VBP approach not because they wish to maximize profit—obviously, profit *optimization* is an important driver—but because they want to develop better business and do so in a manner that encourages all parties to continue the relationship. VBP should lead to win-win situations. There is no intention, certainly by the authors of this book, to position VBP as an exploitative (or as an exclusionary) pricing method. All parties to a genuine VBP transaction are engaged in a search for real economic and emotional value. This process demands careful study of the economic and emotional aspects of the transaction with the objective of identifying specifically areas of gain that can be shared. When VBP is applied properly, it cannot fail to enhance the welfare of all parties.

Importance of Differentiation

Every VBP transaction is unique because it is designed on the basis of a specific assessment of the buyer's real needs. This assessment is made from an analysis of market contextual factors as well as factors internal to the client's organization, usually through careful examination of the client's value chain—the client's own value-adding processes. Such assessments are made through direct observations and by a consultative approach adopted by the vendor's representatives. The vendor then creates, using her own specific skills and capabilities, a unique solution for the buyer. This solution is differentiated from competitive offers because it is based firmly on the vendor's unique capabilities and the purchaser's unique requirements. This solution will be an assembly of products and/or services, some elements of which *individually* may be similar to those offered by competitors. This is incorporated into a well-structured solution and a unique value proposition created and presented explicitly to the customer. This offers complete transparency, in which both parties are crystal clear on the entire nature of the offer. Taken as a whole, the solution is unique and difficult or impossible for a competitor to replicate. The price structure also will be different in every case because it is based on a unique offer (see Figure A.1).

Perfect Customer Knowledge

The concept of *perfect customer knowledge* is central to the economist's (and the legislator's) ideal of perfect competition. If every supplier possessed perfect knowledge of every customer (and of competitors), then inevitably all products and services on offer would be identical—and probably priced identically as well. The reality is, however, that most modern markets are not perfect, although the Internet has put in place some of the necessary factors for perfect competition in some industries (e.g., ready access to detailed market data and the ability to communicate instantaneously with customers). In most cases, however, the more market and customer information that can be collected, the greater is the competitive edge that it potentially offers its owner because it enables the vendor to customize offers specifically to customers' real needs. In VBP, we deliberately set out to collect as much market and customer data as we can, with the express purpose of quantifying the economic (and emotional) benefits our product or service can deliver and thus assessing as precisely as possible the customer's real willingness to pay through knowledge-based negotiation. This approach helps us to capture as much of the consumer surplus as possible and should lead to higher (but not excessive) prices because the prices are linked directly to the benefits delivered to the customer. A final agreement is reached by both parties negotiating at arms' length and equipped with all the facts that are available to each.

Market Segmentation

Every customer is different—with different needs, pressures, expectations, contexts, and so on. Most market-oriented businesses recognize this simple fact and respond to it by means of market segmentation, in which they seek to define discrete, mutually exclusive categories of customers with specific needs and wants in common that can be addressed by a differential marketing strategy. Most successful companies segment their markets and address these submarkets with distinct and different marketing strategies—even for a product or service that is invariant between segments. The collection of market data helps us to identify categories of market segments whose price sensitivity (and sensitivity to other elements of the marketing mix) we can judge. Inevitably, this will lead to first-degree price discrimination. The nature of the VBP process, however, is that there is no injury.

Many aspects of pricing are of interest to both the European Commission and the courts. Most of the directly price-related matters have arisen under Article 102 TFEU: "It is abusive for a dominant undertaking to apply dissimilar conditions to equivalent transactions with other trading parties, thereby placing them at a competitive disadvantage."

In terms of Article 102 TFEU, dominance needs to be demonstrated by means of the tests and procedures referred to earlier. The reality is that most undertakings in a given market will enjoy dominance in some form, albeit not at the level envisioned by legislation. This is normal competitive behavior in which companies seek to gain, retain, and exploit competitive advantage. Their economic reward arises from their ability to use this attribute to achieve some form of differentiation that is sufficiently attractive to customers that they prefer to purchase from one company rather than another. This can hardly be described as disadvantaging the customer—quite the opposite, in fact—but it certainly can be seen as disadvantaging competitors. This is the whole point.

In its judgment in the *United Brands* case, the ECJ offered the following statement in relation to excessive pricing:

> … charging a price which is excessive because it has no reasonable relation to the economic value of the product supplied would be … an abuse. … This excess could, inter alia, be determined objectively if it were possible for it to be calculated by making a comparison between the selling price of the product in question and its cost of production, which would disclose the amount of the profit margin.

From the point of view of VBP, this statement completely misses the point. Economic value to the customer has nothing whatsoever to do with the economics of the manufacturing process. There is no guaranteed correlation between manufacturing cost and value delivery to the consumer. Value has to do with the measurable economic benefits, as well as the less readily measurable emotional benefits, that a customer gains through his use of a product or service. A product or service can be created and delivered at high cost but offer little or no demonstrable benefit to the user. If there is no measurable benefit to the customer, then any price would be excessive. This presumed correlation lies at the very heart of the flawed nature of cost-based pricing.

By contrast, a price that is genuinely based on real, measurable, and demonstrable benefit to the customer and which creates advantages to the customer in which both vendor and customer share cannot conceivably be described as excessive—whether employed by a dominant undertaking or otherwise and whether perceived as discriminatory or otherwise—because economic and emotional benefits have been employed in its construction, and an arm's-length negotiated approach between parties with equal contractual capacity has led to a mutually acceptable agreement.

Perhaps the principal reason why the courts thus far seem to have failed to offer clear guidance on economic value is because they have been considering the wrong thing—*manufacturing economics*—rather than *objective customer value delivery*. This has been the subject of this whole book to this point.

Additional material (particularly commentary on a number of important landmark cases) is included on the Axia Value Solutions Web site at www.axiavalue.com/VBP.

Case Studies for Chapter 10

CASE STUDY 1: ALPHA

Background Market-leading speciality chemicals company with locations in the United States and the European Union

Change drivers Chief executive under pressure to improve results and generate better return on investment (ROI). Identified value-based pricing (VBP) as a means of achieving the necessary results. He communicated his enthusiasm for the VBP approach and drove it strongly through sales management and product management teams.

Current methods Current methods were classic cost plus, and deals were won through brand and discounting. Eighty percent of the sales team were technical and primarily order takers. They saw no real need to change the approach because it was working. This sales approach was normal in the industry, and the sale was technical.

Customer value	Alpha's products generally were perceived by the industry to deliver great value for money that was being given away by discounting-on-demand practices. Through the use of external consultants, the company undertook an extensive project to quantify this value as a basis for arguments to bring the sales team on board and also to present to customers.
Changes required	Senior management, product management, and marketing all were bought in. Salespeople were fiercely resistant. It was recognized that if the initiative were to succeed, sales teams would have to buy in fully and change their behavior. A deep challenge to the change was that salespeople perceived themselves to be scientists and sales discussions to be scientific conversations with peers. The move to VBP would alter that dynamic permanently. Another challenge was that the initiative was perceived as a marketing initiative and all about increasing prices, in the process taking away the only tool salespeople thought they had—flexibility on pricing. A final challenge was the perception that customers would never accept the arguments anyway, so why bother.
Opposition	Although management was bought in, in the case of sales management, this was "skin deep," and the idea was never really fully accepted. Therefore, it was not reinforced through coaching or example in the field. People gave it lip service, but there was no real commitment. Aggressive driving by the CEO and by product management solidified the resistance. Although the company spent a fortune on collateral and case studies, the lack of buy-in meant that the sales team used them at best half-heartedly. The intensive and extremely costly value-based selling (VBS) training failed because it did not address the powerful underlying forces of

Implementation

resistance. Notwithstanding the opposition from some members of the sales organization, others (between 10 and 20 percent) did recognize the validity of the approach and welcomed the change. This was an example of the "Jean Luc Picard syndrome." The CEO said, "Make it so," but provided no other support in the form of strategy, communications processes, or consultation. This was a major change program that went well beyond pricing arithmetic (the easy part) to a culture change in the whole company. Premature communication to the market that the company was adopting VBP resulted in significant pushback by customers, reinforcing the worst expectations of the sales force and vindicating their opposition.

Lessons

- Bring everyone on board before launching the initiative.
- Recognize it is a journey—not a project.
- Segment markets very carefully to select the right customers and deals.
- Get buy-in from salespeople by understanding and resolving their opposition.
- Go slowly, and do not communicate too much too soon to customers.

CASE STUDY 2: BETA

Background

Major supplier of polymers for construction industry with locations throughout the European Union.

Change drivers

Change in top-management team brought the realization that continued cost cutting was not improving profit margins and that a new approach was required. Management fully bought into the need for change, and VBP/VBS were seen as the strategy of choice. General recognition was that the company could do much better than it was and had the qualities to be a specialty products provider rather than a commodity supplier. Most of the industry was heading toward commodities. Business owners also were pressing for better results.

Current methods   Beta was production/technology-oriented and was willing to invest heavily in manufacturing technology and product development. The cost-plus nature of pricing in the industry drove the company to be very creative in driving down costs across the business. In the added-value parts, Beta was achieving acceptable margins; in commodities, margins were almost nonexistent and price negotiations always acrimonious. Cost savings achieved were lost because salespeople were "obliged" to discount to win the deals.

Customer value   Beta invested carefully in product and service differentiation, but from a technical perceptive—not from the customer's. The combination of technological differentiation and poor sales skills meant that a lot of money was left on the table. The company found it very difficult to identify, measure, and communicate its value both generally and in particular on a customer-by-customer basis principally because of obsession with product technology. Customer metrics also were a problem. The company had a world-class understanding of the key metrics and drivers for its own organization but no clear understanding of how customers defined value. This made it virtually impossible to create suitable customer value measures or to communicate them credibly to clever buyers.

Changes required   Beta was very careful in selecting and recruiting technologists, in creating proper work practices, and in developing its professionalism. This discipline did not extend to the commercial functions. Salespeople were recruited from technology streams in the business and, although technically extremely proficient and often highly qualified, were not sufficiently competent in deal selecting, selling, and negotiation. A major problem was that salespeople were "beaten up" on a regular basis by buyers and seemed powerless to resist. Huge changes were needed to bring the team to the same high level of professionalism as its technical colleagues. Management recognized fully the need for this change and initiated a number of programs to make the change happen. The culture needed to move from technology-driven to market-led.

Opposition   Because of the way in which the changes were introduced, there was relatively little pushback from salespeople. They recognized the need to change and that the right change would help them in their territories. If there was opposition, it was from technical people in middle management, who were nervous about the shift toward a more commercial culture.

Implementation   Beta invested in intelligent and integrated information systems to support commercial activities. This provided sound market, customer, and competitor data networked across the whole company so that a user could pick up and track customer orders history and other relevant market data. In parallel, Beta initiated intensive training of salespeople in both VBS and negotiation. VBS did not achieve the hoped-for results because it was too theoretical and did not build on an adequate grounding. Sales skills were too low for the more sophisticated ideas in VBS to work properly. Also, some of the salespeople were of the wrong type, and this too needed to be addressed. Salespeople need practical tools and processes, particularly in measuring customer impacts of product purchase. Negotiation training was very practical and hence very successful.

Lessons
- Management must recognize that change is necessary and possible.
- VBP involved a culture change in Beta and takes time.
- Top-management support is utterly crucial.
- A clear understanding of customer value is essential.
- The company needs to have the right salespeople.
- Training programs need to deliver practical, usable results.

CASE STUDY 3: GAMMA

Industry and background

Market-leading business services company headquartered in the United Kingdom

Change drivers

The principal driver for a change in pricing strategy in this company was a strategic plan objective to double turnover during the upcoming five years. This company enjoys many strengths, but pricing is perceived by management to be weak and needs to become more scientific and information-driven.

Current methods

Prices are published to internal staff on a price list. The prices are set at a high level to provide sales staff with the scope to make reductions as necessary to win business. The normal way of winning business is for salespeople to visit the client, understand the need, assess ability to pay, and negotiate the best price they can from the price list consistent with not losing the customer or the business. Salespeople learn how to price from experience on the job, and there is little or no science in how discounts are applied. Pricing decisions are essentially intuitive and lacking in metrics and process, and no reviews of pricing effectiveness are undertaken to improve the process. Consequently, it is difficult to assess value capture. No one in the company "owns" the pricing process, and by default it is picked up by the sales team. If the sale is lost, it is generally assumed that price was too high—not that the offer was wrong, the presentation was unconvincing, or any other matter.

Customer value   Until now, the company has not undertaken rigorous assessments of customer value and is unable specifically to state the exact impact of its services on customer outcome measures. Nevertheless, it is recognized that this is a shortcoming, and steps are being put in place to collect usable customer intelligence, develop pricing tools that salespeople can use in pricing discussions, and create deeper value propositions. Like many companies in the professional and business services sector, Gamma has collected customer satisfaction data and, unusually, employs the net promoter score concept to help management understand how different geographic markets value the company's service. The company recognizes that a deeper understanding of value is needed to be able to create specific deals based on customer value.

Changes required   A process has just been initiated to bring some more science into the decision and to move from intuitive, reactionary pricing to data-informed, intelligent pricing. Apart from data collection and analysis, this move will necessitate other changes, including the need to create a comprehensive pricing approach. The company perceives also the need for "heavy duty" resource analysis of pricing and other data collected to generate real business insights that can be used to deepen relationships with clients.

Opposition   The principal opposition to the changes are the salespeople. They are completely opposed to any process that takes away their ability to control pricing. This opposition is based on the belief that a pricing initiative is about putting prices up and making it harder to sell. The company is undertaking a company-wide consultation exercise to determine what the obstacles are likely to be to a new initiative and how these might be managed.

Implementation   The company recognizes that it is a long way from implementing full VBP, but it also recognizes that this is the way to go because it fits most closely its concept of intelligent, data-driven pricing strategy. The following activities are in process:

- Interviewing salespeople to try to identify where resistance will be to change
- Finding arguments to sell a pricing initiative to salespeople on the basis of improving their personal revenue
- Collecting information to enable the company to roll out the pricing initiative on a region-by-region basis
- Putting in place a company policy to give salespeople a safety net
- Trying it, ensuring that it works, and then rolling it out

Lessons   These are early days for this company, so not too many lessons learned yet

CASE STUDY 4: DELTA

Background   A highly successful UK company in logistics, Delta has been implementing VBP successfully for a number of years and has repositioned itself through a combination of solution development and VBP to the most profitable business in its sector.

Change drivers   The migration to VBP was initiated several years before the time of the interview, and neither interviewee was in post at that time. The main driver, however, was to move away from a commodity business at tiny margins and unrelenting, damaging pressure on prices. Management believed that it was "better than that" and resolved to find a more profitable formula.

Current methods Delta is successfully implementing VBP and is earning the rewards of the approach. The company was originally a player in the one-off-job commodity market. The market was becoming increasingly commoditized, with competitors finding every possible way to cut cost out of their supply chain. This inevitably led to poor service and dissatisfied customers. Delta's business model did not fit this approach because it delivered a quality service. The company searched for ways of providing value-added services and found it in an innovative solution-based approach. This gave the company scope not only to achieve much better margins than competitors but also to structure good, longer-term deals with the right kinds of customers. The company works hard at understanding customer issues and needs and uses experience and know-how to build effective solutions that map into the clients' issues and pain points.

Delta's pricing model is to offer a fixed price that provides a very good margin. However, the company also builds in and contracts to achieving year-on-year efficiencies and shares the savings achieved with clients. This gives clients an incentive to maintain the relationship and Delta to keep improving delivery costs. The relationships established create mutual trust so that future recommendations are readily accepted. As a result of this strategy, almost every deal has to be customized.

Interestingly, for this part of Delta's business, the company employs no salespeople. When the company sells value-added services, it is senior people from the business solutions team who pitch the solution. Furthermore, the company does not sell to buyers but only to the people who will be accountable for the success of the operation. "We need to work with the guy in the company whose head is on the block so that when the solution is implemented successfully, he gets all the credit." If the company is prevented from getting through to this individual, it will not bid for work and is prepared to walk away.

Customer value   Delta sees very clearly that if the value-based approach is to work, it must be based on a fair sharing of the benefits between buyer and seller. The company has found that it can get good margins only if the client "gets a bigger slice of the cake." The company achieves this through a close focus on customer value chains and works to understand as fully as it can what is valuable to its customers in order to provide value that will work for them.

Changes required   No current changes are envisaged, apart from improving the efficiency of company processes.

Opposition   There are no salespeople, so there is no opposition from that quarter. The nature of the team selling process means that all the customers' questions are answered authoritatively by the executive responsible for delivering the service, so there is little customer opposition.

Implementation   The process is working well and enables the company to achieve two to three times the margins achieved by its competitors.

Lessons
- Do not be satisfied with mediocre business performance.
- Look for ways to assemble a real solution.
- Sell the solution professionally by using senior people in the company.
- Select the deals and clients and be prepared to walk away.
- Refuse to be "nickel and dimed" by procurement.

CASE STUDY 5: EPSILON

Background	Epsilon is a global specialty chemicals company headquartered in Europe. The company is a mature user of VBP and has evolved a pricing organization to support it.
Change drivers	VBP was introduced about 14 years ago, a little before the time of the respondent. The principal reason for introducing VBP was to capture more of the value created for the company's clients. Clients are distributed throughout Europe and in general focus on a narrow area of industry in which products are seen as commodities and thus production yields are very important. Epsilon produces a range of chemicals that can enhance customers' productivity dramatically. The company now operates in a "sweet spot" in many of its markets in which manufacturing costs are very low but value created for customers is very high. VBP is strongly driven by management.
Current methods	Management recognized at an early stage in implementing VBP that the collection of performance data was useful not only to improve products but also to provide irrefutable evidence of product effectiveness. Normally, selling is done after completion of product trials, and the data collected form part of that selling process. The company also has created decision tools that can be used by salespeople to create different scenarios of product use in order to facilitate informed discussion and decision. Pricing has evolved into an important function in the company globally, and Epsilon has created a regional organization with common methods, metrics, and language.
Customer value	Epsilon put a great deal of effort and investment into assessing and measuring customer value. There are several methods in use. First, conjoint/

tradeoff and mapping methods are used to collect perceptual data from a large cohort of end users both on an in-country basis and across several countries. The data collected assess not only what is important qualitatively but also how Epsilon's offer compares with those of competitors, especially the customer's next-best alternative. Customer-facing staff (i.e., sales, technical, and service) are debriefed regularly in order to pinpoint current thinking and detect early trends. More formal financial and "hard" data metrics (from trials and evaluations) are used to measure economic impact. These data also provide comparative benchmarks.

Customer relationships in this industry are very important, and price negotiation often can be counterproductive for all parties. Accordingly, the data collected all form part of an ongoing dialogue with customers that minimizes the need for negotiation but also ensures that customers are fully informed of the results they can expect from the use of Epsilon's products. Epsilon is very dependent, as are the end users, on channel partners, and much effort is put into integrating partners into the pricing calculation, as well as ensuring contribution to value delivery.

Changes required   The process is working well, although occasional adjustments are required to optimize results. These changes are made through the global pricing manager working with his team of six country pricing managers.

Opposition   The company encounters very little opposition either from internal sales staff or from customers.

Implementation   The value-measurement methods facilitate the creation of a value-based list price. This is then adjusted to accommodate local country requirements and the needs of channel partners depending on the services provided to end users.

Epsilon has implemented VBP fully in the company. There can occasionally be significant challenges to align all the various business functions so that they are all "pointing in the same direction." It's a journey that this company started 14 years ago, and there is still room to improve. It cannot possibly be implemented in six months.

Lessons
- Top management can help by removing obstacles and not looking for too much too soon.
- Top management can help by reinforcing its importance.
- VBP is a journey that may take several years to implement fully.
- It's not just a case of changing the arithmetic.
- The company needs the right kind of salespeople—open-minded and willing to learn.
- The company needs to give salespeople correct data and tools—and train them in their use.

CASE STUDY 6: ZETA

Background
Zeta is a relatively young (30-year-old) technical consultancy company that has grown spectacularly from startup to well over 1,500 people and operates in 15 countries. Zeta has applied VBP from startup, and the highly profitable operations have fueled the company's fast growth.

Change drivers
The company has always applied VBP, principally on a shared-savings basis, so there was little to say in terms of change drivers. Conventional consultancy fees are hard to justify upfront and are among the first to be cut during recessionary times. Zeta's business model, in contrast, generates immediate and obvious value. This ensures loyalty and continuity of the client relationships over time.

Current methods   The starting point for every engagement is to find the individual who "owns" the problem. Usually these are senior executives with corporate profit-and-loss responsibility. Zeta consultants then work with these individuals to develop a relationship based on trust and mutual respect. The preferred arrangement is a longer term one in which both parties can benefit fully from the work done. Historically, the company operated on the basis of selling one-off, short-term deals. This meant that salespeople were always under pressure to win business, which became harder and harder to replace.

In most large firms, there are specialists whose job is to look for opportunities to improve efficiency. While these specialists can identify opportunities successfully, they do not have the industry-wide experience nor the detailed information databases that Zeta possesses and therefore achieve generally poorer results. Zeta management is very careful to establish trust with clients, and this means finding ways to work with in-company specialists and not "showing them up" to be ineffective. In fact, Zeta encourages companies to do everything they can for themselves before getting started. This gives management comfort when it takes over. The normal approach is for Zeta to put in some effort upfront free of charge. The company gives clients a taster, demonstrates some attractive early results, and watches the reaction. If at this point clients find excuses, then they are not serious, and Zeta walks away.

Wherever possible, engagements are made on a shared-savings basis over a three-year period with a rolling contract. Although there is a very precise work process, Zeta never works on a time basis and never gives an indication of the number of days' work any job entails. The issue is not the number of days worked. It is the successful achievement of results for the client that matters. When customers object, the work is sold on the basis of "we want to do the right job and not be under time constraints," which is what would happen using a time-sheet approach. Upfront commercials are done by the consultants and analysts who will do the work—not by salespeople.

Customer value   Selling is about what drives the customer and starts with a deep discovery process. To put together the right deal, Zeta needs to understand the full context of client information, psychology, decision-making processes, how the client assesses capital investments, and so on.

In this work, "We must stay close to the client—we can't do it by fax/e-mail. It's not a correspondence course."

Changes required   Apart from adjustments for different types of work or new geographies, for instance, occasionally fixed-price contracts, the process works well.

Opposition   The engagement process is a dialogue with the client in which all the benefits are fully laid out and both parties are fully bought in. The process largely eliminates opposition and price negotiation.

Implementation   As described earlier.
Lessons
- Engagement is a dialogue in which the people delivering the service work with the individual who "owns" the problem.
- Longer-term arrangements are preferred.
- The company provides low-cost, high-impact tasters to demonstrate value and assess seriousness.
- The company avoids committing to a specific number of hours or days.
- The company stays close to the client through the life of the project.

CASE STUDY 7: ETA

Background   Eta, a long-established manufacturer, is part of a global engineering enterprise. The products of this company are very technical machines used as components in a wide range of final products across many sectors. Eta has implemented Six Sigma, which is a respected process in the company.

Change drivers   Historically, products in this industry could look forward to a 30-year life. Competition and increasing government regulation have reduced life cycles to 3 years. Companies must introduce new products more frequently and achieve adequate ROI faster. This also means price increases and cost reductions that are very difficult to justify in a mature market such as Eta's. Cost-based is the incumbent pricing method in this industry but cannot achieve the necessary returns quickly enough. Top management has not really bought in fully to VBP. Senior executives do understand it but rapidly revert to discounting if they feel that a deal is at risk. Therefore, there is inadequate support at the top level of the company. This explains in large part the implementation problems experienced by pricing management.

Current methods   The company is in transition from a full cost-based approach to VBP.
                     Products are sold by traditional sales engineers, many of whom have been in the company many years. Some younger members of the sales team have business degrees. Salespeople are used to selling on engineering attributes rather than on value, and it is proving a challenge to get them to move to a new approach. The company also employs applications engineers who can help colleagues understand the value of the products. VBP approaches lead to price increases of 20 percent or

more compared with conventional methods. Sales and marketing "own" the price, and there are difficult tensions around price across these functions.

Customer value Eta uses a number of tools to assess customer value and uses the information derived as the basis of price setting, particularly value mapping (Marketing War-Room by Customer Value Inc) and the analytic hierarchy process. AHP is well accepted and has enabled some progress to be made in value measurement. These tools are particularly useful in providing sound arguments for salespeople to use. Whenever a deal is lost, it is automatically that the price was too high. There is no attempt to assess other reasons (e.g., poor proposition, inadequate information collection, or poor product execution). This is used as justification for further discounts and to resist pricing innovations. It is recognized at senior executive level that the sales team needs to be retrained, but since such training is expensive, it has never been sanctioned. Therefore, things continue as normal even though they are not working well.

Changes required VBP is not really understood yet, although headway is being made slowly. The sales team consists predominantly of engineers, and most have been with the company for many years. They are most difficult to convert to the new way of thinking.

Opposition This is the second attempt to introduce VBP into this company. The first attempt failed because it was impossible to overcome internal resistance primarily from the sales organization, which perceived VBP to be a marketing attempt to wrest control of pricing from them, inevitably leading to much higher prices for salespeople to sell. Six Sigma tools in this environment can help legitimize the process. This has worked to a degree. Customers have accepted the price changes more

Implementation

readily than anticipated—superior technology and regulatory pressure have an inevitable impact. The company is on the journey but facing many obstacles on the road. Faster progress could be made if there were more drive and support from top management, but for the moment, this is not in place. The opposition from the sales organization is difficult to overcome because salespeople perceive that VBP will make their lives much more difficult. Some get it and can see how focus on value might make selling more effective. The remainder of team members are vehemently opposed to this initiative.

Lessons

- Top-management buy-in and support are essential.
- Transition from cost-based business to full VBP implementation is a long process.
- Sales buy-in is crucial but demands a softly-softly approach.
- The company needs the right kind of salespeople.
- Quantification and trust in the quantification will catalyze implementation.

CASE STUDY 8: THETA

Background

Theta is part of an international company with headquarters in the European Union. The history of VBP goes back to 1984, and our respondent has been implementing VBP since that time at the senior executive level. This discussion is different from the other cases reported here because it is an overview based on practical experience of some of the key issues in making VBP work.

Change drivers

Drivers included the need to generate greater profit as well as to exploit significant capabilities and value-added services as fully as possible. In a previous company that marketed an engineering consumable, the company realized that selling the item by weight (cost-plus) was unlikely ever to generate attractive returns. Furthermore, the practice at the time of giving away valuable services (pretechnical audits) free of charge was not only eroding meager margins but also leaving potentially huge sums of money on the table. Customers, the company discovered, were fully prepared to pay premium prices for the services hitherto provided for free.

Current methods The business model was loss-making. The executives were under pressure to create a new business with greater potential for margin. The approach was to provide a contracted-out machine management and maintenance service. By ensuring that all a client's machines were maintained in tiptop performance, the company was able to generate savings of staff, time, and maintenance materials, as well as support and improve productivity, by reducing downtime. The service provider carried all the costs and levied a fee to the customer. This was a win-win formula.

Customer value Key skills for salespeople to acquire and that were completely different from "box shifting" were the ability to look carefully for value and to link cost savings and productivity gains with proposed prices.

Changes required This type of proposition went way beyond the normal selling skills of most salespeople because it has to take into account a much larger impact on the business than just commoditized service consumables. Not all salespeople are able to handle this kind of work, and the company needed to train salespeople in auditing premises, in measuring and analyzing costs, and in building customized propositions as well as up-skilling to value-based selling.

Training also was required at management levels to ensure that the new approach would be supported properly by other functions. Value-based marketing training was delivered to all senior people—operations, supply chain, information technology (IT), and finance—to ensure that they understood and bought into the new approach.

Additional Reading

Anderson JC, Kumar N, Narus J. 2007. *Value Merchants: Demonstrating and Documenting Superior Value in Business Markets*. Boston: Harvard Business School Press.

Baker RJ. 2006. *Measure What Matters to Customers: Using Key Predictive Indicators*. Hoboken, NJ: Wiley.

CIO Council, Best Practices Committee. 2002. *Value-Measuring Methodology: How-to Guide*. Washington DC.

Hanan M, Karp P. 1991. *Competing on Value*. New York: Amacom.

Hubbard DW. 2007. *How to Measure Anything: Finding the Value of Intangibles in Business*. Hoboken, NJ: Wiley.

Kim WC, Mauborgne R. 1997. "Value Innovation: The Strategic Logic of High Growth." *Harvard Business Review*, January–February.

Miller R.B., Heiman S.E., Tuleja T. 1985. *The New Strategic Selling: The Unique Sales System Proven Successful by the World's Best Companies*. New York: Warner Books.

Parmenter D. 2007. *Key Performance Indicators: Developing, Implementing, and Using Winning KPIs*. Hoboken, NJ: Wiley.

Rackham N. 1995. *SPIN Selling*. New York: Gower.

Reilly T. 2003. *Value-Added Selling: How to Sell More Profitably, Confidently, and Professionally by Competing on Value Not on Price*. New York: McGraw-Hill.

Scott MC. 1998. *Value Drivers: The Manager's Guide to Driving Corporate Value Creation*. Hoboken, NJ: Wiley.

Thomas J. 2006. *Value Selling: Driving Up Sales One Conversation at a Time*. New York: VVA Publishing.

Yankelovich D, Meer D. February 2006. "Rediscovering Market Segmentation." *Harvard Business Review*.

Notes

Chapter 1

1. Sam I. Hill, Jack McGrath, and Sandeep Dayal, "How to Brand Sand." *Strategy-Business Editors*, Second Quarter, 1998.

2. Ian C. MacMillan and Rita Gunther McGrath, "Discovering New Points of Differentiation," *Harvard Business Review*, July–August 1997.

3. Geoffrey A. Moore, *Crossing the Chasm, Marketing and Selling High-Tech Products to Mainstream Customer*, rev. ed. New York: HarperCollins, 1999.

Chapter 2

1. Clayton M. Christensen and Michael Raynor, *The Innovator's Solution*. Boston: Harvard Business School Press, 2003.

2. Joseph L. Bower and Clayton Christensen, "Disruptive Technologies: Catching the Wave," *Harvard Business Review On Point,* 2000.

3. Bradley T. Gale and Donald Swire, *Positioning and Pricing Product Lines in Recessionary Times.* Boston: Customer Value, Inc., March 2009.

4. Article can be found at www.google.co.uk/search?source=ig&hl=en&rlz=1R2WZPA_en&q=staycationing+ uk&aq=3v&oq=staycationing.

5. See www.fruitweb.com/fc/?p=133

6. Bradley T. Gale, *How Much Is Your Product Really Worth?* Boston: Customer Value, Inc., 2002.

7. Benson Shapiro and Robert J Dolan, *Performance Curves: Costs, Prices, and Value.* Boston: Harvard Business School Press, 1989.

8. Steven Forth, "Are Value Maps Leading You Astray?" Available at leveragepoint.typepad.com/ … /what-do-we-mean-when-we-say-**value**.htm.

Chapter 3

1. B. Atkin, R. Skinner. (1977) *How British Industry Prices*, London: Industrial Market Research Ltd., 1977.

2. R.W. Mills, C. Sweeting. *Pricing Decisions in Practice: How Are They Made in U.K. Manufacturing and Service Companies?* London: Chartered Institute of Management Accountants, 1984.

3. S. Fabiani, C. Loupias, F. Martins, and R. Sabbatini, *Pricing Decisions in the Euro Area*. Oxford, U.K.: Oxford University Press, 2007.

4. John Lawrence Day, *Pricing for Profitability: Activity-Based Pricing for Competitive Advantage*. New York: John Wiley and Sons, 2002.

Chapter 4

1. S. Fabiani, C. Loupias, F. Martins, and R. Sabbatini, *Pricing Decisions in the Euro Area*. Oxford, U.K.: Oxford University Press, 2007.

2. John Gourville and Dilip Soman, "Pricing and the Psychology of Consumption," *Harvard Business Review*, September 2002.

3. For a most interesting case study in the area of hot-wiring, visit www.solidwastemag.com/issues/story.aspx?aid=1000109436&type=Print%20Archives.

Chapter 5

1. James C. Anderson and J. A. Narus, "Business Marketing: Understand What Customers Want," *Harvard Business Review*, November–December 1998;

2. *Quantifying Outsourcing Intangible Benefits*, A Glomark-Governan White Paper. August 2006. Available at www.glomark.com

3. K. N. Thompson, B. J. Coe, and J. R. Lewis, "Gauging the Value of Suppliers' Products: Buyer Side Applications of Economic Value Pricing Models," *Journal of Business & Industrial Marketing* 9(2):29–40, 1994.

4. Thomas L. Saaty, "Decision Making with the Analytic Hierarchy Process," *International Journal of Services, Economics, and Management* 1(1):83–98, 2008.

Chapter 6

1. Thomas T. Nagle and J. E. Hogan, *The Strategy and Tactics of Pricing: A Guide to Growing More Profitably*, 4th ed. Philadelphia: Pearson/Prentice-Hall, 2006.

2. "Innovative Lawyers: Billing and Fees," *Financial Times*, October 23, 2009.

Chapter 7

1. Ronald J. Baker, *2001 Professionals Guide to Value Pricing*, 3rd ed. Harcourt Brace, 2001.

2. *Ibid.*

3. *Ibid.*

4. *Ibid.*

5. Philip Kotler, G. Armstrong, J. Saunders, and V. Wong, *Principles of Marketing: The European Edition*. Philadelphia: Pearson/Prentice-Hall, 2008.

6. Nessim Hanna and H. R. Dodge, *Pricing: Policies and Procedures*. New York: Macmillan Business, 1995.

7. Arvind Sahay, "How to Reap Higher Profits with Dynamic Pricing," *MIT Sloan Management Review*, Summer 2007.

8. Benson P. Shapiro, "Performance-Based Pricing Is More Than Pricing," *Harvard Business School Note*, 2002.

9. Robert J. Dolan, "How Do You Know the Price is Right?" *Harvard Business Review*, September–October 1995.

10. Adam Brandenburger and V. Krishna, "Bundling," *Harvard Business School Note*, 1995.

11. Stefan Stremersch and Gerard Tellis, "Strategic Bundling of Products and Prices: A New Synthesis for Marketing," *Journal of Marketing* 66:65–72, 2002.

12. Robert J. Dolan and H. Simon, *Power Pricing*. New York: Free Press, 1996.

13. Carl Shapiro and Hal R. Varian, "Versioning: The Smart Way to Sell Information," *Harvard Business Review*, November–December 1998.

14. Kent B. Munroe, *Pricing: Making Profitable Decisions*, 2nd ed. New York: McGraw-Hill International Editions, 1990.

15. Nessim Hanna and H. R. Dodge, *Pricing: Policies and Procedures*. New York: Macmillan Business, 1995.

16. Robert J. Dolan and H. Simon, *Power Pricing*. New York: Free Press, 1996.

Chapter 8

1. Michael J. Lanning, *Delivering Profitable Value*. New York: Basic Books, 1998.

2. James C. Anderson, James A. Narus, and Woutter van Rossum, "Customer Value Propositions in Business Markets," *Harvard Business Review*, March 2006.

3. Gerry Johnson, Kevan Scholes, and Richard Whittington, *Exploring Corporate Strategy*. Boston: Pearson Education, 2008.

4. Arik R. Johnson, "Competitive Intelligence and Competitor Analysis as Knowledge Management Applications," *The Knowledge Management Yearbook 2000–2001*. Boston: Butterworth-Heinemann, 2001.

5. Michael Porter, *Competitive Advantage: Creating and Sustaining Superior Performance*. New York: Free Press, 1985.

6. Harry Macdivitt, *Constructive SWOT Analysis*. London: BPP Professional Module, October 2010.

Chapter 10

1. John Hogan, "Building a World-Class Pricing Capability: Where Does Your Company Stack Up?" *Monitor Group Perspectives*, 2010. Available online at http://www.monitor.com/Portals/0/MonitorContent/imported/MonitorUnitedStates/Articles/PDFs/Monitor_Bldg_WorldClass_Pricing_Capability.pdf

2. Robert J. Dolan, "How Do You Know When the Price Is Right?" *Harvard Business Review*, September–October 1995.

3. ManMohan Sodhi and Navdeep Sodhi, "Six Sigma Pricing," *Harvard Business Review Toolkit*, May 2005.

4. Robert J. Dolan, "How Do You Know When the Price Is Right?" *Harvard Business Review*, September–October 1995.

5. *Ibid.*

6. Hogan, "Building a World-Class Pricing Capability (2010).

7. ManMohan Sodhi and Navdeep Sodhi, "Six Sigma Pricing," *Harvard Business Review Toolkit*, May 2005.

8. Hermann Simon, "Pricing—Where Is It Heading?" available at www.managementfirst.com/articles/pricing.htm.

9. Hogan, "Building a World-Class Pricing Capability," (2010).

10. Robert J. Dolan, "How Do You Know When the Price Is Right?" *Harvard Business Review*, September–October 1995.

11. Hermann Simon, "Pricing—Where Is It Heading?" available at www.managementfirst.com/articles/pricing.htm.

12. *Ibid.*

13. Walter Baker, M. Marn, and C. Zawada, "Building a Better Pricing Structure," *Journal of Professional Pricing* 19(4), 2010.

14. Andreas Hinterhuber, "Customer Value-Based Pricing Strategies: Why Companies Resist," *Journal of Business Strategy* 20(4):41–50, 2008.

15. *Ibid.*

16. ManMohan Sodhi and Navdeep Sodhi, "Six Sigma Pricing," *Harvard Business Review Toolkit*, May 2005.

CHAPTER 11

1. Ian C. MacMillan and Rita Gunther McGrath, "Discovering New Points of Differentiation," *Harvard Business Review*, July–August 1997.

2. Richard Anthony D'Aveni, *Beating the Commodity Trap: How to Maximize Your Competitive Position and Increase Your Pricing Power.* Cambridge, MA: Harvard Business Press, 2010.

3. "How to Fight a Price War," *Harvard Business Review*, March–April 2000.

4. James C. Anderson, James A. Narus, Woutter van Rossum, "Customer Value Propositions in Business Markets," *Harvard Business Review*, March 2006.

5. Richard Anthony D'Aveni, *Hypercompetition.* New York: Free Press, 1994.

Appendix A

1. B. J. Rodger and A. MacCulloch, *Competition Law and Policy in the EU and UK.* London: Cavendish Publishing, 2004.

2. EU Notice of Market Definition 1997 (OJ C372/3, [1998] 4 CMLR177).

3. Guidance on the Commission's enforcement priorities in applying Article 82 of the EC Treaty to abusive exclusionary conduct by dominant undertakings. *Official Journal of the EU*, 24.2.2009, C 45/7.

4. D. W. Carlton and M. Israel, "Price Discrimination," in *Handbook of Competition Economics,* 2009. Law Business Research Limited, 87 Lancaster Road, London, W11 1QQ, United Kingdom.

Index

About the Authors

Harry Macdivitt served as marketing director in a leading electronic controls company, with specific responsibility for strategic management, new product marketing, and development for U.K. and international markets (United States, Russia). He has run training programs for corporations in the United Kingdom, European Community, North America, and China and works regularly with growth-oriented small- and medium-sized businesses.

Mike Wilkinson works worldwide with clients across a diverse range of industries and business sectors focusing on value and value selling. He has worked in a wide range of senior sales positions and has experience with fast-moving consumer goods as well as business-to-business sales.